Biblical Hermeneutics

An Introduction to Basic Concepts of Bible Study

THE BOOKE OF THE Prophet Ezekiel.

CHAP. I.

1 The time of Ezekiels prophecie at Chebar. 4 His vision of foure Cherubims, 15 Of the foure wheeles, 26 and of the glory of God.

Now it came to passe in the thirtieth yeere, in the fourth moneth, in the fifth day of the moneth, (as I was among †the captiues by the riuer of Chebar) that the heauens were opened, and I saw visions of God.

2 In the fifth day of the moneth, (which was the fifth yeere of king Iehoiakins captiuitie,)

3 The word of the LORD came expresly vnto †Ezekiel the Priest, the sonne of Buzi, in the land of the Caldeans, by the riuer Chebar, and the hand of the LORD was there vpon him.

4 ¶ And I looked, and behold, a whirlewinde came out of the North, a great cloude, and a fire †infoulding it selfe, and a brightnesse was about it, and out of the midst thereof as the colour of amber, out of the midst of the fire.

5 Also out of the midst thereof came the likenesse of foure liuing creatures, and this was their appearance: they had the likenesse of a man.

6 And euery one had foure faces, and euery one had foure wings.

7 And their feet were †straight feet, and the sole of their feet was like the sole of a calues foot, and they sparkled like the colour of burnished brasse.

8 And they had the handes of a man vnder their wings on their foure sides, and they foure had their faces and their wings.

9 Their wings were ioyned one to another, they turned not when they went: they went euery one straight forward.

10 As for the likenesse of their faces, they foure had the face of a man, and the face of a lyon on the right side, and they foure had the face of an oxe on the left side: they foure also had the face of an eagle.

11 Thus were their faces: and their wings were ‖ stretched vpward, two wings of euery one were ioyned one to an other, and two couered their bodies.

12 And they went euery one straight forward: whither the spirit was to goe, they went: and they turned not when they went.

13 As for the likenesse of the liuing creatures, their appearance was like burning coles of fire, and like the appearance of lamps: it went vp and downe among the liuing creatures, and the fire was bright, and out of the fire went foorth lightning.

14 And the liuing creatures ranne, and returned as the appearance of a flash of lightning.

15 ¶ Now as I beheld the liuing creatures: behold one wheele vpon the earth by the liuing creatures, with his foure faces.

16 The appearance of the wheeles, and their worke was like vnto the colour of a Berill: and they foure had one likenesse, and their appearance and their worke was as it were a wheele in the middle of a wheele.

17 When they went, they went vpon their foure sides: and they returned not when they went.

18 As for their rings, they were so high, that they were dreadful, and their ‖ rings were full of eyes round about them foure.

19 And when the liuing creatures went,

†Hebr. captiuitie.

†Hebr. Iehezkel.

†Heb catching it selfe.

†Hebr. a straight foot.

‖Or, diuided aboue.

‖Or, strakes

The 1611 King James Version

BIBLICAL HERMENEUTICS

AN INTRODUCTION TO BASIC CONCEPTS OF BIBLE STUDY

Lee Roy Martin

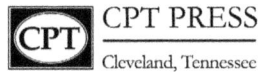

CPT PRESS
Cleveland, Tennessee

Biblical Hermeneutics
An Introduction to Basic Concepts of Bible Study
Published by CPT Press
900 Walker ST NE
Cleveland, TN 37311
USA
email. cptpress@pentecostaltheology.org
website. www.cptpress.com

ISBN-13: 978-1-953358-47-9

Copyright © 2024 CPT Press

Unless otherwise noted, Scripture quotations are from the New King James Version.

All rights reserved. No part of this book may be reproduced or translated in any form, by print, photoprint, microfilm, microfiche, electronic database, internet database, or any other means without written permission from the publisher.

Contents

Preface.. viii

1. The Importance of the Bible
   The Value of Bible Study 1
   The Role of the Bible in the Christian Life............................ 2
   The Characteristics of a Faithful Interpretation..................... 6

2. The Inspiration of Scripture
   The Bible Testifies to Its Divine Origin................................ 11
   The Bible Has a Message for Us.. 11
   The Meaning of 'Verbal Inspiration'..................................... 12

3. The Value of Biblical Hermeneutics
   What is Biblical Hermeneutics?.. 29
   Why Should We Study Hermeneutics?................................. 30
   Transmission and Translation of Scripture 35
   The Relevance of the Old Testament 36
   Preparing to Receive the Message of the Bible 42

4. Basic Concepts in Hermeneutics
   The Clarity of Scripture.. 47
   The Significance of Context... 51
   Historical Backgrounds.. 53
   The Unity and Diversity of Scripture.................................... 55
   The Witness of the Church 57
   The Witness of the Holy Spirit... 62

5. The Bible and Christian Affections
   Burning Hearts... 69
   The Sanctifying Effect of Scripture...................................... 70
   The Christian Affections 70
   Case Studies 74

6. Interpreting Figures of Speech
- Literal Meaning and Figurative Language 77
- The Most Important Figures of Speech 79
- Other Figures of Speech 88
- How to Understand Figures of Speech 89

7. Interpreting the Proverb, Riddle, and Fable
- Words of Wisdom 91
- The Proverb 92
- The Riddle 98
- The Fable 101

8. Interpreting Parables
- The Definition of The Parable 105
- Parables in the Old Testament 106
- Parables in the New Testament 107
- Study the Background 116
- Observe the Occasion 116
- Analyze the Characters and Events 120
- Search the Surrounding Passage 122
- Conclusion 123

9. Interpreting Allegories and Types
- The Allegory 127
- The Type 132

10. Interpreting Biblical Poetry
- The Nature of Poetry 135
- Poetry in the Bible 140
- Poetry in the Psalms 141
- Steps for Interpreting the Poetry 150

11. Interpreting Biblical Narrative
- Narrative in the Bible 155
- The Elements of Narrative 155
- Common Literary Devices 161
- Narrative Theology 163
- Practical Application of Biblical Narrative 164

12. Interpreting Prophecy
Characteristics of Prophecy 167
Historical Context of the Old Testament Prophets 174
Keys to Interpreting Old Testament Prophecy 176
Daniel and Revelation 177

13. A Method for Systematic Bible Study
Approaches to Bible Study 181
Outline of the Exegetical Process 183
Detailed Instructions for Exegetical Bible Study 185
Biblical Commands and Cultural Context 196

14. From Research to Presentation
Converting Research into a Sermon or Lesson 203
Converting Research into an Academic Exegesis Paper 209

Appendix: Resources for Hebrew and Greek Word Studies 216
Bibliography 219

Preface

There is no shortage of books on biblical hermeneutics. So, why would I write another one? I have written this short introduction because I see the need for fresh approach to the subject. A fresh approach is needed for three reasons:
1. Many books on hermeneutics are too long and complex.
2. The short books on hermeneutics are incomplete.
3. Current treatments are heavy on theory, but they lack concrete examples from the Bible.

In response to these shortcomings, I have attempted to write a clear, concise (but thorough) description of guidelines for interpretation. Furthermore, with every theory, I have included biblical examples.

This second edition, published by CPT Press, is a revision and expansion of a previous version published by Senda de Vida Publishers in Miami, FL. Much appreciation is due to Marco Calderon, who was willing to publish my first edition in both English and Spanish.

I am grateful for all of my students at the Pentecostal Theological Seminary, who have used my book over the last 13 years. Their kind words and suggestions have encouraged me to revise and to expand the work. I am also grateful for my colleague Chris Thomas, who is the finest example of a Christian scholar.

As always, I thank God for my family and for my church. They support all of my endeavors with much enthusiasm. My wife Karen works diligently to edit all of my writings.

Lee Roy Martin
Cleveland, Tennessee
April 23, 2024

1

THE IMPORTANCE OF THE BIBLE

The Value of Bible Study

What prevents us from learning how to play a musical instrument, to speak a foreign language, or to write a novel? Perhaps it is the daunting nature of the task. We know that we cannot master these abilities in a week or even in a month – they require much effort, practice, and self-discipline over a long period of time. Similarly, we would love to know more about the Bible, but cannot become a Bible expert in a few days, weeks, or months. And yet, the comprehensive study of the Bible is well worth the work and the time that it requires. The purpose of this book is to help you begin a plan of Bible study that you can continue for years to come.

It does not matter if you are twenty years old, fifty years old, or eighty years old, the time is always right to study the Bible. For example, even the Apostle Paul saw the need for continuing education. When Paul was imprisoned in Rome, soon to be executed, he wrote a letter to Timothy, his young friend and fellow minister, his son in the faith, and he says this:

> I have fought the good fight, I have finished the course, I have kept the faith; in the future there is laid up for me the crown of righteousness, which the Lord, the righteous Judge, will award to me on that day; and not only to me, but also to all who have loved his appearing. Make every effort to come to me soon; ... When you come bring the cloak which I left at Troas with

Carpus, and the books, especially the parchments (2 Tim. 4.7-13 NASB).

Paul's last request was this: 'bring my cloak, and the books, especially the parchments'. Now, I understand why Paul says, 'bring my cloak', because a person can get cold in a Roman prison; but what about the phrase 'and the books, especially the parchments'? The Greek word for 'books' (*biblia*) means papyrus scrolls; and the word 'parchment' (*membranas*) means scrolls made of animal skins. These were the two forms of books in that day. It is likely that what he called 'books' were copies of the Gospels and other books found in the New Testament. These were originally written on papyrus. What he called 'parchments' were probably leather scrolls of the Old Testament books.

Do you see this picture? Paul is in a Roman prison awaiting execution. He knows that his time is short.

Paul has finished his course – why does he need his books?

Paul has fought a good fight – why does he need to study?

Paul has done his work, and he is only months away from death, so why does he say, 'bring me the parchments'?

I submit to you that as long as there was a breath remaining in Paul's body, he was intent on following his own counsel to 'preach the word, be instant in season, out of season' (2 Tim. 4.2). Therefore, Paul's ministry from prison gave him reason to search the Scriptures, to study a bit more, and to learn how to minister in the cosmopolitan city of Rome. He asked that Timothy bring him the books of Scripture so that he could improve his preaching, deepen his relationship with God, and minister more effectively in the final hours of his life.

I am asking you to follow the example of Paul. I am asking you to make a commitment to study the Word of God regularly. May God bless you as you serve him and minister to his people.

The Role of the Bible in the Christian Life

Christians agree that the Bible has a vital and indispensable role in the Christian life. However, our agreement about the importance of Scripture and our constant affirmation regarding the inspiration of the Bible do not necessarily mean that we fully understand the function and purpose of the Bible in the Church. As Pentecostals, we want to do *more* than affirm biblical truth, we want our lives to be transformed and guided by biblical truth.

Let me begin with a question: 'Why do we read, teach, and preach the Bible?' Obviously, we utilize Scripture because it is God's Word to us, but I am asking about the Bible's purpose, role, and function in the church and in our individual lives.

The Lord says,

> So shall My word be that goes forth from My mouth;
>   It shall not return to Me void,
> But it shall accomplish what I please,
>   And it shall prosper in the thing for which I sent it.
>   (Isa. 55.11)

God's Word will 'accomplish' something, but exactly WHAT does the Lord accomplish through his word? The Word will 'prosper', but in what way does it prosper? What effect does the Scripture have on the hearer? We could make a long list of specific results that come from hearing the Word, things like knowledge of the truth, conviction of sin, salvation, love, courage, hope, gratitude, joy, healing, blessing, sanctification, wisdom, encouragement, strength, deliverance, direction, peace of mind, fruitfulness, patience, anointing, faith, and communion with God.

However, let us take a look at the Apostle Paul's comments regarding the usefulness of Scripture. In his second letter to Timothy, Paul writes the following:

> … from childhood you have known the sacred writings which are able to give you the wisdom that leads to salvation through faith which is in Christ Jesus. All Scripture is inspired by God and profitable for teaching, for reproof, for correction, for training in righteousness; that the man of God may be adequate, equipped for every good work. I solemnly charge you … preach the word (2 Tim. 3.15-4.2 NASB).

Taking the lead from Paul's passionate presentation, I would suggest at least four benefits that we obtain from Scripture: Doctrine, Discipleship, Deepened Relationship, and Development in Ministry.

1. Doctrine – To Improve Our Understanding of God

First and foremost, Paul states that Scripture is profitable for teaching doctrine. That is, we study the Bible to learn what we should believe. The full gospel teaches that Jesus Christ is Savior, Sanctifier, Spirit-baptizer, Healer, and Soon-coming King. These doctrines are founded on the study of Scripture. The neglect of Bible study and Bible preaching will result in an erosion of these key doctrines.

2. Discipleship – To Increase Our Likeness to God

The second reason or purpose for reading Scripture is for Christian formation, that is, discipleship. Paul states that all Scripture 'is profitable for teaching, for reproof, for correction, for training in righteousness.' He is describing discipleship. What are the elements of discipleship?

KNOWING—Beliefs and attitudes
BEING—Affections and character
DOING—Practices and behaviors

How does discipleship happen? How are we formed in the faith? This is an important question for the church. Paul states that Scripture contributes to our Christian formation.

3. Deepened Relationship – To Enhance Our Communion with God

On a daily basis, we often read the Bible for a third reason – to encounter the presence of God. Reading the Bible should be an act of worship. It is a form of fellowship with God, communion with God, spending time with God. We may not be reading in order to determine a doctrinal question or to develop specific character traits but only to experience God's presence as he speaks to us through his Word.

As we worship, we should meditate in the Word of God. The Lord said to Joshua, 'This book of the law shall not depart out of your mouth, but you shall meditate on it day and night, that you may be careful to do according to all that is written in it' (Josh. 1.8). In Psalm 1.2 tells us that we are blessed if our 'delight is in the law of the LORD, and in his law' we meditate day and night. See also Psalm 119.15, 'I will meditate in thy precepts, and have respect unto thy ways;' and Psalm 119.148, 'My eyes are awake before the watches of the night, that I may meditate upon thy Word.'

God gave us the Bible not only to increase our knowledge of him, but also to strengthen our relationship with him. As we hear and receive the Word of God, we will grow in grace and in Christian character (2 Pet. 3.18). Peter advises us: 'long for the pure milk of the word, that by it you may grow in respect to salvation' (1 Pet. 2.2 NASB). As we see ourselves in the Scriptures, we are transformed into the image of Jesus Christ. Paul states it this way: 'being transformed into the same image from glory to glory, just as from the Lord, the Spirit' (2 Cor. 3.18 NASB). As we receive the Word of God, it will sanctify us. Jesus prayed for us to the Father: 'Sanctify them by the truth; your word is truth' (Jn 17.17 NIV; see also Eph. 5.26). Let us pray that we may not only be hearers of the Word but that we may also be doers of the Word (Jas 1.22). Sanctification involves three aspects of the Christian life: the head, the hands, and the heart—knowing, doing, and being. These three can also be described as doctrine, behavior, and the affections.

4. Development in Ministry – To expand Our Effectiveness for God

Not only do the Scriptures teach us and disciple us, they prepare us for ministry to others. Paul tells Timothy that the Scriptures are the ultimate resource for the equipping of the servant of God. A minister may be gifted and competent in many areas, but there is no substitute for the Word of God. Jeremiah preached that Israel had forsaken the fountain of living water and had dug cisterns, broken cisterns that could hold no water (Jer. 2.13). A man-made cistern can never replace a fountain of fresh water.

We may be skilled speakers,
    but without the Scripture, we have no message.
We may be masters of administration,
    but without the Scripture, we accomplish nothing.
We may be great promoters,
    but without the Scripture, lives are not changed.
It is only by the Word of God
    that bondage is broken,
    that sickness is healed,
    that relationships are mended,

that sin is defeated
and that hope is restored.

Through the Scriptures, God's ministers are made 'complete, thoroughly equipped for every good work' (NKJV).

The Characteristics of a Faithful Interpretation

As we read and interpret the Bible, how do we know that our interpretations are valid? The Bible has been used and misused in order to prove an amazing assortment of ideas. For example, the Scriptures have been quoted in order to justify the practice of slavery. Sometimes our prejudice gets in the way of good interpretation. The Bible has provided an excuse to persecute the Jews and other ethnic groups. Brigham Young, a leader in the Mormon church, used the Bible to defend his polygamy. Even today, some interpreters are quoting the Bible to promote their own agendas. So, how do we judge our own views and opinions? As we study the Bible, we must keep in mind the purposes of Scripture as well as these eight qualities of faithful interpretation.

A faithful interpretation of Scripture communicates what the Bible *says*, not what we *wish it said.*

We must be willing to go wherever the Scripture leads us even if what it says seems to go against what we have heard in the past. The ministries of teaching and preaching carry with them great responsibilities. Our interpretations of Scripture should not be merely arbitrary, but they should be informed decisions made with the guidance of the Holy Spirit. We must 'rightly divide the word of truth' (2 Tim. 2.15). That is, we must be diligent to handle the Word of God carefully. Moreover, we must not add or take away from the meaning of the Bible (Deut. 4.2; Rev. 22.19).

A faithful interpretation adheres to the Spirit of the Scripture not just to the 'letter.'

Paul says, 'the letter kills, but the Spirit gives life' (2 Cor. 3.6); and Jesus said, 'my words are Spirit and they are life' (Jn 6.63). The letter says, 'You shall not commit adultery;' but the Spirit of Scripture says, 'He who looks on a woman to lust after her has committed adultery in his heart' (Mt. 5.28). The Holy Spirit will never contradict the teachings of Scripture. However, if the work of the Holy Spirit includes our reproof and correction, then, by necessity the Spirit must sometimes contradict US in our thoughts, will, and behavior. The Spirit's ministry of correction includes confronting our insufficient or errant biblical interpretations.

A faithful interpretation takes into account both the diversity of Scripture and the unity of Scripture.
When we read the Bible, we must remember the two aspects of its composition: 1. The Bible is composed of sixty-six books, and each book has a distinctive message and voice, just as the members of an orchestra play different instruments and different notes. 2. The Bible in its entirety is the Word of God. It is one book that presents to us a unified voice in its teaching much like the orchestra that performs one song. The different musical instruments blend together to form one magnificent sound, and the sixty-six books of the Bible blend together to form one message that God is our creator, redeemer, and king.

A faithful interpretation conforms to Christ as the 'word made flesh' (Jn 1.14).
Jesus is the ultimate expression of God's Word to us. We read in Heb. 1.1-2 that 'God spoke many times and in many ways to our ancestors through the prophets. And now in these final days, he has spoken to us through his Son'. Therefore, the ultimate test of our interpretation is its conformity to the Word as revealed in Jesus.

A faithful interpretation will produce love for God and love for neighbor.
Therefore, it will generate worship of God, it will strengthen the body of Christ, and it will encourage ethical behavior.

A faithful interpretation will stand up to the scrutiny and discernment of the Church.
Sensationalist and idiosyncratic interpretations are rarely faithful interpretations.

A faithful interpretation focuses on the teaching of the text, not peripheral elements.
The words of Scripture are presented in terms of ancient culture, habits, traditions, practices, dress, and politics. Sometimes, these

elements are just part of the ancient context but not a part of the message itself. For example, Jesus and all of his disciples wore robes and sandals, but that does not mean we should be wearing robes and sandals.

A faithful interpretation understands that the Bible is one story in two parts.

As part one, the Old Testament provides the foundation for the story. The New Testament is part two, and just as a story progresses through time, so God's relationship to humanity progresses. However, in its unity, the Bible is the story of God's relationship to humanity as revealed in creation, human sin, God's promise of redemption, the people of Israel, Jesus Christ, and the coming of God's kingdom.

The unity of Scripture is demonstrated by the consistency of teachings about God and about God's plan. For example, in both the Old and New Testaments:

Salvation is by grace through faith.
Forgiveness is through the shedding of blood.
God relates to his people through Covenant.
God is sovereign.
God creates a people.
The Holy Spirit forms the believing community.
The Holy Spirit empowers leaders for service.
The greatest commandment is love.

The Bible is a single story, and we can point to many ways that the story moves forward as we transition from the Old Testament to the New Testament. Some progressions include the following:

In the OT, Israel conquers by violence,
but the 'weapons of our warfare are not carnal'.

In the OT, God's temple was a building,
but in the NT, the Church is God's temple.

In the OT, God's teachings were written in tables of stone,
but in the NT, God's word is written on our hearts.

The OT kingdom was physical,
but the NT kingdom is spiritual.

The OT focused on the nation of Israel,
but the NT includes all nations.

In the OT, the Holy Spirit came upon only a few, select leaders, but in the NT, the Holy Spirit is poured out on everyone.

The OT required ongoing sacrifices,
but Jesus is the final sacrifice.

The life, death, and resurrection of Jesus mark the decisive turning point in the biblical story. Therefore, the Mosaic covenant has been replaced by the New Covenant in Jesus Christ (Heb. 8.13). Therefore, Christians must conform to God's moral law, but they are not obligated to follow the OT ceremonial laws or ritual laws.

For Review and Study

1. How does the Apostle Paul serve as an example to us regarding the importance of Bible study?
2. Explain the value of the Bible for the establishing of sound doctrine.
3. Explain the value of the Bible for discipleship.
4. Explain the value of the Bible for deepening our relationship with God.
5. Explain the value of the Bible for the minister.
6. Discuss the eight characteristics of a faithful interpretation of Scripture.

He dieth. Iudah made captaine. Chap.j. Three sonnes of Anak slaine. 96

m Rather then mans dissimulation should not be punished, the dumbe creatures shal cry for vengeance.

Gene.19,50. iudges 2,9.
n Such are the people commonly as their rulers are,

Beholde, this stone shall be a witnesse vnto vs: for it ᵐ hath heard all the wordes of the Lord which he spake with vs, it shal be there for a witnesse against you, lest you denie your God.

28 Then Ioshua let the people depart euery man vnto his inheritance.

29 And after these things, Ioshua the sonne of Nun, the seruant of the Lord died, being an hundred and ten yeeres old.

30 And they buried him in the border of his inheritance in * Timnath serah, which is in mount Ephraim, on the North side of mount Gaash.

31 And Israel ⁿ serued the Lord all the dayes of Ioshua, and all the dayes of the Elders that ouerliued Ioshua, and which had knowen all the workes of the Lord that hee had done for Israel.

32 And the * bones of Ioseph, which the children of Israel brought out of Egypt, buried they in Shechem, in a parcell of ground which Iaakob bought of * the sonnes of Hamor the father of Shechem, for an hundreth pieces of siluer, and the children of Ioseph had them in their inheritance.

33 Also Eleazar the sonne of Aaron died, whom they buried in the † hill of Phinehas his sonne, which was giuen him in mount Ephraim.

Gene.50,25.
Exod.13,19.
Gene.33,19.

† Ebr. Gibeath.
Phinehas.

The booke of Iudges.

THE ARGVMENT.

Albeit there is nothing that more prouoketh Gods wrath, then mans ingratitude: yet is there nothing so displeasant and hainous that can turne backe Gods loue from his Church. For now when the Israelites were entred into the land of Canaan, and saw the trueth of Gods promise performed, in stead of acknowledging his great benefits, and giuing thanks for the same, they fel to most horrible obliuion of Gods graces, contrary to their solemne promise made vnto Ioshua, and so prouoked his vengeance (as much as in them stood) to their vtter destruction. Whereof as they had most euident signes by the mutabilitie of their state: for hee suffered them to bee most cruelly vexed and tormented by tyrants; he pulled them from libertie, and cast them into slauery, to the intent they might feele their owne miseries, and so call vnto him and be deliuered; so to shew that his mercies endure for euer, he raised vp from time to time (such as should deliuer them and assure them of his fauour and grace, if they would turne to him by true repentance. And these, deliuerers the Scripture calleth Iudges, because they were executers of Gods iudgements, not chosen of the people, nor by succession, but raised vp as it seemed best to God for the gouernance of his people. They were fourteene in number besides Ioshua, and gouerned from Ioshua to Saul the first king of Israel. Ioshua and these vnto the time of Saul, ruled 377 yeeres. In this booke are many notable points declared, but two especially: first the battell that the Church of God hath for the maintenance of true Religion against idolatrie and superstition, next, what great danger that common wealth is in, when as God giueth not a magistrate to retaine his people in the pureues of Religion, and his true seruice.

CHAP. I.

1 After Ioshua was dead, Iudah was constituted captaine. 6 Adoni-bezek is taken. 14 The request of Achsah. 16 The children of Keni. 28 The Canaanites are made tributaries, but not destroyed.

a By the iudgement of Vrim: read Exod.28. 30,num.27,21. 1.Sam.28,6.
b Who shalbe our captaine?

c For the tribe of Simeon had their inheritance within the tribe of Iudah, Iosh. 19,1.
|| Or, the lord of Bezek,
d This was Gods iust iudgement, as the tyrant himselfe confesseth, that as he had done, so did he receiue, Leuit. 24,19,20.

After that Ioshua was dead, the children of Israel ᵃ asked the Lord, saying, ᵇ Who shall goe vp for vs against the Canaanites, to fight first against them?

2 And the Lord sayd, Iudah shall goe vp: beholde, I haue giuen the land into his hand.

3 And Iudah saide to Simeon his ᶜ brother, Come vp with me into my lot, that we may fight against the Canaanites, and I likewise wil go with thee into thy lot: so Simeon went with him.

4 Then Iudah went vp, and the Lord deliuered the Canaanites, & the Perizzites into their handes, and they slew of them in Bezek ten thousand men.

5 And they found || Adoni-bezek in Bezek: and they fought against him, and slew the Canaanites and the Perizzites.

6 But Adoni-bezek fled, and they pursued after him, and caught him, and ᵈ cut off the thumbes of his handes and of his feete.

7 And Adoni-bezek said, Seuenty kings hauing the thumbes of their hands and of their feete cut off, gathered bread vnder my table: as I haue done, so God hath rewarded me: so they brought him to Ierusalem, and there he died.

8 (Now the children of Iudah had fought against Ierusalem, and had taken it, and smitten it with the edge of the sword, and had set the ᵉ city on fire.)

9 Afterward also the children of Iudah went downe to fight against the Canaanites, that dwelt in the mountaine, and toward the South, and in the low countrey.

10 And Iudah went against the Canaanites that dwelt in Hebron, which Hebron beforetime was called * Kirjath-arba: and they slew ᶠ Sheshai, and Ahiman, and Talmai.

11 And from thence hee went to the inhabitants of Debir, and the name of Debit in old time was Kiriath-sepher.

12 And Caleb said, Hee that smiteth Kiriath-sepher, and taketh it, euen to him will I giue Achsah my daughter to wife.

13 And Othniel the sonne of Kenaz, Calebs younger brother tooke it, to whom he gaue Achsah his daughter to wife.

14 And when she came to him, she mooued him to aske of her father a field, and she lighted off her asse, and Caleb said vnto her, ᵍ What wilt thou?

15 And

e Which was afterward built againe and possessed by the Iebusites, 2.Sam. 5,6.

Iosh.15,14.
f These three were giants, and the children of Anak.

g Reade Iosh. 15,18.

The Geneva Bible 1560

2

THE INSPIRATION OF SCRIPTURE

The purpose of this book is to help you understand the Bible. In general terms, the process of interpreting the Bible is much like interpreting other books – we read the text and we inquire about the meaning of the text. As we read, we search for clues that will direct us toward meaning. The Bible, however, stands in a class by itself, because it is the Word of God.

The Bible testifies to its divine origin.

Biblical writers claim inspiration when they use introductory formulas like 'saith the LORD,' which is found 815 times. The phrases 'Word of God' and 'Word of the LORD' occur 303 times. Claims that God 'spoke' or 'said' the words are found 440 times. Just as Jesus is God's Word in human form (Jn 1.14), the Bible is God's Word in written form.

The Bible has a message for us.

Therefore, since the Bible is a special book, God's Word, when we read the Bible we not only ask the question, 'What does this text mean?' but we ask also, 'What does this text mean to me?' And, if we are a teacher or preacher, we ask further questions, such as, 'What does this text mean to my congregation, or to my class?' Hermeneutics helps us to understand the meaning and message of the Bible.

The Meaning of 'Verbal Inspiration'

So, what do we mean by 'inspiration'?[1] What, exactly, is the meaning of 'inspiration' as it is expressed by 2 Tim. 3.16 ('all scripture is inspired')? In everyday speech, 'inspiration' may refer to a moment of insight, a flash of creativity, a timely idea, or a feeling of motivation. Almost anything that catches our attention and makes an impression on us can be described as inspired.[2] However, when we say that the Bible is inspired, we mean much more. Inspiration attributes to the Scripture a unique origin, a unique authority, and a unique power. The divine origin of Scripture ensures that every word of the Bible is true, from Genesis to Revelation.

Furthermore, we might ask, 'Is God's inspiration of Scripture an action accomplished in the past, or is inspiration an ongoing and contemporary work of Spirit?' Does inspiration relate only to the writing of Scripture, or is inspiration also related also to the process of reading and hearing Scripture today? What is the relationship of 'inspiration' to 'revelation'? In this chapter, I suggest six important theological implications of a Pentecostal approach to verbal/plenary inspiration.

1. Inspiration Implies that God is Speaking.

First and foremost, the doctrine of verbal inspiration means that the God of the Bible is the God who speaks. God desires to communicate with his people in a living relationship. Renowned theologian Karl Barth writes, 'God's Word means that 'God speaks,' and all else that is to be said about it must be regarded as exegesis and not as a restriction or negation of this statement.'[3]

God speaks so that humanity might know him, love him, serve him, and live in constant communion with him. In the beginning, God spoke openly and freely to Adam and Eve (Gen. 1.28); but after they sinned, their relationship with God was broken. They were cast out of the garden, and humanity was no longer able to

---

[1] This section is adapted from my academic article, 'A Pentecostal Perspective on Theological Implications of the Verbal Inspiration of Scripture', *Dunamis: Jurnal Teologi dan Pendidikan Kristiani* (*Dunamis: Journal of Theology and Christian Education*) 8.1 (October 2024); published in Spanish in HECHOS 6.2 (2024).

[2] J. Ben Wiles, *A Believing People* (Living What We Believe; Cleveland, TN: Church of God Adult Discipleship, 2018), p. 14.

[3] Barth, *Church Dogmatics: Volume I. The Doctrine of the Word of God*, p. 133.

enjoy perfect fellowship with God. However, God was not completely silent. In order to enact his plan of redemption, he would speak to people like Noah, Abraham, Hagar, and Rebecca (Gen. 7.1; 12.1; 16.18; 25.23). God 'spoke to Moses face to face' (Exod. 33.11). He spoke to the people of Israel 'from the midst of the fire' (Deut. 5.24). Sometimes, God would speak through dreams and visions (Gen. 15.1; 28.12; 37.5); and, at other times, he would speak through the prophets. In the Old Testament alone, it is stated more than 2000 times that God spoke. Many of God's Old Testament messages promised a future restoration of the perfect communication that had existed between God and humanity before the Fall. For example, the prophets declared that the day would come when 'the earth shall be full of the knowledge of the Lord as the waters cover the sea' (Isa. 11.9; see also Isa. 25.6-9; 65.17-24; Zech. 2.5-12; 14.9, 16).

God's plan of restoration became much clearer when God came to earth in the person of Jesus Christ. Jesus is the Word of God made flesh (Jn 1.14); therefore, in Jesus, God was speaking face to face with humanity once again. Therefore, the writer of Hebrews could declare, 'God, who at various times and in various ways spoke in time past to the fathers by the prophets, has in these last days spoken to us by His Son' (Heb. 1.1-2). In Jesus Christ, the Word of God was revealed clearly, openly, freely, and fully.

At the end of his earthly ministry, Jesus ascended back to heaven; but Jesus continues to speak to humanity from heaven through the Spirit (Heb. 12.25). The Holy Spirit speaks through dreams, visions, and other revelatory gifts of the Spirit (Acts 2.17; 1 Cor. 12.7-11). Pentecostals insist that God speaks today and that what God says through the gifts of the Spirit will always be consistent with what God says in the Scripture. The revelatory gifts did not cease with the death of the apostles, because the death of the apostles did not bring about the death of the Holy Spirit! Pentecostals would argue that God also speaks through faithful testimonies, through sound teaching, and through music (Acts 4.31; 15.35; Rom. 12.7; Eph. 5.18-20; 1 Thess. 2.13; 2 Tim. 4.2; Rev. 6.9.[4] God communicates through anointed preachers 'who have spoken the word

---

[4] French L. Arrington, *Exploring the Declaration of Faith* (Cleveland, TN: Pathway Press, 2003), p. 20.

of God' to us (Heb. 13.7). Also, God continues to speak today through the Old Testament (Heb. 12.5).

God is speaking to humanity, but humans only 'know in part' (1 Cor. 12.9). 'For now we see in a mirror, dimly,' but when Christ returns, we will see him 'face to face' (1 Cor. 12.10-12). When Jesus returns, he will restore the perfect conditions of the Garden of Eden; and 'God himself will be with' us (Rev. 21.3). Until then, however, God has provided three primary means of speaking to humanity. First, as mentioned above, he speaks directly through the Holy Spirit; and second, he speaks through other members of the Body of Christ.

There is still a third way that God speaks, and that is through his written Word, the Holy Scriptures. Throughout Old Testament times, whenever God spoke through his prophets, he would move upon them to record his words in writing. For example, after the Lord spoke his commandments to Israel from Mt. Sinai, 'Moses wrote all the words of the Lord' (Exod. 24.4). Later, the prophet Jeremiah ministered as a preacher for forty years; but one day, the Lord told him, 'Take a scroll of a book and write on it all the words that I have spoken to you' (Jer. 36.2). Similarly, the Lord commanded the prophet Habakkuk, 'Write the vision and make it plain on tablets' (Hab. 2.2; see also 1 Chron. 28.19; Isa. 38.9; Jn 5.46-47).

The inspired writings of Moses, the prophets, and other people were collected to form the Old Testament. The Old Testament was the Bible that Jesus read, studied, and taught. Furthermore, it was the Bible of the early church for many years. About 20 years after Pentecost, the apostles were led of the Spirit to begin writing the four gospels and the other books of the New Testament, a process that required about 45 years. Finally, the books of the Old Testament and the New Testament were gathered together and organized into one sacred book that Christians call 'The Holy Bible.'

The collecting and merging of the 66 books into the Bible was a huge step forward for God's people. For the first time, the authoritative writings of the prophets and apostles were available in one sacred book. However, very few Bibles were available, because each copy was handwritten on parchment and because making a copy of the Scriptures was time-consuming and expensive. Therefore, until the invention of the printing press (around 1450), the Bible was accessible only to scholars and church leaders, while ordinary Christians heard the Word of God only when the Scriptures were read in the churches. The printing press made the Bible more affordable; and soon after its invention, the Bible was translated into many different languages, including German, Italian, French, Spanish, and English.

The doctrine of the Bible as the speech of God leads to the necessary corollary that Scripture is 'subject' not an 'object.' In modern biblical studies, the scholar functions as the subject; and the Bible is the object of study. Scripture is studied 'objectively,' like any other text. The text is poked, prodded, dissected, and analyzed, just like the frog in biology class or the meteorite at the Arecibo Science Museum. Approaching the Bible as subject, however, requires the 'reader' to become a 'hearer.'

2. Inspiration Implies that God Utilizes People.

Pentecostals understand that the Holy Spirit uses people to fulfill God's work in the world, and one aspect of that work was the creation of Scripture. Christians today able to acquire and to read the Bible in their own languages. The common availability of the Bible is due to the work of Spirit-led prophets, apostles, scribes, and translators. The inspiration of Scripture does not mean that the Bible came down from heaven on a silver platter, red-letter edition, thumb-indexed, and bound in genuine leather. Instead, the Bible was produced through a lengthy, painstaking process. In a few cases, God gave the exact words that were to be written down (Exod. 34.1). More often, however, there were at least six steps involved in producing the Scriptures.

First, God revealed his Word to the prophets through dreams, visions, the Word of the Lord, or through other means. Revelation, however, is only the first step in the process that leads to the writing of Scripture. As Herman Bavinck points out, 'Revelation and inspiration are distinct ... [they] have to be distinguished.'[5]

Second, the prophet who received the revelation from God would often preach or teach the message to God's people.

---

[5] Herman Bavinck, *Reformed Dogmatics* (trans. John Vriend; 4 vols.; Grand Rapids, MI: Baker Academic, 2003), I, p. 426.

Third, the Holy Spirit would motivate the prophets and scribes to write down God's revelation. As French Arrington explains, 'Revelation is an act that makes the truth known. Inspiration preserves the truth revealed through revelation.'[6] The Old Testament was written in Hebrew and Aramaic, and the New Testament was written in Greek. The gospel writers wrote from their experience as eyewitnesses to the ministry of Jesus (Jn 21.24; 1 Pet. 1.16); and they recorded the words of Jesus, which they had heard with their own ears. Luke reported in the book of Acts the sermons of Peter, Stephen, and Paul.

Biblical writers sometimes conducted research, incorporating oral traditions and material from other written documents.[7] A Pentecostal writer explains: 'The Spirit did not use these writers as machines but employed their personal qualities. He ... enabled them to use traditions, documents and history ....'[8] For example, the Old Testament mentions at least thirteen non-biblical documents that were consulted by the biblical writers, including the Book of Jasher (Josh. 10.13), the Acts of Solomon (1 Kgs 11.41), the Prophecy of Ahijah (2 Chron. 9.29); the Sayings of Hozai (2 Chron. 33.19), and the Book of the Wars of the Lord (Num. 21.14).

At the beginning of Luke's Gospel, he explains his procedure for researching and writing his two-volume work (Luke–Acts). I would draw your attention to four important elements of Luke's introduction. First, he states that the gospel of Jesus was 'handed down' (*paradidosan*, παρέδοσαν) to him. This means he did not start with a blank slate. Before he wrote the first word, he already knew the basic facts of the gospel. Second, his information was given to him by 'eyewitnesses' (*autoptai*, αὐτόπται), that is, by the apostles of Jesus and by other disciples of Jesus who were interviewed by Luke. Third, Luke declares that he 'carefully investigated' (*parekolouthekoti*, παρηκολουθηκότι) the details of the gospel story. Many fictional accounts of Jesus' life were circulating at that time, and Luke was careful to separate fact from fiction. Luke wants his reader Theophilus to know the 'certainty' (*asphaleian*, ἀσφάλειαν) of the truths that he had been taught. Luke's process of research, discernment, and

---

[6] Arrington, *Exploring the Declaration of Faith*, p. 15.
[7] Conn, *The Bible: Book of Books*, pp. 55-56.
[8] *Church of God Evangel* (July 17, 1943), p. 3.

prayer was aimed at producing a gospel that was TRUE in every point. The doctrine of inspiration suggests that the Holy Spirit guided Luke's research and his writing of the Gospel.

When the prophets and apostles put their messages into written form, they were not always instructed to include everything that God had shown them. Thus, the inspiration of Scripture also means that the Spirit guided the writers in their selection of material. The Bible tells us that Solomon knew three thousand proverbs (1 Kgs 4.32); yet the Scriptures include only eight hundred out of those three thousand. He also knew more than one thousand songs, but only two of them are found in the Bible (Psalms 72 and 127). The process of selectivity is described in the verse that says Solomon 'pondered and sought out ... many proverbs' (Eccl. 12.9). In Solomon's time, all the peoples of the near east collected and recited proverbs—we have thousands of examples from Mesopotamia and Egypt. Solomon, therefore, would have heard these proverbs; and he even 'sought' them out. After seeking out many proverbs, he then 'pondered' (*azan*, אזן) them, which means he evaluated their truthfulness. A Pentecostal doctrine of inspiration would imply that when Solomon sat down to write the book of Proverbs, the Spirit gave him the wisdom to choose only the ones that contained truths vital for the Kingdom of God. Proverbs chapters 30 and 31 contain examples of sayings that Solomon had 'sought out.' Although they were written by Agur (Prov. 30.1) and by Lemuel (Prov. 31.1), not by Solomon himself, the Spirit guided Solomon to include these non-Israelite proverbs because they contained truth. It is possible, as well, that Solomon modified these two chapters so that they conformed to the wisdom that had been given to him by God.

Other examples of selectivity can be found in the New Testament. John heard the words of the seven thunders; and he says, 'I was about to write; but I heard a voice from heaven saying to me, "Seal up the things which the seven thunders uttered, and do not write them"' (Rev. 10.4). Also, the Apostle Paul told us that he was 'caught up into Paradise and heard inexpressible words, which it is not lawful for a man to utter' (2 Cor. 12.4). Furthermore, the Apostle John declared that he wrote only a small portion of what could be said about Jesus. John stated, 'the world itself could not contain the books that would be written' (Jn 21.25, see also Jn 20.30).

Therefore, when we say that the Bible is the Word of God, we do not mean that the Bible contains ALL of God's Word or EVERYTHING that God has revealed to His servants. However, the Bible contains the truth that we need for 'life and godliness' (2 Pet. 1.3).

Fourth, the priests and scribes would guard the Scriptures, preserve them, and make handwritten copies generation after generation.

Fifth, the religious leaders (at first Jewish then Christian) would carefully examine the content, impact, and reception of individual writings to decide which documents should be included within the biblical canon. Pentecostals would argue that the Holy Spirit was a work in the community of faith to discern the genuineness and universal relevance of the writings.

Sixth, dedicated scholars, most of them ministers of the Gospel, would translate the Bible from its original Hebrew, Aramaic, and Greek into all the languages of the world.

3. Inspiration Implies that God is the Origin of Scripture.

The Bible is God's self-revelation, which teaches God's nature, character, and plan of redemption. It is the Word of God, written under the direction of the Holy Spirit. God moved upon the writers of Scripture in a variety of ways, but they did not explain the exact methods of inspiration. In the case of John, when the risen Lord appeared to him in a vision, John was told, 'What you see, write in a book ...' (Rev. 1.11). Apparently, John was given the freedom to use the words that seemed most appropriate to describe his vision. The Apostle Peter explains that 'no prophecy of Scripture is a matter of one's own interpretation, for no prophecy was ever made by an act of human will, but men moved by the Holy Spirit spoke from God' (2 Pet. 1.20-21 NASB). Peter's statement means that Scripture originates in the will of God, not in the 'human will.' Furthermore, the human writers were 'moved by the Holy Spirit' as they wrote the Scriptures.

Peter's comments indicate that the writing of Scripture was a divine-human cooperation, although the exact nature of inspiration remains somewhat of a mystery.[9] There were times when the Holy

---

[9] Arrington, *Exploring the Declaration of Faith*, p. 18. The 'Chicago Statement on Biblical Inerrancy' agrees; it says, 'The mode of divine inspiration remains largely a mystery to us' (Article VII).

Spirit gave to the prophets the exact words to write, such as at Mount Sinai (Exodus 20-23; cf. Rev. 14.13). At other times, as was stated earlier, the writers utilized their own vocabularies and styles to record what they had seen in a dream or vision, or to describe events that they had witnessed.[10] Therefore, the writers expressed their own personalities and wrote with their own literary styles[11] and from within their own cultures; but, at the same time, the Holy Spirit revealed the truth to them.[12] Therefore, as Emil Brunner states, 'God himself actually speaks, using human words.'[13]

Within the pages of the Bible, we find different kinds of written material, including songs, proverbs, epistles, poetry, narratives, genealogies, census lists, parables, and more. God moved upon the writers of Scripture to record the truth in a wide variety of forms, and everything in Scripture is inspired by the Holy Spirit.

Throughout its history, the Pentecostal movement has been committed to the inspiration and authority of Holy Scripture. At no point has the inspiration of Scripture been questioned or its

---

[10] Conn, *The Bible: Book of Books*, pp. 58-59.

[11] Arrington, *Exploring the Declaration of Faith*, p. 18. Cf. the 'Chicago Statement on Biblical Inerrancy' (Article VIII).

[12] The 'Chicago Statement on Biblical Inerrancy' (Article XIII) states that inerrancy is not negated by 'biblical phenomena such as a lack of modern technical precision, irregularities of grammar or spelling, observational descriptions of nature, the reporting of falsehoods, the use of hyperbole and round numbers, the topical arrangement of material, variant selections of material in parallel accounts, or the use of free citations.' The Exposition of the statement goes on to include the following disclaimer.

> Differences between literary conventions in Bible times and in ours must also be observed: since, for instance, non-chronological narration and imprecise citation were conventional and acceptable and violated no expectations in those days, we must not regard these things as faults when we find them in Bible writers. When total precision of a particular kind was not expected nor aimed at, it is no error not to have achieved it. Scripture is inerrant, not in the sense of being absolutely precise by modern standards, but in the sense of making good its claims and achieving that measure of focused truth at which its authors aimed. The truthfulness of Scripture is not negated by the appearance in it of irregularities of grammar or spelling, phenomenal descriptions of nature, reports of false statements (e.g., the lies of Satan), or seeming discrepancies between one passage and another.

[13] Brunner, *The Christian Doctrine of God*, p. 22. Barth agrees, stating that 'the biblical word of man is [God's] own Word' (*Church Dogmatics: Volume I. The Doctrine of the Word of God*, p. 110). Using a different phrase, Barth declares that Scripture is 'the Word of God and the word of man' (p. 265).

importance diminished. For example, the authority of Holy Scripture was the first doctrinal statement adopted by the Church of God. At the organizational meeting of the group that would become the Church of God, Richard Spurling gave an invitation for membership to those who were willing to take the New Testament as their 'only rule of faith and practice' (Aug. 19, 1886). Then, the first publication of the Church of God teachings in the *Evangel* (Aug. 15, 1910) began with the statement, 'The Church of God stands for the whole Bible rightly divided.' This statement on the Bible, along with a list of other teachings, was adopted by the 1911 General Assembly of the Church of God.[14] Thirty-seven years later (1948), the Church of God adopted their Declaration of Faith, which includes the statement, 'We believe in the verbal inspiration of the Bible.'[15]

4. Inspiration Implies that Scripture is Alive and Life-giving.

Because of inspiration, the Bible is more than letters on a page; 'it is a living book' that gives and sustains life.[16] Thus, 'The Word of God is primarily spiritual.'[17] The English word 'inspire' is a combination of the Latin words 'in' and 'spirare'—meaning 'the act of breathing into any thing.'[18] Thus, to be 'inspired' means to be breathed into by God. The *Middle English Dictionary* defines inspiration as 'filled with divine spirit or power.' The word 'inspiration' occurs in the Bible only in 2 Tim. 3.16. The Greek word translated 'inspired' is *theopneustos* (θεόπνευστος), which means 'God-

---

[14] *The Evening Light and Church of God Evangel* (Aug. 15, 1910), p. 3; and *Minutes of the Sixth Annual Assembly of the Churches of God Held at Cleveland, Tennessee, January 3-8, 1911* (Cleveland, TN: Church of God Publishing House, 1911), pp. 6-7.

[15] Other Pentecostal denominations state similar positions. The Assemblies of God uses the phrase 'verbally inspired of God.' The Church of God in Christ states their belief in 'full inspiration,' and the Church of Pentecost prefers the term, 'divine inspiration.' The Church of God of Prophecy believes that Scripture is 'inspired, inerrant, and infallible.' Similarly, the Elim Pentecostal Church states, 'We believe the Bible, as originally given, to be without error, the fully inspired and infallible Word of God.' The Foursquare Church uses the terms 'inspired' and 'inbreathed by the Holy Spirit.' The International Pentecostal Holiness Church declares the Bible 'to be the inspired, inerrant, and authoritative Word of God.' These statements are available on the denominational websites.

[16] Conn, *The Bible: Book of Books*, pp. 39-40.

[17] Barth, *Church Dogmatics: Volume I. The Doctrine of the Word of God*, p. 135.

[18] Noah Webster, *An American Dictionary of the English Language,* https://webstersdictionary1828.com.

breathing.'[19] Pentecostal New Testament scholar John Poirier has shown that the word *theopneustos* was used in ancient times to mean 'life-giving,' or 'having divine qualities' (e.g. *Sibylline Oracles* 5.308-311).[20] This meaning of *theopneustos* is consistent with the context of 2 Tim. 3.16, where Paul declares the life-giving power of Scripture for Timothy. The life-giving breathing of God can be illustrated by Gen. 2.7, where we read that God breathed into Adam. The Scripture says, 'Then the Lord God formed man of dust from the ground, and breathed into his nostrils the breath of life; and man became a living being' (Gen. 2.7 NASB). Just as the breath of God created life in Adam, the breath of God in the Scriptures creates life in all who receive the Word of God. Accordingly, John Poirier states, 'If we consider what the image of 'divine breathing' signifies in Scripture, the answer is clear and obvious: the *giving of life*.'[21]

The life-giving power of God's Word was recognized in the Old Testament by Moses, who wrote that 'man shall not live by bread alone; but man lives by every word that proceeds from the mouth of the Lord' (Deut. 8.3). Therefore, Scripture itself is likened to food: 'desire the sincere milk of the word, that ye may grow thereby' (1 Pet. 2.2; also Heb. 5.12-14). The nourishing qualities of the Word are also illustrated in God's command to Ezekiel to devour the Scriptures (Ezek. 2.8-3.4). The same command was given to John (Rev. 10.9). The living quality of the Word of God was perfectly embodied in Jesus Christ, and he also spoke God's living Word. He

---

[19] Hermann Cremer, *Biblisch-theologisches Wörterbuch der neutestamentlichen Gräcität* (Gotha: Friedrich Andreas Perthes, 1866), insists that *theopneustos* has an active sense; that is, Scripture imparts the Spirit. For Cremer, Scripture is 'God-breathing' rather than 'God-breathed.' The translation of *theopneustos* as 'inspired by God' is derived from the fourth-century Latin translation of St. Jerome and today is consistently defined by the lexicons as 'inspired.' See *The Theological Dictionary of the New Testament*, VI, p. 455; *The Brill Dictionary of Ancient Greek*; *A Greek-English Lexicon* (BDAG), pp. 449-50; Louw-Nida, *Greek-English Lexicon*, I, p. 417; Liddell-Scott, *Greek-English Lexicon*, p. 791; and *Exegetical Dictionary of the New Testament*, II, p. 140.

[20] John C. Poirier, *The Invention of the Inspired Text: Philological Windows on the Theopneustia of Scripture* (The Library of New Testament Studies; New York: T&T Clark, 2021).

[21] John C. Poirier, 'Is 'All Scripture … Inspired'?: The Meaning of θεόπνευστος in 2 Timothy 3.16' (Paper presented at the 39th Annual Meeting of the Society for Pentecostal Studies; Seattle, WA; March 2013), p. 3 (emphasis original).

declared, 'The words that I speak to you are spirit, and they are life' (Jn 6.63). Furthermore, the living nature of God's Word is affirmed in the book of Hebrews: 'For the word of God is living and powerful, and sharper than any two-edged sword, piercing even to the division of soul and spirit, and of joints and marrow, and is a discerner of the thoughts and intents of the heart' (Heb. 4.12). The Word of God is 'living;' it is 'powerful;' and it 'is a discerner' of our innermost thoughts and desires. According to the Apostle Paul, the written Scripture is creative and life-giving because it is infused with the Spirit—'for the letter kills, but the Spirit gives life' (2 Cor. 3.6).

5. Inspiration Implies that Scripture Brings Salvation.
Because the Scripture is alive with the Spirit, it transforms everyone who will hear its message. The Apostle Paul writes the following to Timothy.

> from childhood you have known the Holy Scriptures, which are able to give you the wisdom that leads to salvation through faith which is in Christ Jesus. All Scripture is inspired by God and is profitable for teaching, for reproof, for correction, for training in righteousness; that the minister of God may be qualified, equipped for every good work. I charge you therefore ... Preach the word! (2 Timothy 3.15-4.2)

Paul's statement to Timothy indicates seven overall truths about the inspiration of Holy Scripture.

First, the inspiration of Scripture means that its ultimate purpose is to lead us to salvation in Christ.

God did not give the Scriptures for purposes of entertainment or to teach ancient history. Poirier writes, 'the description of Scripture as 'God-breathing' denotes that it has a life-giving aspect. The question naturally follows: In what sense might Scripture have a life-giving aspect? The answer is simple: Scripture contains the life-giving gospel.'[22] The Scriptures touch the heart, move the conscience, and convince the mind—they are the 'power of God unto salvation' (Rom. 1.16). Barth observes that the Bible 'does not say how we are

---

[22] Poirier, 'Is 'All Scripture ... Inspired'?, p. 5.

to find our way to [God], but how God has sought and found the way to us.'[23]

Second, inspiration is the quality of 'All Scripture.'

The entire phrase 'verbal inspiration' means that every word in the Bible, from the beginning of Genesis to the end of Revelation, is inspired by the Spirit.[24] Therefore, Pentecostals, such as the Church of God, have stated from early days that they stand 'for the whole Bible rightly divided.' The term 'verbal' signifies the words of the Bible, not just the thoughts or ideas. Verbal inspiration is strongly implied by God's command that no one should add to Scripture or take away from it. God said to Israel, 'You shall not add to the word which I am commanding you, nor take away from it' (Deut. 4.2 NASB, see also Rev. 22.18-19). Verbal inspiration means that readers are not free to pick and choose which parts of the Bible they will accept and believe. Even the most obscure stories and lengthy genealogies have teaching value.

Third, the inspiration of Scripture is a present, abiding quality. Inspiration is normally defined in connection to the original writing process. A common view of Fundamentalists and other Evangelicals is that inspiration concerns only the original manuscripts. For example, prominent Evangelical scholar Charles C. Ryrie writes that inspiration is 'God's superintendence of the human authors so that, using their own individual personalities, they composed and recorded … the original autographs.'[25] Ryrie's insufficient definition is based in part on the English phrase 'given by inspiration' (2 Tim. 3.16 KJV). The words 'given by' would seem to suggest God's oversight of the writing process. However, the words 'given by' are not found in the Greek text. The Greek says simply, 'All Scripture is inspired.' The mistranslation, 'given by,' is not found in the earliest English translation (Wycliffe 1382). The unwarranted addition of

---

[23] Karl Barth, *The Word of God and Theology* (trans. Amy Marga; London; New York: T&T Clark, 2011), 25. The German is 'wie er den Weg zu uns gesucht und gefunden hat'; Karl Barth, *Das Wort Gottes und die Theologie: Gesammelte Vorträge* (München: Chr. Kaiser, 1925), p. 28.

[24] 'Verbal inspiration' is first mentioned in the *Church of God Evangel* Aug. 8, 1936, p. 6.

[25] Charles C. Ryrie, *A Survey of Bible Doctrine* (Chicago: Moody Press, 1972). Ryrie's definition is problematic for other reasons as well. For example, if inspiration applies only to the original autographs, then how can we say that our Bible is inspired? We do not have any of the original autographs.

the words 'given by' was apparently introduced first by William Tyndale (1525) and was continued in the Geneva Bible (1560), the Bishop's Bible (1568), and the King James Version (1611). The mistranslation seems to be limited to English versions. Spanish, Italian, and Latin translations omit the words 'given by.' They are in agreement that the translation should read, 'All Scripture is inspired by God…'.

Therefore, Paul's point is not that the Scripture *was given* by God, but that the Scripture *is filled with the breath of God* and that it is lifegiving and salvific. Yes, the Bible is the Word of God; and according to 2 Pet. 1.21, it came through the prophets who were 'moved by the Holy Spirit' to write down the revelations that God had given to them. In describing what the Spirit did in the past, Peter explains the origin of Scripture as a work of the Holy Spirit. However, in 2 Tim. 3.16, the Apostle Paul uses the word 'inspired' to explain the Spirit's present work in Scripture, not only the Spirit's past work. Paul does not say that Scripture *was* inspired (past tense); he says that Scripture *is* inspired (present tense).[26] Even now, the Holy Spirit moves and breathes through the words of Scripture, making them dynamic, alive, and directed toward this present generation. Although the Bible was written centuries ago, it is not only God's word for the *past*, it is God's word for the *present*.[27] When the apostles quote the Scriptures, they almost always use the present tense of 'to say,' as in 'the Spirit says…' not 'the Spirit said…' (see Acts 7.48; Rom. 11.9; Gal. 4.30; Heb. 1.6; 3.7; Jas. 4.5, 6).

In agreement with Paul, early Pentecostals taught that the present inspiration of Scripture applies also to translations, that is, to the Bible that we read today.[28] Unfortunately, many definitions of 'inspiration' limit the Spirit's work of inspiration to the original Hebrew and Greek manuscripts. The fact that the apostles quoted from the Greek translation of the Old Testament indicates that Paul would consider translations to be infused with the Spirit just like

---

[26] The sentence lacks a verb, which is a common construction in the Greek present tense of *eimi* (εἰμι).

[27] Cf. Barth, *Church Dogmatics: Volume I. The Doctrine of the Word of God*, p. 111.

[28] See *The Book of Doctrines: Issued in the Interest of the Church of God* (Cleveland, TN: Church of God Publishing House, 1922), pp. 6-7, where the trustworthiness of translations is affirmed by the Church of God. The book's readers are advised to consult the article on the Bible in the *Encyclopedia Britannica*.

the original Hebrew and Greek. Although translations may appear imperfect, the Holy Spirit uses contemporary translations to reveal the truth. This is possible because the Holy Spirit is the Spirit of truth. Of course, Pentecostals affirm that Bible translations should adhere as closely as possible to the meaning of the original Hebrew and Greek Scriptures and that interpretations of Scripture must be based on the Hebrew and Greek texts.

Fourth, the inspiration of Scripture means that it has a vital role in Christian discipleship.

To reiterate a point we made earlier, Paul says that Scripture is useful for 'doctrine' (*didaskalian*, διδασκαλίαν); that is, what to believe. Scripture teaches doctrine related to God, humanity, sin, salvation, sanctification, the Holy Spirit, divine healing, and the return of Jesus. Also, Paul says that Scripture gives 'reproof,' which is to show someone where they have gone wrong; and Scripture offers 'correction,' which is to set a person on the right path. Furthermore, Scripture provides 'Training in righteousness,' which is to give instruction in the proper way of living the Christian life. Thus, according to Paul, the Holy Scriptures address the three aspects of effective Christian discipleship. 1. Knowing—Beliefs and attitudes, 2. Being—Affections and character, and 3. Doing—Practices and behaviors. As the primary source for discipleship, the Scriptures lead to spiritual growth, moral and ethical formation, sanctification, and a deepening of one's relationship with God.

Fifth, the inspiration of Scripture means that it is part of the equipping of ministers.

Paul reminds Timothy that the Scriptures are an important aspect of ministry. The minister may be a gifted leader, talented, intelligent, a great speaker, and an efficient administrator; but it is the Scriptures that make the minister qualified and well-equipped to preach, teach, lead, and make disciples.

Sixth, the inspiration of Holy Scripture means that its message is missional.

Thus, Paul says to Timothy, 'preach the Word' (4.2) Paul insists that the message of Scripture should form the content of Christian preaching. Paul knew that false teachers would arise who would twist the Scriptures, conform to ungodly culture, and attract many followers. To those who are deceived, the truth is relative, and the straightforward meaning of the Scripture is rejected. However, only the preaching of the unadulterated Word of God will produce salvation and spiritual fruit.

The missional message of Scripture flows out of its universal relevance. Although the Old Testament is addressed specifically to the Hebrew people, it is God's Word to all people, everywhere, and in every time period. Israel was called by God to be a 'light to the nations' and to bring blessing and salvation to all people (Gen. 12.3; Isa. 2.3; 49.6; Ps. 67.2; 96.1-13), and Israel's light continues to shine by means of the Scriptures. Similarly, many of the New Testament books were written to specific churches or individuals. The book of Acts was written to a man named Theophilus, and the book of Philippians was written to the church at Philippi; nevertheless, because these books are inspired apostolic writings, they are authoritative for all churches and for all believers. The universal authority of Scripture is captured in the theological term 'canon,' which means 'rule' or 'standard' (Gal. 6.16, Greek *kanon*, κανών). Therefore, when we say that the book of James is canonical, we mean that it is accepted as part of the Christian Bible and that it is authoritative as a rule and standard for the church.[29]

Seventh, the inspiration of Holy Scripture applies to both Old and New Testaments.

When Paul wrote to Timothy, the New Testament did not exist; therefore, his statement about the inspiration of Scripture applies to the Old Testament books. However, the writings of the apostles were later recognized as Scripture. Like the prophets of the Old Testament, the apostles spoke with divine authority. Therefore, the Apostle Peter classified Paul's epistles as Scripture. Peter states,

> as also our beloved brother Paul, according to the wisdom given to him, has written to you, as also in all his epistles, speaking in them of these things, in which are some things hard to understand, which untaught and unstable people twist to their own destruction, as they do also the rest of the Scriptures (2 Pet. 3.15-16).

Here, Peter states that Paul wrote his epistles 'according to the wisdom given to him,' which indicates that God, through the Holy

---

[29] Conn, *The Bible: Book of Books*, p. 73.

Spirit, gave Paul the wisdom necessary to write the epistles. Furthermore, the writings of Paul are classified as Scripture, inasmuch as they are compared to 'the rest of the Scriptures.' The word 'rest' (Greek *loipos*, λοιπός) means 'the other,'[30] 'pertaining to the part of a whole,'[31] 'the rest of any number or class under consideration.'[32] Therefore, Paul's writings are Scripture, in the same category as the 'other Scriptures,' which would include the Old Testament and the Gospels.

6. Inspiration Implies that the Scripture and the Holy Spirit Work as One.

Pentecostals affirm strongly that there is no conflict between the Word and the Spirit. God's Word is truth (Jn 17.17), and the Holy Spirit is the 'Spirit of truth,' who guides us 'into all truth' (Jn 14.17; 16.13). God the Father, God the Son, and God the Holy Spirit have eternally existed as One God, the personification of truth. In the beginning, the Spirit was hovering over the waters; and God spoke the Word, 'Let there be light, and there was light' (Gen. 1.2-3). By God's Word, all things were created (Heb. 11.3); yet, the psalmist says to God, 'You send forth Your Spirit, they are created' (Ps. 104.30). God's Word and God's Spirit always work in unison to accomplish God's purposes on earth. Jesus is the Word of God, but He was anointed by the Holy Spirit (Lk. 4.18). The Holy Spirit anointed the writers of Scripture; and the Holy Spirit presently inspires the Scriptures, making them alive and powerful. Furthermore, the same Spirit that 'moved' upon the writers of Scripture also moves upon the readers and hearers of Scripture today. The Spirit 'teaches' us the things of God (1 Cor. 2.13-14) and removes the 'veil' that hinders us from receiving the truth of Scripture (2 Cor. 3.8-17).

---

[30] Frederick W. Danker, Walter Bauer, and William Arndt, *A Greek-English Lexicon of the New Testament and Other Early Christian Literature* (Chicago: University of Chicago Press, 3rd edn, 2000), p. 602.

[31] J.P. Louw and Eugene Albert Nida, *Greek-English Lexicon of the New Testament: Based on Semantic Domains* (2 vols.; New York: United Bible Societies, 2nd edn, 1989), I, p. 613.

[32] Joseph Henry Thayer, *A Greek-English Lexicon of the New Testament: Being Grimm's Wilke's Clavis Novi Testamenti* (New York: Harper & Brothers, 1889), p. 382. Cf. Frederick W. Danker and Kathryn Krug, *The Concise Greek–English Lexicon of the New Testament* (Chicago: The University of Chicago Press, 2009), p. 218, 'being part of a class in addition to the entity or entities just mentioned.'

Responding to the Inspired Word of God

Karl Barth asserts that the Bible is unique. He writes, 'Of no other word can it be said that this word has decisively the power of truth.'[33] Pentecostals agree with Barth's assessment, and because of the Bible's unique origin, unique authority, and unique power, it deserves a unique response from its readers.

First, we must spend quality time reading, studying, and meditating in the Word.

Second, we must receive God's Word with faith. As we receive the Word by faith, we must allow it to discern the 'thoughts and intents' of our hearts. It is easy for us to point the finger at everyone else, but God gives us his Word so that OUR hearts may be transformed into the likeness of Jesus Christ.

Third, we must follow through with obedience to God's Word: 'But be doers of the word, and not hearers only, deceiving yourselves' (Jas. 1.22).

Fourth, we must share the Word of God with others. As we study the Scriptures and then teach them to others, God will work in the lives of people. Through his Word, he will move people to repentance (Acts 2.37-38; Rom. 1.16). Through his Word, he will sanctify and purify people's hearts (Jn 17.17). Through his Word, God will heal the sick (Ps. 107.20). Through hearing God's inspired Word, the congregation will grow in faith (Rom. 10.17).

For Review and Study

1. What makes the Bible a special book?
2. How does inspiration represent the speech of God?
3. In what ways did God use people in the writing of Scripture?
4. Explain the concept of selectivity in the writing of Scripture.
5. What was God's role in the writing of Scripture?
6. Describe the life-giving nature of Scripture.
7. How does the Bible lead a person to salvation?
8. Discuss the cooperation between the Word and the Spirit.

---

[33] Barth, *Church Dogmatics: Volume I. The Doctrine of the Word of God*, p. 136.

3

THE VALUE OF HERMENEUTICS

What is biblical hermeneutics?

The word 'hermeneutics' is an academic term that means 'interpretation'. You may not realize it, but you have been involved in hermeneutics virtually all of your life. Soon after you were born, you learned the meaning of your mother's smile. Later, you learned the meaning of language. You listened, and you interpreted. Then, you began to read; and with every sentence that you read, you practiced hermeneutics.

Biblical hermeneutics is the act of interpreting Scripture. The word 'hermeneutics' comes from the Greek verb *hermeneuo*, which means 'to explain, to interpret.' Therefore, biblical hermeneutics teaches the most effective methods and rules for interpreting and explaining the message of the Bible.

For sake of discussion, we can divide the process of biblical study into three parts: (1) exegesis, which reveals what the Scripture *says*; (2) interpretation, which reveals what the Scripture *means*; and (3) application, which reveals the *significance* of Scripture for the present context. In theory, we may talk about exegesis, interpretation, and application as separate activities; but, in practice, the three elements often overlap and intersect. Furthermore, as we engage in reading and hearing the Scriptures, the three activities may appear in cyclical, rather than linear, fashion. That is, as we study the Bible, our thoughts may move back-and-forth between the text, our context, and what we sense that God is saying to us at that moment.

The Bible is written communication between God and humanity, and communication operates according to certain rules. On a day-by-day basis, we rarely think about those rules, because frequent communication is a natural human activity. However, learning the rules of communication for biblical study will help us to understand the Bible more effectively.

Why should we study hermeneutics?

As Christians, we are encouraged to search God's Word (Acts 17.11), to desire it (1 Pet. 2.2), and to keep it (1 Jn 2.5). As we stated earlier, the Bible teaches us what we should believe, what kind of people we should be, and how we should live (2 Tim. 3.16). Therefore, it is of supreme importance that we understand the Bible, 'rightly dividing the word of truth' (2 Tim. 2.15). Our calling may also involve sharing the Scriptures with other people. The ministries of teaching and preaching carry with them great responsibilities. Interpretations of Scripture should not be merely arbitrary, but they should be informed decisions made with the guidance of the Holy Spirit.

The need for guidelines in our study

We need guidance in understanding and explaining the Bible. We must be careful to handle the Word of God carefully. The Apostle Peter writes about the Scripture saying, 'as also in all his epistles, speaking in them of these things, in which are some things hard to understand, which untaught and unstable people twist to their own destruction, as they do also the rest of the Scriptures' (2 Pet. 3.16). In this text he tells us two things: (1) There are many things in the Scripture that are hard to understand, and (2) Some interpreters will *twist* the Scriptures, thus leading to their own destruction.

We must not twist the Scripture

To twist the Scripture is to distort its meaning, bending it and forcing it to mean what we want it to mean. Similarly, the Apostle Paul warns us against the misuse of the Word of God, when he says 'For we are not like many who *corrupt* the Word of God ...' (2 Cor. 2.17). To *corrupt* the Word is to use it for personal gain, to interpret it so that it benefits our own aims and purposes rather than the aims and purposes of God. We are also given a warning not to handle the 'Word of God *deceitfully*' (2 Cor. 4.2). That is, we must not distort it or attempt to change its meaning. Furthermore, Paul encourages Timothy to 'rightly divide' the Word of God (2 Tim. 2.15). The words 'rightly divide' mean to cut straight, as a carpenter cuts a straight board, or a tentmaker cuts a straight piece of canvas. Paul contrasts the one who cuts straight the Word of God to the false teachers who lead people astray with their detours and worthless talk (2 Tim. 2.16-18).

The devil himself uses Scripture, but he twists it and misuses it for his own evil purposes. When Jesus was in the wilderness for forty days, Satan came to him and tempted him. He said to Jesus, 'If You are the Son of God, throw Yourself down. For it is written: he shall give his angels charge over you, and, In their hands they shall bear you up, Lest you dash your foot against a stone' (Mt. 4.6). Jesus, knowing that Satan is the father of lies, replied with the correct interpretation of Scripture. He answered, 'It is written again, You shall not tempt the LORD your God' (Mt. 4.7).

Hermeneutics enhances our understanding

Peter also tells us that there are many things in the Scripture that are hard to understand. It seems clear that some kind of guidelines are needed for the interpretation of Scripture. The rules of hermeneutics help us to understand the Bible. Hermeneutics teaches us how to avoid incorrect and dangerous interpretations. Hermeneutics provides rules and guidelines so that we may interpret the Bible correctly.

The value of hermeneutics

Have you ever been misunderstood? Have you ever misunderstood someone else? Of course you have. Interpretation is an everyday process. Every day we attempt to understand spoken or written ideas. And we all know how easily misunderstandings creep into our communication, resulting in a lack of communication. The following topics illustrate the value of hermeneutics for improving our understanding of the Bible.

Understanding the languages of the Bible

If we find it so easy to misunderstand one another under the best of circumstances, then it should come as no surprise that understanding the Bible is often difficult. Interpretation of the Bible is complicated by several factors. First of all, we must recognize the original languages of the Bible. The Bible was originally written in Hebrew, Aramaic, and Greek. These languages spanned a period of 1500 years. These ancient languages used terminology and symbolism that is very foreign to the modern world. It is true that we have translations, but translations do not solve every difficulty. Each translation involves interpretation because languages cannot be translated mechanically, word for word.

Understanding the culture of biblical times

Secondly, we must understand the culture of biblical times. There is a culture gap of 4000 years from Adam to Jesus. Then, there is another 2000-year gap from Jesus to our time. This culture gap relates to almost every part of life. Over the centuries, almost every category of culture has seen radical changes, including daily habits, political structures, religious customs, family relationships, educational patterns, work environments, and social traditions. It has been a long time since we took a daily walk to the well in order to bring home our drinking water. We no longer offer sacrifices of lambs, goats, or bulls. Very few people work the soil with their bare hands. We think it extremely archaic, even oppressive, that women would be required to wear veils over their faces or for a father to decide whom his daughter should marry. But these are the kinds of customs that we read about in the Bible.

Understanding important geographical references

Thirdly, we must understand geographical and political references in Scripture. The geography of the Bible reaches from Mesopotamia to Palestine to Egypt to Greece and to Rome. Most of us have never heard the names of the biblical kings and generals. They are ancient history. Could the person on the street today tell you anything about Sennacharib, Darius, or Cyrus the Great? Many of the biblical cities are completely unknown today. The nations and peoples that we find in Scripture have long been forgotten, people such as the Hittites, the Amalekites, the Philistines, the Moabites, the Babylonians, and the Medes and the Persians.

Understanding the religious tradition of biblical times

The Gospels tell us that Jesus was often misunderstood. On the basis of their tradition, the Pharisees and the Sadducees were continually opposing the message of Jesus. In Mk 12.18-24, the Sadducees confronted him regarding the resurrection of the dead. They quoted Scriptures to Jesus, reminding him of the law that required a man to marry his brother's widow. They wanted Jesus to explain whose wife she would be in the resurrection. Jesus replied, 'Are you not therefore mistaken, because you do not know the Scriptures nor the power of God?' The Sadducees had certainly *read* the Scriptures, but Jesus insisted that they did not *know* the Scriptures. Furthermore, their misinterpretation of Scripture was due in part to their lack of faith in the power of God.

On another occasion, when Jesus was confronted by the scribes, he asked them the question, 'Have you not read' the Scripture? (Mt. 12:3-7) Of course, they had read the Scriptures. They had read them over and over and over. They had counted every word, and they had observed the position of every dot. Yet, Jesus accused them of misunderstanding the Scripture when he said, ' if you had known what this means.' So, they had read without understanding. They had read the letters, but they had not been taught by the Holy Spirit.

Perhaps their misunderstanding was due in part to an unwillingness to change their tradition. Those who hear the Word of God sometimes construct inner barriers in their own hearts. It may be that they are unwilling to hear the message. For example, in Jer. 11.6-12, The Lord is speaking to his people, but they do not listen. The Lord says, 'they do not obey, nor incline their ear . . . they refuse to hear my words' (See also Jer. 13.8-11). Instead, they preferred to worship idols. In Zech. 7.9-14, we read that Israel 'refused to hear' God's Word; they 'stopped their ears that they should not hear.' Their hearts were as hard as stone, so that they would not hear God.

On some occasions, the listener may have been willing to understand, but the message was confusing to them, possibly because it was contrary to their established beliefs or traditions. For example, when Jesus spoke of the one who had 'sent' him, his disciples did not understand that he spoke of the Heavenly Father (Jn 8.26,27). When he described himself as the door of the sheepfold, they did not understand what he meant (Jn 10.1-6). When he entered

Jerusalem riding upon a donkey, the disciples did not recognize the significance of the event. (After the resurrection, however, they did understand) When Jesus declared that he would be crucified and raised from the dead, the Gospels tell us that his disciples did not understand what he was saying (Mk 9.32; Lk. 18.31). They were expecting the Messiah to be a victor who would deliver the Jews from the oppression of the Romans and establish an earthly kingdom. If Jesus' own disciples were confused by his words, then it is no wonder that we are sometimes confused as well.

Understanding the variety of books in the Bible

The Bible sometimes appears difficult because of its diversity. Our English Bible has 66 books written over a time span of more than 1000 years. The books of the Bible stand together as a unity, but each book stands on its own. Each book of the Bible has its own distinct message and emphasis. Some Bible scholars have viewed this distinction of message and emphasis more as a contradiction. They would claim that one writer contradicts another. For example, the four Gospels present the life of Jesus from four different perspectives. We should not attempt to remove the individual aspects of each of the four Gospels, any more than we would want to view a beautiful sculpture from only one angle. Each gospel writer has his own message of Jesus, and we should celebrate each of those messages. Another example of diversity would be the approaches of Paul and James to the question of works and faith. Paul emphasizes that we are 'justified' by faith, not by works (Gal. 2.16); and James stresses the point that 'faith without works is dead' (Jas 2.20). On the other hand, we affirm that those diverse messages are complementary, not contradictory. There is an underlying unity throughout all of Scripture. This unity provides the basis for our Christian worldview and our Christian theology.

We need hermeneutics

There have always been disagreements in the interpretation of Scripture. The prophet Jeremiah's interpretations were very different from the standard interpretations of his day. Jesus departed frequently from interpretations of the scribes. Even the Apostle Peter admitted that in Paul's writings are some things 'hard to understand'

(2 Pet. 3.16). Job declared, 'I have uttered what I did not understand, things too wonderful for me, which I did not know' (Job 42.3).

For whatever reasons, understanding the Bible has been and continues to be a real challenge. That is why we need principles for Biblical interpretation – hermeneutics.

The questions of hermeneutics may be illustrated by an episode in the book of Acts. In chapter 8, we read about Philip's encounter with the Ethiopian eunuch, a court official of Candace, queen of the Ethiopians. This Ethiopian official was reading from the prophet Isaiah. Philip the evangelist asks the question, 'Do you understand what you are reading?' (v. 30) The Ethiopian replied, 'How can I, unless someone guides me?' (v. 31) He admitted that he needed help; he needed guidance. Although he understood the words, he did not understand the message. He understood what the writer Isaiah had said, but he did not understand the significance of the words. Reading the words of the Bible does not necessarily lead to an understanding of the message of the Bible. He did not realize that Isaiah could be speaking of the Messiah Jesus.

Furthermore, the Ethiopian did not understand what the text meant for his life, and neither did he realize that this prophetic text was about to change his life. The question from Philip is the same question that I ask you today, 'When you read the Bible, do you understand what you are reading?'

Transmission and translation of Scripture

Because the Bible is readily available in most any bookstore, we may not realize the long process that was necessary in bringing the Bible to us. To reiterate what was stated in the previous chapter, our Bible came to us in three steps.

The books of the Bible were written by the prophets and apostles.
Beginning with Moses and the other prophets of the Old Testament, God revealed his Word through dreams, visions, and prophetic revelations. These prophets recorded the revelations in written form on leather scrolls. Similarly, the New Testament Apostles recorded the Gospels of Jesus and the letters to the churches on scrolls made of leather and papyrus.

The books of the Bible were handed down from generation to generation.
Over the years, the scrolls were collected by God's people, who copied them by hand, generation after generation. The inspired scrolls were collected together to form the Holy Scriptures, what we now call the Bible. For many centuries, every copy of the Bible was handwritten. Only after the invention of the printing press in 1440 did the Bible became available in large numbers.

The Bible was translated into our native languages.
The books of the Bible were originally written in the Hebrew, Aramaic, and Greek languages. As the Church spread across the world, it brought in converts who spoke different languages. These new Christians could not read Hebrew, Aramaic, and Greek; therefore, the Bible had to be translated so that everyone could understand it. Sometime around AD 400, Saint Jerome translated the Scriptures into Latin. His Latin version (called the Vulgate) became the official Bible of the Roman Catholic Church. However, the Greek Orthodox Church continued to use the Greek version called the Septuagint (abbreviated LXX).

During the Protestant Reformation, the Bible was translated into several languages and became more widely available because of Johannes Gutenberg's printing press (invented in 1440). The first translation of Bible into English was done by John Wycliffe (1382), and the first English printed version was the William Tyndale Bible (1525). The earliest translation of the complete Bible into Spanish was the *Biblia del Oso*, published in 1569. It was revised in 1602 and became known as the Reina-Valera version.

The Relevance of the Old Testament

Christians often appeal to the Old Testament to support their views on important issues. Some of these issues are related to beliefs about God (doctrinal/theological issues), and some of them are related to the Christian lifestyle (moral/ethical issues). However, whenever the Old Testament is employed as a source of authority, opponents will invariably challenge the relevance of the Old Testament. They will argue that the Old Testament is outdated culturally and that it was written only for the ancient Jewish people.

Opposition to the Old Testament takes a number of different forms, including (1) moral relativism and (2) biblical misinterpretation. First, moral relativism essentially refuses to accept the moral authority of Scripture, preferring instead socially constructed morals that can change according to time and place. Second, biblical misinterpretation causes some people to discard the Old Testament. Prominent Christian leaders such as Andy Stanley have stated that even the Ten Commandments are not binding upon believers today. He writes, 'The Ten Commandments have no authority over you. None. To be clear: Thou shalt not obey the Ten Commandments.'[34] Stanley's view relegates the Ten Commandment to times long past and makes them irrelevant for Christians. A similar view is held by so-called 'progressive Christianity' and by teachers who espouse what might be called 'hyper-grace,' a doctrine that trivializes faithfulness, obedience, and holiness of life.

In this section, we will show that the Old Testament, when properly interpreted, is not outdated. Furthermore, it continues to hold significance and universal relevance for today. It offers deep insights into the nature of God, as well as moral and ethical principles that continue to guide Christian approaches to life.

1. We affirm the authority of the whole Bible.
Today's culture is divided on many moral and ethical issues, because the culture as a whole has no agreed-upon source of moral authority. The Church, however, agrees that God is the ultimate source of authority on all issues of truth and ethics. Furthermore, the Church trusts the Bible as the revealed Word of God that addresses all cultural issues either directly or indirectly.

2. We affirm the unity of the Bible.
The Old Testament and the New Testament are two parts of one story. Jesus, the Apostles, and the early Church did not refer to the books of Genesis through Malachi as the 'Old Testament' but as

---

[34] Andy Stanley, *Irresistible : Reclaiming the New That Jesus Unleashed for the World* (Grand Rapids, MI: Zondervan, 2018), p. 136. Opposition to the Old Testament is not a new phenomenon. Throughout history, several prominent leaders made the serious error of discarding the Old Testament. These include Marcion, whose views in the second century were judged to be heretical; Adolf von Harnack, a liberal 19th-century church historian; and Rudolf Bultmann, a prominent liberal New Testament scholar of the 20th century.

'Scripture,' a word found fifty-two times in the New Testament. The term 'Old Testament' is unfortunate and misleading, making the first Scriptures sound outdated and irrelevant. **Misunderstanding arises in part by the failure to distinguish between the old 'covenant' and the older Scriptures.** It is true that the old covenant enacted at Mt. Sinai (Exodus 20-24) has been revised by the new covenant, as was predicted by the prophet Jeremiah (31.31-34; Heb. 8.7-13). The new covenant was ratified by the blood of Jesus Christ (Mt. 26.28), and it is a 'better covenant' (Heb. 7.22; 8.6), making the covenant of Moses 'obsolete' (Heb. 8.13).

The Old Testament books remains valid and authoritative for two reasons. First, although there are distinctions between the old covenant and the new covenant, commonalities between the two demonstrate that the new covenant is a revision, not a complete replacement, of the old covenant. For example.

1. Both Jeremiah's prophecy and Hebrews 8 state that the two covenants have the same participants—God and God's People.

2. Also, both covenants hold the parties accountable to God's 'laws.' According to Jeremiah, the essential difference between the old and new covenants is that the old covenant wrote God's law on tables of stone, but the new covenant writes God's law on the heart and in the mind. Therefore, the law of God is present in the new covenant, and obedience is required. Jesus said, 'If you love me, keep my commandments' (Jn 14.15; see also Jn 15.10 and 1 Jn 2.3, 4; 3.22; 5.2, 3). In the new covenant, however, the knowledge of God is internalized by the Holy Spirit; and obedience is facilitated through living in the Spirit (Rom. 8.1; Gal. 5.16).

3. The writer of Hebrews adds a third point. The old covenant utilized the tabernacle and the priesthood as means of intercession, but the new covenant utilizes the heavenly tabernacle and the High Priest Jesus as means of intercession (Hebrews 9). The old tabernacle and priesthood were fulfilled in Christ.

4. The way of salvation is the same in both covenants—salvation is received by grace through faith. The characterization of the Old Testament as 'law' and the New Testament as 'grace' is incorrect. We read that 'Noah found grace in the eyes of the Lord,'

and he was saved from the flood (Gen. 6.8). The Apostle Paul cites the Old Testament example of Abraham as proof that righteousness is granted by faith (Gen. 15.6; see also Hab. 2.4 and Hebrews 11). Numerous other examples could be given, but we will just point out that the Ten Commandments (that is, 'law') were not the basis for Israel's salvation. Their deliverance from Egypt came *before* they received the commandments (Exodus 20). Their salvation came because God 'remembered his covenant with Abraham,' a covenant of grace (Exod. 2.24).

The second reason that the Old Testament is authoritative despite the institution of the new covenant is that the phrase 'old covenant' refers to the ceremonial and ritual laws that were required. Yet, the books of the Old Testament consist of much more than the ceremonial and ritual laws. For example, the book of Genesis and the first part of Exodus reveal important truths that come prior to the Sinai covenant. In fact, the greater part of the Old Testament teaches us not through laws but through stories, through songs, through prophecy, and through wisdom writings.

3. We affirm the need for good interpretation of Scripture.
The Apostle Paul writes to Timothy and says, 'Be diligent to show yourself approved unto God, a worker that is not ashamed, rightly dividing the word of truth' (2 Tim. 2.15). The Old Testament is sometimes rejected because the reader does not understand the ancient context, the cultural references, the figures of speech, or the different genres that are found there. Understanding the Old Testament requires good exegesis of the biblical text.

4. We affirm the priority of the New Testament.
In matters of interpretation, the Old Testament must be read in the light of the New Testament. The Old Testament is not inaccurate, but it is incomplete. For this reason, Jesus and the Apostles often talked about how Scriptures are 'fulfilled' in Christ. The word 'fulfilled,' however, does not mean that the Old Testament can now be discarded.

5. We affirm the Inspiration of the Old Testament.
Those who would discard the Old Testament stand in sharp contrast to Jesus and his Apostles. The New Testament itself affirms

the indispensable role of the Old Testament. The Apostle Paul, in his second letter to Timothy, writes,

> ... from childhood you have known the Holy Scriptures, which are able to give you the wisdom that leads to salvation through faith which is in Christ Jesus. All Scripture is inspired by God and is profitable for teaching, for reproof, for correction, for training in righteousness; that the minister of God may be qualified, equipped for every good work (2 Tim. 3.15-17; translation from the Greek by Dr. Lee Roy Martin).

When Paul speaks of 'the Holy Scriptures,' he is speaking about the books that we call the Old Testament. At the time Paul is writing to Timothy, the New Testament did not yet exist. Therefore, Paul's statement to Timothy indicates several key reasons that the Old Testament continues to be relevant.

1. The Old Testament is Relevant because It Points to Jesus Christ.

According to Paul, the ultimate purpose of the Old Testament is to lead us to salvation in Christ. When Paul insists that the Old Testament points to Jesus Christ, he is echoing the teaching of Jesus. After his resurrection, Jesus talked with two disciples on the road to Emmaus, and 'beginning at Moses and all the Prophets, he expounded to them in all the Scriptures the things concerning himself' (Lk. 24.27 NKJV).

2. The Old Testament is Relevant because It is the Inspired Word of God.

Paul states that 'all Scripture (OT included) is inspired.' He uses the word 'inspired' to explain the Spirit's *present* work in Scripture, not just the Spirit's past work. Even now, the Holy Spirit moves and breathes through the words of the Old Testament, making them dynamic, alive, and directed toward this present generation. Although the Bible was written centuries ago, it is not only God's word for the *past*; it is God's word for the *present*. God continues to speak to us through the Old Testament.

3. The Old Testament is Relevant because It Teaches Sound Doctrine.

The inspiration of Scripture means that it has a vital role in Christian discipleship. In terms of discipleship, Paul says that Scripture is useful for 'doctrine;' that is, what to believe. In the Old Testament we learn about God, creation, humanity, sin, salvation, sanctification, the Holy Spirit, divine healing, the last days, and many other doctrines.

In regard to cultural issues of today, the book of Genesis teaches the sovereignty of God, the role of humanity, the nature of the family, and the origin of sin. In God's original creation, all humans are equal and are created in God's image. It follows that all racism is antithetical to God's plan. In God's original creation, men and women were both given the same command to exercise 'dominion' over all creation (Gen. 1.28). It follows that abuse of women does not accord with God's plan. In God's original creation, the family consisted of a male and a female. It follows that homosexual acts and same-sex marriage do not conform to God's plan. All of these teachings from Genesis are affirmed in the New Testament.

4. The Old Testament is Relevant because It Forms Christian Character.

Also, Paul says that the Old Testament gives 'reproof,' which is to show someone where they have gone wrong; and it offers 'correction,' which is to set a person on the right path. The 'reproof' and the 'correction' that emerge from the Old Testament often challenge today's pervasive immorality. This challenge, of course, explains why many people want to set aside the Scriptures.

5. The Old Testament is Relevant because It Guides Our Morals and Behavior.

Furthermore, the Old Testament provides 'training in righteousness,' which is to give instruction in the proper way of living the Christian life. In this context, the word 'righteousness' means living in right relationship with God and with other people. Because we are born in sin, we do not know by nature how to live righteously. We must be trained in righteousness; that is, we must learn how to love God and love our neighbor.

Thus, according to Paul, the Old Testament addresses the three aspects of effective Christian discipleship. 1. Knowing—Beliefs and attitudes, 2. Being—Affections and character, and 3. Doing—Practices and behaviors. As the primary source for discipleship, the Old Testament Scriptures lead to spiritual growth, moral and ethical formation, sanctification, and a deepening of our relationship with God.

Throughout the Old Testament, we learn the importance of compassion, justice, and righteousness. For example, the command to care for the widow, orphan, and stranger (Exod. 22.22-24) underscores the responsibility to protect and support vulnerable members of society. Proverbs, a book of wisdom literature, provides practical advice for living with integrity, humility, and self-discipline.

Preparing to receive the message of the Bible

We must have a willing heart.
Distance in time and culture are not the only reasons for misunderstanding. Those who hear the Word of God sometimes construct inner barriers in their own hearts. It may be that they are unwilling to hear the message. For example, in Jer. 11.6-12, the Lord is speaking to his people, but they do not listen. The Lord says, 'they did not obey or incline their ear, but everyone followed the dictates of his evil heart' (see also Jer. 13.8-11). Instead, they preferred to worship idols. In Zech. 7.11, we read about Israel, 'But they refused to heed, shrugged their shoulders, and stopped their ears so that they could not hear.' Their hearts were as hard as stone, so that they would not hear God's Word.

We must be receptive to God's Word.
Hermeneutical rules and principles are helpful, but mastery of these rules does not guarantee that we will arrive at the correct interpretation. We require the wisdom and understanding that is given by the Holy Spirit. Whenever we approach the Scripture, either to read, to teach it, or to preach, we should begin with three actions that will prepare us to hear the Word of God: (1) We should pray that God will give us receptive hearts. Jesus said, 'My sheep hear My voice, and I know them, and they follow Me' (Jn 10.27). That is, we should ask God to open our ears to hear his Word and open our eyes to see his wonders; (2) Realizing that God is present in his Word, we must come to the study of his Word with an attitude of worship and praise; (3) We must be hungry to receive the milk and the meat

of his Word. As Peter said, 'as newborn babes, desire the pure milk of the word, that you may grow thereby' (1 Pet. 2.2).

Humility is Essential in Bible Study.
The Apostle Paul wrote these words to the church at Corinth:

> For now we see in a mirror, dimly, but then face to face. Now I know in part, but then I shall know just as I also am known. And now abide faith, hope, love, these three; but the greatest of these is love (1 Cor. 13.12-13 NKJV).

We stated earlier that we study the Bible with at least four goals in mind:
1. to improve our understanding of God (knowledge),
2. to enhance our communion to God (relationship),
3. to increase our likeness to God (discipleship),
4. to expand our effectiveness for God (ministry).

As we study Scripture, and seek to grow spiritually, we are confident in many areas of doctrine and practice. Without any doubt, we believe in the authority of Scripture. Without any doubt, we 'contend earnestly for the faith which was once for all delivered to the saints' (Jude 1.3 NKJV). However, although the essential doctrines of Scripture are clear, many passages of Scripture are difficult to understand (2 Pet. 3.16).

Undergirding all of our goals for Bible study should be a sincere desire to hear the voice of God. Knowledge, relationship, discipleship, and ministry require that we come to God and to God's Word with an attitude of openness to God, hunger for God, fear of God, and humility in the presence of God.

Therefore, the attitude of humility must permeate all of our biblical study. If we learn Greek and Hebrew, but do not have humility, our interpretations will be a dead letter, lacking in Spiritual power, for 'the letter kills, but the Spirit gives life' (2 Corinthians 3.6). Arrogance will doom our Bible study to mediocrity and irrelevance.

The Apostle Paul addresses the need for humility. He confesses that he did not possess perfect understanding. Let us look closely at what Paul is saying here. Paul is an Apostle of Jesus Christ. The Lord Jesus appeared to him in a vision, a vision that was so bright that it blinded him for three days. Then, according to Galatians

1.17-18, Paul was in Arabia for three years being taught by the Lord himself. Paul was caught up into the third heaven and saw things that he was not permitted to tell. If there was anyone in the world that knew God, it was Paul. If there was anyone in the world that new the Gospel it was Paul. If there was anyone who understood correct theology, it was Paul and yet he admitted that his knowledge was only 'in part.' He did not know everything. He did not have perfect understanding. He did not have perfect knowledge. Paul declare that someday we will stand before God, and we will know God perfectly. God will reveal everything to us, and there will be no hindrance to our understanding. But for now, we only know in part. We must maintain humility.

In 1 Corinthians 13, Paul also makes the point that whatever we do must be motivated by love. If it is not motivated by love, then it is not worth anything. Without love we can have all the gifts, but we are no more than a gong or a clanging cymbal. Without love, we are just noise makers. So, let our biblical study be motivated by love, and also let our interpretations produce love. Our biblical interpretations should reflect our love for God and our love for other people. Our interpretations should cause our hearers to love God and love their neighbor. I'm connecting this now back to the Old Testament Deuteronomy Chapter 6, 'Hear O Israel, the Lord our God the Lord is one and you shall love the Lord your God with all your heart with all your soul, with all your strength and you shall teach these commandments unto your children. You shall bind them on the post of your doors write them on the palms of your hands engraved them on your forehead you when you go out and when you come in teach them to your children when you're walking by the way so that they may learn to love the Lord.' That is why God gave us the Scripture; God gave us a Scripture to teach us how to love God and love one another. Let us read the Scriptures with humility and with the motivation of love.

For Review and Study

1. What is the origin of the name 'hermeneutics'?
2. What does biblical hermeneutics teach us?
3. Mention the three parts of biblical study.
4. 2 Pet. 3.16 tells us two things. What are these two things?

5. Peter warns us not to 'twist' the Scripture. What does he mean by the word 'twist'?
6. Explain how hermeneutics enhances our understanding of the Bible.
7. Enumerate the three languages that were originally used to write the Bible.
8. Describe the 'culture gap' between the Bible times and our time.
9. Explain ways in which the religious traditions of the Bible times might be different from our time.
10. Discuss the five reasons for the contemporary relevance of the Old Testament.
11. The Bible has a message for us. In addition to the question, 'What does this text mean?', what other questions should we ask?
12. Describe how the books of the Bible were written and handed down to us.
13. List the three actions we must do that will prepare us to hear the Word of God.
14. Discuss the role of humility in Bible study.

Hearing the Living Word of God
A prayer to precede Bible Study
—by Martin Luther

Lord God, Heavenly Father,
Govern and guide us
Through your Holy Spirit
That we hear your Word
With our whole hearts, receive it,
And become sanctified through it,
so that we may put all our trust and
hope in Jesus Christ, your Son,
be protected from all offenses and pride,
and finally be saved through your grace in Christ;
through your son, Jesus Christ our Lord.
Amen.

Allgemeines evangelisches Gesang- und Gebetbuch zum Kirchen und Hausgebrauch, Hamburg, 1846, p. 428 #1.

ρϞ

ΟΤΙΟΥΔΕΙϹΕΝΠΝΙ ΘΥ ΛΑΛΩΝ ΛΕΓΕΙ
ΑΝΑΘΕΜΑ ΙΗΝ ΚΑΙ ΟΥΔΕΙϹ ΔΥΝΑΤΑΙ
ΕΙΠΕΙΝ ΚϹ ΙΗϹ ΕΙ ΜΗ ΕΝ ΠΝΙ ΑΓΙΩ ΔΙ
ΑΙΡΕϹΕΙϹ ΔΕ ΧΑΡΙϹΜΑΤΩΝ ΕΙϹΙΝ ΤΟ
ΔΕ ΑΥΤΟ ΠΝΑ ΚΑΙ ΔΙΑΙΡΕϹΕΙϹ ΔΙΑΚΟ
ΝΙΩΝ ΕΙϹΙΝ ΚΑΙ Ο ΑΥΤΟϹ ΚϹ ΚΑΙ ΔΙ
ΑΙΡΕϹΕΙϹ ΕΝΕΡΓΗΜΑΤΩΝ ΕΙϹΙΝ ΚΑΙ
Ο ΑΥΤΟϹ ΘϹ Ο ΕΝΕΡΓΩΝ ΤΑ ΠΑΝΤΑ
ΕΝ ΠΑϹΙΝ ΕΚΑϹΤΩ ΔΕ ΔΙΔΟΤΑΙ Η ΦΑ
ΝΕΡΩϹΙϹ ΤΟΥ ΠΝϹ ΠΡΟϹ ΤΟ ϹΥΜΦΕΡΟΝ
Ω ΜΕΝ ΓΑΡ ΔΙΑ ΤΟΥ ΠΝϹ ΔΙΔΟΤΑΙ
ΛΟΓΟϹ ϹΟΦΙΑϹ ΑΛΛΩ ΔΕ ΛΟΓΟϹ
ΓΝΩϹΕΩϹ ΚΑΤΑ ΤΟ ΑΥΤΟ ΠΝΑ
ΕΤΕΡΩ ΔΕ ΠΙϹΤΙϹ ΕΝ ΤΩ ΑΥΤΩ
ΠΝΙ ΑΛΛΩ ΔΕ ΧΑΡΙϹΜΑΤΑ ΙΑΜΑΤΩΝ
ΕΝ ΤΩ ΠΝΙ ΑΛΛΩ ΔΕ ΕΝΕΡΓΗΜΑΤΑ
ΔΥΝΑΜΕΩϹ ΑΛΛΩ ΠΡΟΦΗΤΕΙΑ
ΑΛΛΩ ΔΙΑΚΡΙϹΕΙϹ ΠΝΩΝ ΕΤΕΡΩ
ΓΕΝΗ ΓΛΩϹϹΩΝ ΕΤΕΡΩ ΔΕ ΕΡΜΗΝΙΑ
ΓΛΩϹϹΩΝ ΤΑΝΤΑ ΔΕ ΠΑΝΤΑ ΕΝΕΡ
ΓΕΙ ΤΟ ΕΝ ΚΑΙ ΤΟ ΑΥΤΟ ΠΝΑ ΔΙΑΙΡΟΥΝ
ΕΚΑϹΤΩ ΚΑΘΩϹ ΒΟΥΛΕΤΑΙ ΚΑΘΑ
ΠΕΡ ΓΑΡ ΤΟ ϹΩΜΑ ΕΝ ΕϹΤΙ
ΚΑΙ ΜΕΛΗ ΠΟΛΛΑ ΕΧΕΙ ΠΑ

Greek Manuscript on papyrus from the second century (1 Cor. 12.3ff)

4

BASIC CONCEPTS IN HERMENEUTICS

This chapter introduces the basic principles necessary for the correct interpretation of the Bible. These basic principles will be expanded and explained more thoroughly in subsequent chapters.

The clarity of Scripture

The Bible is God's Word written in human words that we can understand. It is not written in a special language but in normal human language, using words, grammar, and literary standards in their straightforward meanings. In order to become better interpreters of Scripture, it is important that we learn how to become better readers. We will be able to recognize the clarity of Scripture if we follow these six guidelines.

Observe the plain meaning of the text.

The Bible is not a puzzle.

Although the Bible is a special book, we should read it naturally, and we should interpret its words as we would in ordinary daily use. God did not intend that the Bible should be a puzzle or a secret message. Parts of the Bible are difficult for us to understand because of the great distance between us and the times in which it was written, but most of the Bible is written in a form that is plain and easy to understand if we study the original setting and times.

The Bible does not contain secret, hidden messages.

When reading the Bible, we should first observe the literal, plain meaning of the text. That is, we should not seek out some new mystical, hidden or secret interpretation. The message of the Bible is not hidden; it is available to ordinary people. False teachers often claim to have secret knowledge, and they deceive their followers and create a false religion. The Apostle Paul warns us against these false teachers who disseminate the 'doctrines of demons' (1 Tim. 4.1).

The meaning of the Bible is not hidden from us.

The Lord tells us that his Word is not hidden; it is near at hand— 'For this commandment which I command you today is not too mysterious for you, nor is it far off. It is not in heaven, that you should say, 'Who will ascend into heaven for us and bring it to us, that we may hear it and do it?' Nor is it beyond the sea, that you should say, 'Who will go over the sea for us and bring it to us, that we may hear it and do it?' But the word is very near you, in your mouth and in your heart, that you may do it' (Deuteronomy 30.11-14).

The Bible contains mysteries.

To say that the Bible should be read in a straightforward manner is not to deny the difficulty of some passages of Scripture. Some of these difficult passages contain what H.C. Trumbull called a 'paradox.' According to Trumbull, Christianity

> is made up of seeming contradictions. All its teachings are contrary to the common opinions of humanity. According to this law, giving is getting; scattering is gaining; holding is losing; having nothing is possessing all things; dying is living. It is the one who is weak who is strong.[35]

I would prefer the biblical term 'mystery' rather than the modern word 'paradox.' It is a mystery how God can be one, yet three. It is a mystery how Jesus could be God 'manifest in the flesh' (1 Tim. 3.16), so that Jesus is both fully God and fully human at the same time. It is a mystery how the dead can be raised to life again.

---

[35] H. Clay Trumbull, *Practical Paradoxes or Truth in Contradictions*, 1889, p. 9.

Philosophers and theologians have attempted to explain the mysteries of God, but God's ways are beyond our capacity to grasp. The mind of God operates on a higher level than the human mind. Isaiah said of God, 'his understanding no one can fathom' (Isa. 40.28 NIV). The human mind is limited, but God's knowledge and wisdom are unlimited. The Lord declares, 'For my thoughts are not your thoughts, neither are your ways my ways, saith the LORD. For as the heavens are higher than the earth, so are my ways higher than your ways, and my thoughts than your thoughts' (Isa. 55.8-9).

Observe the common usage of words.
The study of Scripture begins with the study of words as they are commonly used. It bears repeating that the words of Scripture do not have secret, hidden meanings. We can use a good Bible dictionary or commentary to find meanings for the words that we do not understand. For example, Jesus speaks of a man who called his servants to him and 'And to one he gave five talents, to another two, and to another one, to each according to his own ability; and immediately he went on a journey' (Mt. 25.15). The Bible dictionary will explain that a 'talent' is a measure of money; it is not a measure of abilities. Sometimes it is helpful to consult with Greek and Hebrew dictionaries in order to illuminate the meaning of the original languages.

Observe the grammatical meaning of sentences.
When we read the Bible, we are using the rules of grammar that are a natural part of our language. The writers of Scripture followed these same general rules of grammar. We should learn to identify the parts of speech, such as the noun, pronoun, verb, adverb, adjective, conjunction, and interjection. We should learn to identify the parts of a sentence, which include the subject, the verb, and the object. As we read the Bible, we should take note of any changes from one speaker to another, from one audience to another, and from one verb tense to another.

Recognize any figurative language.
Figurative language is the symbolic use of words to convey a meaning that is different from the literal meaning. Our everyday use of language is saturated with figurative, symbolic language. We may say of a man that he is as 'strong as an ox.' We may describe a good

Christian as 'a pillar of the Church.' Within the bounds of normal speech, we find frequent use of figurative language, and the Bible is no different. Many passages in the Bible contain figurative language. Types of figurative language include parable, metaphor, hyperbole, anthropomorphism, and simile. For example, in Jn 7.38, Jesus says, 'He who believes in Me, as the Scripture has said, out of his heart will flow rivers of living water.' The 'rivers of living water' signify the Holy Spirit, but that does not mean the Holy Spirit is literally 'water.' The water is a symbolic representation (a metaphor) of the life-giving power of the Holy Spirit.

Much of the Bible utilizes figurative, symbolic language. In order to become better interpreters of Scripture, it is important that we learn how to recognize and interpret figurative language. We will study figures of speech in greater detail in Chapter 4.

Interpret according to the genre of the text.
In our daily lives we encounter many different genres of written communication. If we pick up a newspaper or magazine, we may read news items, advertisements, editorials, and wedding and birth announcements. While reading the newspaper, we may be listening to music or talk radio, two other genres of communication. Each genre calls for us to interpret according to different attitudes and rules. The Bible contains a variety of literary genres, each of which has its own characteristics that must be taken into account as we read and interpret. Much of the Bible is written in the form of story, which we call 'narrative' (Genesis, Exodus, Numbers, Joshua, Judges, Ruth, Samuel, Kings, Chronicles, Esther, Ezra, Nehemiah, the Gospels and Acts). Another large part of the Bible is written in poetic form (Psalms, Ecclesiastes, Song of Solomon and much of the prophetic material). Other genres include legal material (Leviticus), wisdom literature (Job, Proverbs), apocalyptic (Daniel and Revelation), and epistle (e.g., Romans, Corinthians, Colossians, Ephesians, etc.). Each of these parts of Scripture must be interpreted according to the rules that govern that particular genre.

Interpret according to logic and natural reasoning.
God communicates to us in ways that make sense; that is, he expects us to use our minds and our ability to reason. Jesus commanded us to love God with all of our 'mind' (Mt. 22.37). As we interpret the Scriptures, we should use all available resources to investigate and

to study. John Wesley's method of interpretation included these four elements: (1) Scripture, (2) experience, (3) church tradition, and (4) logic. Saint Luke informs us that he conducted investigation as he prepared to write his gospel account of the life of Jesus. Luke says, 'It seemed good to me also, having had perfect understanding of all things from the very first, to write to you an orderly account, most excellent Theophilus' (Lk. 1.3).

The significance of context

Meaning is found in context.

Although we affirm the fundamental clarity of Scripture, we also recognize that every biblical word and verse must be interpreted in light of its context. The context is the material that surrounds the word or verse being studied. Those who disregard the context can make the Bible mean anything they want it to mean. The story is told of a man who was seeking God for direction, and he decided to let his Bible be his guide. Therefore, with his eyes closed, he opened his Bible at random and pointed to the page. The verse that he found said that Judas 'departed, and went and hanged himself ' (Mt. 27.5). Hoping for a better result, he tried again, and the verse that he found said, 'Go and do likewise' (Lk. 10.37). He decided to try one more time, and when he pointed to the page he saw the words, 'What you do, do quickly' (Jn 13.27). This story is humorous, but it illustrates the danger of reading verses without considering their context.

An example from Paul

A more serious example would be 1 Cor. 15.32, where Paul says, 'Let us eat and drink, for tomorrow we die.' Taken by themselves, these words might suggest that Paul is advocating a careless lifestyle. However, if we read the preceding words, we will learn that Paul is speaking of the life that is lived by those people who do not believe in the resurrection. He is saying this: 'If there is no resurrection, then we may as well eat and drink, for tomorrow we will die, and that will be the end of us.' Paul, of course, does believe in the resurrection, and he does not advocate a careless and immoral lifestyle.

Levels of context

The correct interpretation of any passage of Scripture depends upon its context, especially the immediate context. The idea of context can be divided into various levels. The first level of context that we must consider is the sentence. The meaning of every word depends in part upon the sentence in which it is found.

Circles of Context

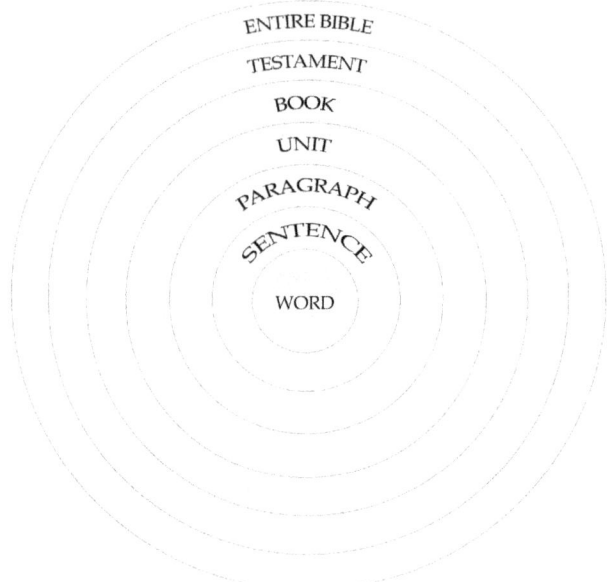

The second level of context is the verse or paragraph. Sentences are joined together to form verses and paragraphs that aim for a particular point. The third level of context we call a unit. Several paragraphs are joined together to form larger units of information. Sometimes these units will be episodes within a Gospel or another narrative book. The fourth level of context is the book. Several units come together to form a biblical book. The fifth level of context is the testament, either the Old Testament or the New Testament. The sixth and final level of context is the entire Bible. The meaning of each passage, therefore, depends upon its relationship to the surrounding paragraph, unit, and book of the Bible in which it is found. The more we learn about the whole Bible, the better able we are to interpret each verse and passage.

The progress of revelation

The place that a passage occupies within the Testament and within the entire Bible relates to a concept called the *progress of revelation*. The Bible was not written all at once, rather it was revealed over a period of over a thousand years. Adam and Eve, for example, knew very little about the plan of God. They were told to keep the garden of Eden and to be fruitful and multiply, and they were allowed to eat of all of the trees except for one tree. Later on, Abraham received a deeper understanding of God's plan when God appeared to him and promised to him the land of Canaan. Still later, Moses met God on Mount Sinai and received a more complete revelation of God than that of Abraham. David received more light than Moses. Isaiah was given a deeper understanding than David. John the Baptist had a more complete revelation than the Old Testament prophets, and the Apostles received an even fuller revelation after the resurrection of Jesus and after the Day of Pentecost. Each passage of the Bible must be interpreted in light of its place within the ongoing process of divine revelation. On the one hand, as a foundation is incomplete without the house, the earlier Scriptures are incomplete without the later Scriptures. On the other hand, just as a house needs a foundation; the later Scriptures need the earlier Scriptures as their foundation.

Historical backgrounds

Not only must we consider the place of a Scripture within the progress of revelation, but we must also consider the historical background of the passage that we are studying. The Bible was written many years ago, in a time when social customs, family traditions, and political systems were different from those of today. The Old Testament background includes the Ancient Near Eastern cultures of Egypt and Mesopotamia, and the New Testament is set against a background where the Jews are looking for a Messiah who will free them from the oppression of the Roman Empire.

An example from the Old Testament

The importance of understanding the historical background can be illustrated through the example of the prophet Jonah. The Lord spoke to Jonah and commanded him to preach to the city of

Nineveh in the land of Assyria. Jonah, however, ran from his assignment. The Lord gave Jonah a second chance and he obeyed. Jonah's preaching caused the Assyrians of Nineveh to repent of their wickedness, and the Lord was merciful and did not send judgment. Jonah was very angry that the Lord would have mercy upon the Assyrians (Jon. 4.1). Why was he angry? He was angry because the Assyrians were a source of Israel's suffering, beginning when Adad-Nirari III invaded Palestine and continuing when the Assyrian rulers invaded the area five times between 773 and 754 BC. Assyria, therefore, of which Nineveh was a major city, was already known in Jonah's day as a dangerous and mortal enemy; it stood as the epitome of everything that was cruelly hostile to Israel. Jonah, therefore, desired judgment—not forgiveness—upon his enemies. This is why Jonah was angry.

Pharisee and publican
Jesus tells the story of two men who went to the temple to pray.

> one a Pharisee and the other a tax collector. The Pharisee stood and prayed thus with himself, 'God, I thank You that I am not like other men—extortioners, unjust, adulterers, or even as this tax collector. I fast twice a week; I give tithes of all that I possess.' And the tax collector, standing afar off, would not so much as raise his eyes to heaven, but beat his breast, saying, 'God, be merciful to me a sinner.' (Lk. 18.10-13)

Jesus declared that it was the publican whose prayer was accepted by God. This story is made powerful when we understand that the pharisees were religious leaders of the people and were considered to be very holy. The publicans, however, worked for the Roman government and were considered to be traitors to the Jewish people. The original hearers of this story would have expected the pharisee to be the one who was justified, yet it was the publican who was accepted by God because his prayer was humble.

New Testament people groups
In the Gospels we read about various certain groups of people; some were called pharisees, others were saduccees, others were publicans, and still others were called scribes. Who were these groups and what did they believe? Why did they oppose the ministry of Jesus? In order to learn the answers to these questions and

to learn more about the times and customs of the Bible, we should consult commentaries, Bible dictionaries, Bible encyclopedias, and Study Bibles. Also, the Study Bible published by Senda de Vida includes introductions and explanatory notes that include historical backgrounds.

The unity and diversity of Scripture

When we read the Bible, we must remember the two aspects of its composition: (1) The Bible is composed of sixty-six books, and each book has a distinctive message and voice, just as the members of an orchestra play different instruments and different notes. (2) The Bible in its entirety is the Word of God. It is one book that presents to us a unified voice in its teaching much like the orchestra that performs one song. The different musical instruments blend together to form one magnificent sound, and the sixty-six books of the Bible blend together to form one message that God is our creator, redeemer, and king.

The unity of Scripture

The Apostle Paul writes, 'All Scripture is inspired by God, and is profitable for doctrine, for reproof, for correction, for instruction in righteousness' (2 Tim. 3.16). From Genesis to Revelation, every part of the Bible is the Word of God, and every part of the Bible is given to us by the Holy Spirit for our benefit.

The Scripture principle

Because the Bible is divinely inspired, we believe that every verse of Scripture must be interpreted in light of the whole teaching of Scripture. The verses of the Bible should not be read in isolation from each other. We should compare Scripture with Scripture. Interpreting the Bible in light of its unity is sometimes called the 'Scripture principle' or the 'analogy of Scripture.'

Accepting the whole Bible

Moreover, the unity of Scripture requires that we be open to hearing the whole Word of God, not just a part of the Word. The unity of Scripture prevents us from reading only our favorite verses while ignoring other parts of Scripture. Some parts of the Bible will comfort us while other parts of the Bible will challenge and confront us. Some parts of the Bible will move us to weep and repent, and other parts will inspire us to rejoice and shout.

The diversity of Scripture

The uniqueness of the biblical books

Although we affirm the unity of all Scripture, we also recognize that the books of the Bible were written by many different authors over a very long period of time. Each book of the Bible is written to a particular audience, and it is written to address a particular theme or topic. Each biblical writer brings to the writing his or her own personality, writing style, and vocabulary.

The example of the four Gospels

The best example of the diversity of Scripture is the fact that God gave us four Gospels that tell the life and ministry of Jesus. Why do we need four Gospels instead of only one? Interpretation would have been much simpler if we had only one Gospel. The answer is that the Gospels tell the story of Jesus in ways that speak to different audiences. Each of the four Gospels tells the story from a unique perspective. Matthew emphasizes Jesus as the Jewish Messiah whose life is a fulfillment of the Old Testament prophecies. Matthew includes a large amount of Jesus' teachings. Mark devotes most of his attention to the works of Jesus, his miracles, and his healings. Luke emphasizes the ministry of Jesus to the poor, the oppressed, and the sinner. Luke also writes more about the Holy Spirit and prayer than any other Gospel. The Gospel of John is written to show emphatically that Jesus is the eternal Son of God. John mentions only seven miracles, but each of these miracles is strategically placed in order to build suspense until the final miracle, which is the raising of Lazarus from the dead. John states his purpose when he writes, 'but these are written that you may believe that Jesus is the Christ, the Son of God, and that believing you may have life in his name' (Jn 20.31). John, therefore, calls us to 'believe,' while the Gospel of Luke calls us to 'repent' (Lk. 13.3). It is interesting that the word 'repent' is not found at all in the Gospel of John.

Each Gospel provides the immediate context for interpreting the verses within it. That is, when we read a verse in Matthew, we must first determine its place within the book of Matthew before we compare it to Mark, Luke, and John. The same is true of the other Gospels. The four Gospels give us four distinct portraits of Jesus, and yet each portrait is just as true and just as important as the others.

The witness of the Church

The fifth basic criteria for biblical interpretation is the witness of the Church.

The Christological principle

Jesus is the Word of God incarnated

The witness of the Church may be summarized in three principles, the first of which is the 'Christological principle.' The Christological principle means that all of Scripture must be interpreted in light of the nature and work of Jesus Christ. The Scripture is the written Word of God, and Jesus Christ is the incarnated Word of God. The Gospel of John tells us, 'In the beginning was the Word, and the Word was with God, and the Word was God' (Jn 1.1). Jesus Christ is the manifestation of God in human flesh. The written Word of God (the Bible) must be interpreted in light of Jesus Christ, who is the full revelation of God in human form.

Both Old and New Testaments witness to Jesus

Although the Old Testament was written to the Jews, it was written in part to prepare them for the coming of the Messiah, Jesus. When Adam and Eve sinned against God, the plan of salvation was put into effect. That plan was instituted and executed through Abraham and his descendants. The New Testament is the fulfillment of the Old. Therefore, the Old Testament is incomplete without the New Testament, just as a house is incomplete without a roof. However, the New Testament is also incomplete without the Old, because a roof would not be very useful without the house upon which it stands. The Old and New Testaments fit together as one revelation, and both testaments must be understood as witnesses to Jesus Christ and his redeeming work upon the cross.

The principle of love

The great commandment

The witness of the Church includes a second principle—the principle of love. This means that all of Scripture must be read in light of the great commandment. Jesus said, 'You shall love the Lord your God with all your heart, with all your soul, and with all your mind. This is the first and great commandment. And the second is like it: You shall love your neighbor as yourself. On these two commandments hang all the Law and the Prophets' (Mt. 22.37-40). Therefore, the command to love God and love our neighbor encompasses all of the other commandments of the Bible.

Love for the Scripture

After Jesus spoke to two disciples on the road to Emmaus, they said, 'Did not our heart burn within us while he talked with us on the road, and while he opened the Scriptures to us?' (Lk. 24.32). Their hearts burned because of their affection for the Word of God. We should not approach the Bible as if it were an object of scientific inquiry. Rather, our hearts should burn as we study the Word. We read the Bible because we love it. As the psalmist said, God's Word is sweeter than honey (Ps. 119.103); and 'a lamp to my feet and a light to my path' (Ps. 119.105). We come to the Scriptures to hear God's Word, and it is impossible to hear God's Word unless we love God. We love God and we love his Word. Our hearts, our affections are vital to hermeneutics. The golden text of the Jews says, 'Hear, O Israel: The Lord our God, the Lord is one! You shall love the Lord your God with all your heart, with all your soul, and with all your strength' (Deut. 6.4-5).

Fire in our bones

Biblical interpretation involves not only the intellect but also the affections. Jeremiah did not say that God's Word was 'thought provoking' or 'a really great idea.' He said, 'But his word was in my heart like a burning fire shut up in my bones' (Jer. 20.9). We must be concerned with the intellect and also the affections.

The principle of the faith

The witness of the Church includes a third principle—the principle of the faith. Interpreting by the 'rule of faith' means that we take into consideration the Church's past and present interpretations. That is, we should accept that we are not alone in our interpretations—we are part of the body of Christ.

We are part of the history of interpretation

We stand within a long tradition of biblical interpretation that begins with Moses. The law of Moses was interpreted by the Old Testament prophets. Later, the prophets were interpreted by the New Testament apostles. Afterwards, both the Old and New Testaments were claimed by the Church as its Scripture, and the Church fathers began to interpret the Scripture as a whole. The Protestant Reformation brought new perspectives on the Bible and its meaning. Therefore, we are not the first believers to read and interpret the Bible. We owe a debt of gratitude to all of those who have gone before us and who have handed down to us a great body of Christian teaching about the Bible. This is the witness of the Church.

We are part of a local congregation

Interpreting by the rule of faith means also that we consider our immediate context and the Church to which we belong. Acts 15 tells us that the believers joined together in their interpretation of the Scripture in an attempt to discern the place of the Gentiles within God's plan of salvation. We must not attempt a private interpretation of the Bible in isolation from our faith community. Peter wrote, 'knowing this first, that no prophecy of Scripture is of any private interpretation' (2 Pet. 1.20). God has placed us within the body of Christ, and we must all come to the Scripture together to read and study. We should gather together for Sunday School, worship, and other Bible classes and study the Word of God together. We should allow our faith community to inform, confirm, and judge our interpretations of Scripture. The Holy Spirit at work to reveal the Word of God in and through the body of Christ.[36]

---

[36] For further study on the role of the faith community in biblical interpretation, see John Christopher Thomas, *The Spirit of the New Testament* (Blandford Forum, UK: Deo Publishing, 2005), and Kenneth J. Archer, *A Pentecostal Hermeneutic: Spirit, Scripture and Community* (Cleveland, TN: CPT Press, 2009).

We are part of a theological tradition

A biblical approach to hermeneutics, taken from Acts 15, relies on the triad of Scripture, the Spirit, and the community;[37] and recent Pentecostal forays into hermeneutics have expanded the role of the community to incorporate reception history.[38] The reception history method was developed largely from the works of Hans Georg Gadamer and Hans Robert Jauss. Gadamer highlighted the effects of the text (*Wirkungsgeschichte*),[39] and Jauss emphasized the reception of the text (*Rezeptionaesthetik*) by its readers.[40] While these two approaches obviously overlap each other, 'Gadamer's term stresses the *effect* of a work, in that the focus is on the text and the influence it has in history. Jauss's term stresses the *reception* of a work, in that the focus is on the way a particular audience interprets a work.'[41] Subsequent practitioners of reception history have defined and implemented the methodology in a variety of ways.[42]

Studies in Pentecostal reception history focus on periodical literature for three reasons. First, most of the early theological discussions were carried on within the pages of numerous periodicals. Second, the periodicals, published by Pentecostal leaders and often representing the various newly formed denominations, are the nearest equivalent to authoritative theological voices. Third, the periodicals include diverse voices of ground-level theological reflection that previously have been marginalized. These rarely-heard voices

---

[37] Kenneth J. Archer, *A Pentecostal Hermeneutic: Spirit, Scripture and Community* (Cleveland, TN: CPT Press, 2009). See especially Archer's study of early Pentecostal hermeneutics (pp. 89-169).

[38] Regarding the Pentecostal utilization of reception history, see John Christopher Thomas, 'The Spirit, the Text, and Early Pentecostal Reception: The Emergence of a Discipline', in *Receiving Scripture in the Pentecostal Tradition* (ed. Daniel D. Isgrigg, et al.; Cleveland, TN: CPT Press, 2021), pp. 49-92; Martin W. Mittelstadt, 'Receiving Luke–Acts: The Rise of Reception History and a Call to Pentecostal Scholars', *PNEUMA* 40.3 (2018), pp. 367-88.

[39] Hans Georg Gadamer, *Truth and Method* (New York: Crossroads, 1989).

[40] Hans Robert Jauss, *Toward an Aesthetic of Reception* (2; trans. Timothy Bahti; Minneapolis: University of Minnesota Press, 1981).

[41] Robert Berg, '"All Men Are Created Equal": An Introduction to Reception History', in *Receiving Scripture in the Pentecostal Tradition: A Reception History* (ed. Daniel D. Isgrigg, et al.; Cleveland, TN: CPT Press, 2021), p. 12 (emphasis original).

[42] For a critique of recent developments and variations on the method, see Thomas, 'The Spirit, the Text, and Early Pentecostal Reception: The Emergence of a Discipline', pp. 49-51.

speak in the form of prayers, songs, poems, testimonies, sermons, lessons, revival reports, missionary reports, and letters to the editor. According to historian Walter J. Hollenweger, the first ten years are crucial for establishing the 'heart' of the Pentecostal tradition;[43] therefore, it is important to examine periodicals from the beginning of 1906 (the start of the Azusa St. revival) to the end of 1925.

Pentecostal reception history aims to locate the Bible within the Pentecostal context and to discover its effects on the tradition's theology and practice. Like the prophets of the Old Testament when they encountered God and like Jesus' disciples on the Day of Pentecost, the Pentecostals experienced a dramatic transformation and reorientation when they were baptized in the Holy Spirit. Their encounters with God altered their vision and gave them new insights into the biblical text. Those insights that come from our spiritual forebears add to the richness of the biblical text. Moreover, the act of engaging with the early literature furthers the reader's formation as a Pentecostal interpreter as it instills the Pentecostal dispositions and affections.

Reception history is viewed somewhat like a 'testimony' of the community's past experiences with the text. As testimony, the examples from reception history are placed into conversation with the text and with contemporary interpreters. The reception history does not govern the contemporary interpretation, but it serves as one voice – 'a great cloud of witnesses' (Heb. 12.1) – within the larger Pentecostal community of faith. These early voices help us to shape our Pentecostal understanding of Scripture as we consider how the first generation of Pentecostals struggled with the biblical text.

Many Pentecostal writings can be accessed online at these websites: Flower Pentecostal Heritage Center (https://ifphc.org/), and Consortium of Pentecostal Archives (https://pentecostalarchives.org/). Canadian periodicals are reprinted in Martin W. Mittelstadt and Caleb Howard Courtney, eds., *Canadian Pentecostal Reader: The First Generation of Pentecostal Voices in Canada, 1907–1925* (Cleveland, TN: CPT Press, 2021).

---

[43] Walter J. Hollenweger, *The Pentecostals: The Charismatic Movement in the Churches* (trans. R.A. Wilson; Minneapolis, MN: Augsburg Pub. House, 1972), 551.

The witness of the Holy Spirit

The sixth and final basic criteria for biblical interpretation is the witness of the Holy Spirit. Jesus said, 'The words that I speak to you are spirit, and they are life' (Jn 6.63). For many years, Bible scholars gave their primary attention to the history behind the biblical text, that is, to questions of authorship, date, original readers, and so forth. Then, some scholars began to shift their emphasis toward the text itself, studying the Bible as a work of literature, examining the plot and the characters, etc. Recent, postmodern interpretive models have moved away from an emphasis on the text, to an emphasis on the reader, where meaning is found not in the history behind the text, or in the text itself, but in the modern reader. Some interpreters claim erroneously that the only meaning that we find in the Bible is the meaning that we, ourselves bring to it. A more biblical approach affirms that, in addition to the biblical text and the reader, there is a third party involved in our interpretation—the Holy Spirit. The same Holy Spirit that inspired the Scriptures also moves upon the readers of Scripture to give them understanding and revelation. Although the study of the history behind the biblical text—such as authorship, date, original readers—is valuable, it is even more important that we listen to the voice of the Holy Spirit.

The Holy Spirit gives meaning.
Peter tells us that the Holy Spirit inspired the Scriptures: 'for prophecy never came by the will of man, but holy men of God spoke as they were moved by the Holy Spirit' (2 Pet. 1.21). The authority of Scripture is not in the church and not in the interpreter; the authority is in God the Holy Spirit. The Holy Spirit continues to give revelation, to give new, fresh expressions of God's Word from the living God. God takes the words which he spoke many years ago, and through the Spirit he gives a new application for us today.

We must be dependent on the continuing revelation of God through the Holy Spirit. The Holy Spirit speaks to us in ways that are above the methods of reason. The revelation from the Holy Spirit can come directly to our hearts while reading the Word. The Holy Spirit reveals the deep things of God.

The Holy Spirit teaches us.

Several Scripture passages speak to the necessity of the Holy Spirit in biblical interpretation. Jesus said to his disciples,

> 'But who do you say that I am?' Simon Peter answered and said, 'You are the Christ, the Son of the living God.' Jesus answered and said to him, 'Blessed are you, Simon Bar-Jonah, for flesh and blood has not revealed this to you, but My Father who is in heaven' (Mt. 16.15-18).

Apparently, Simon Peter had received this revelation from the Holy Spirit.

Then there is Jn 14.26: 'But the Helper, the Holy Spirit, whom the Father will send in My name, he will teach you all things, and bring to your remembrance all things that I said to you.' The Holy Spirit will teach us; he will guide us into all truth (Jn 16.33). John makes the statement even stronger in 1 Jn 2.27: 'But the anointing which you have received from him abides in you, and you do not need that anyone teach you; but as the same anointing teaches you concerning all things, and is true, and is not a lie, and just as it has taught you, you will abide in him.' John seems to be saying that the Holy Spirit is the ultimate teacher and his role should never be usurped by any human teacher. Human teachers are needed, but the teaching of the Holy Spirit is needed even more.

The Holy Spirit reveals the things of God.

We can also point to 1 Cor. 2.10-14, which tells us,

> But God has revealed them to us through his Spirit. For the Spirit searches all things, yes, the deep things of God. For what man knows the things of a man except the spirit of the man which is in him? Even so no one knows the things of God except the Spirit of God. Now we have received, not the spirit of the world, but the Spirit who is from God, that we might know the things that have been freely given to us by God. These things we also speak, not in words which man's wisdom teaches but which the Holy Spirit teaches, comparing spiritual things with spiritual. But the natural man does not receive the things of the Spirit of God, for they are foolishness to him; nor can he know them, because they are spiritually discerned.

This passage in 1 Corinthians suggests to us that the Holy Spirit reveals the deep things of God, giving access to the mind of God. He teaches us spiritual things. We know how to judge the truth by the discernment given us through the Holy Spirit.

Finally, 2 Cor. 3.6-18 speaks of God,

> who has made us competent to be ministers of a new covenant, not in a written code but in the Spirit; for the written code kills, but the Spirit gives life. Now if the dispensation of death, carved in letters on stone, came with such splendor that the Israelites could not look at Moses' face because of its brightness, fading as this was, will not the dispensation of the Spirit be attended with greater splendor? For if there was splendor in the dispensation of condemnation, the dispensation of righteousness must far exceed it in splendor. Indeed, in this case, what once had splendor has come to have no splendor at all, because of the splendor that surpasses it. For if what faded away came with splendor, what is permanent must have much more splendor. Since we have such a hope, we are very bold, not like Moses, who put a veil over his face so that the Israelites might not see the end of the fading splendor. But their minds were hardened; for to this day, when they read the old covenant, that same veil remains unlifted, because only through Christ is it taken away. Yes, to this day whenever Moses is read a veil lies over their minds; but when a man turns to the Lord the veil is removed. Now the Lord is the Spirit, and where the Spirit of the Lord is, there is freedom. And we all, with unveiled face, beholding the glory of the Lord, are being changed into his likeness from one degree of glory to another; for this comes from the Lord who is the Spirit.

Therefore, according to the Apostle Paul, without the Holy Spirit, the meaning of the Scripture is veiled—it is hidden from us—but through the Holy Spirit, we are enabled to understand the Scripture.

Conclusion

In regard to the role of the Holy Spirit in interpretation, John Christopher Thomas writes,

> The role of the Holy Spirit may also be discerned in the interpretive paradigm revealed in Acts 15, where one finds evidence

of a dynamic interaction between the biblical text, the interpretive community, and the Holy Spirit. Here the Spirit functions in several ways. First, the Spirit creates the context for the interpretation of Scripture through his actions, namely, the inclusion of Gentiles into the church. Second, based on these actions, the Spirit guides the community in the selection of which texts are most relevant to this particular situation and how best to approach the texts. Third, it appears that the Spirit offers some guidance in the community's dialogue about the Scripture in that the result 'seems good to us and to the Holy Spirit'. Thus in this paradigm the Spirit's activity is not reduced to talk of illumination but is given concrete expression.[44]

The work of the Holy Spirit in biblical interpretation can be summarized by the following statements.

a. The Holy Spirit enables us to hear the Word of God. We encounter the Holy Spirit as we prayerfully and attentively listen to the voice of God speaking through the Scripture (Heb. 3.7-4.2).

The Holy Spirit speaks to the heart of the believer, making explicit what was implicit in the text and making obvious what was unnoticed. That is, the Holy Spirit brings to our attention the words of Scripture that we need to hear.

c. The Holy Spirit forms the character of the interpreter (sanctification) and creates the interpretive community (the Church). It is the Holy Spirit who works in us to develop the character necessary to hear the voice of God. It is the Holy Spirit who works in the midst of the body of Christ to produce an atmosphere conducive to hearing the truth.

d. The Holy Spirit works in the world and in the community in ways that challenge the old interpretations and that prompt us to search the Scriptures for an explanation of our new experiences.

e. The Holy Spirit makes the Word of God relevant to our situation, enabling the reader of the Bible to hear what the Spirit is saying to

---

[44] John Christopher Thomas, 'Ideas about the Role of the Holy Spirit in Interpretation', in *Dictionary of Biblical Criticism and Interpretation* (London: Routledge, forthcoming).

the Church of today. Let us hear what the Spirit is saying to the Church (Rev. 2.7).

For Review and Study

1. Name the six guidelines for recognizing the clarity of Scripture.
2. Explain what we mean by the 'literal meaning of the text.'
3. Enumerate the seven grammatical parts of speech.
4. Define 'figurative language.'
5. Different literary genres have different characteristics. What are some genres that are found in the Bible?
6. Why should we use logic and natural reasoning when we read the Bible?
7. What do we mean by the word 'context'?
8. Explain the levels of context.
9. What do we mean when we talk about the 'progress of revelation'?
10. Considering the historical background of the Bible, what kinds of things have changed since the Bible was written?
11. What are the two aspects of the Bible's composition that we must remember when we read the Bible?
12. Explain what is meant by 'the Scripture principle'.
13. How does our belief in the unity of the Bible affect our interpretations?
14. Regarding the diversity of Scripture, describe the uniqueness of the biblical books.
15. Why did God give us four Gospels instead of only one?
16. The witness of the Church includes three principles. Name them.
17. Explain why the principle of love is important in our interpretation of the Bible.
20. The principle of faith relates to our place in the history of interpretation. How is our local congregation important in the process of interpretation?
18. Describe the value of studying Reception History.
19. What is the relationship between the Holy Spirit and the meaning of the Bible?

EL NVEVO TESTAMENTO,
QVE ES, LOS ESCRIPTOS
Euangelicos, y Apostolicos.

El Sancto Euangelio de nuestro Señor Iesu Christo segun S. Mattheo.

CAPIT. I.

EL linage y decendencia de Christo de los Padres segun la carne. II. Su conception por el Espiritu Sancto, y su nacimiento de vna Virgen conforme à la prophecia deel.

*Luc. 3,24.
2 Decendiente de Dauid y de Abraham segun la carne, como parece por el cathalogo dela genealogia sig.
*Gen. 21,2.
*Gē. 25,24.
*Gē. 29,35.
*Gē. 38,27.
y 1. Chron. 2, 5.
Ruth 4,18.

*1.Sā 16,1. y 17,12.
*2.Sam,12, 24
*1.Rey.11. 43.
y 1. Chrō 3, 10.
*2.Rey.20. 21. y 21,18. y 1.Chrō. 3, 13.
*2.Rey. 23, 34.
y 24,7.
y 2.Chr,36, 4.
y 2 Rey.24, 6.
*2.Chr.37, 9.
y 1.Ch,3,16.
Esd.3,2.
y 5,2.

1 LIBRO * de la generacion de Iesu Christo ᵃ hijo de Dauid, hijo de Abraham.
2 * Abrahá engendró à Isaac. Y * Isaac engendró à Iacob. Y * Iacob engēdró à Iudas, y à sus hermanos.
3 Y * Iudas engendró de Thamar à Phares y à Zaram. Y Phares engēdró à Esrom. Y Esrom engendró à Aram.
4 Y Aram engēdró à Aminadab. Y Aminadab engendró à Naason. Y Naason engendró à Salmon.
5 Y Salmon engendró de Raab à Booz. Y Booz engendró de Ruth à Obed. Y Obed engendró à Iesse.
6 Y * Iesse engendró àl rey Dauid. * Y el rey Dauid engendró à Salomon de la que fue muger de Vrias.
7 Y * Salomon engendró à Roboam. Y Roboam engendró à Abia. Y Abia engendró à Asa.
8 Y Asa engendró à Iosaphat. Y Iosaphat engendró à Ioram. Y Ioram engendró à Ozias.
9 Y Ozias engendró à Ioathā. Y Ioathā engendró à Achaz. Y Achaz engendró à Ezechias.
10 Y * Ezechias engendró à Manasse. Y Manasse engendró à Amō. Y Amon engendró à Iosias.
11 Y * Iosias engendró [à Ioacim. Y Ioacim engendró] à Iechonias, y à sus hermanos en la transmigraciō de Babylonia.
12 Y despues de la transmigracion de Babylonia * Iechonias engendró à Salathiel. Y Salathiel engendró à Zorobabel.
13 Y Zorobabel engendró à Abiud. Y Abiud engendró à Eliacim. Y Eliacim engendró à Azor.
14 Y Azor engendró à Sadoc. Y Sadoc engendró à Achin. Y Achin engendró à Eliud.
15 Y Eliud engendró à Eleazar. Y Eleazar engendró à Mathan. Y Mathan engendró à Iacob.
16 Y Iacob engendró à Ioseph marido de Maria, de la qual nació ᵇ I E S V S, el qual es llamado, el ᶜ C H R I S T O.
17 Demanera que todas las generaciones desde Abraham hasta Dauid, son catorze generaciones. Y desde Dauid hasta la transmigracion de Babylonia, catorze generaciones. Y desde la transmigracion de Babylonia hasta el Christo, catorze generaciones.
18 ¶ Y el nacimiento de IESVS el Christo fue ansi: Que siēdo Maria su madre desposada con Ioseph, antes q̃ se juntassen, fue hallada estar preñada del Espiritu Sácto.
19 Y Ioseph su marido, como era justo, * y no la quisiesse infamar, quisola dexar secretamente.
20 Y pensando el esto, heaqui que el Angel del Señor le apparece en sueños, diziēdo, Ioseph ᵈ hijo de Dauid, ᵉ no temas de recebir à Maria tu Muger: porque lo que en ella es engēdrado, del Espiritu Sácto es.
21 Y parirá hijo, * y llamarás su nombre ᶠ I E S V S: porque * el saluará à su Pueblo de sus peccados.
22 Todo esto ʰ acōteció paraque se cũpliesse lo que fue dicho por el Señor por el Propheta que dixo,
23 * Heaqui que vna Virgen será preñada, y parirá hijo, y llamarás su nombre Emmanuel, que es, si lo declàres, Con nosotros Dios.
24 Y despertado Ioseph del sueño, hizo como el Angel del Señor le auia mandado, y recibió à su muger.
25 Y no la conoció ⁱ hasta que parió à su hijo Primogenito: y llamó su nōbre IESVS.

CAPIT. II.
LOs Magos enseñados de Dios vienen de las partes del Oriente en busca de Christo a Ierusalē, dōde

b Aba.v.11.
c El Messias.
Vngido.
Electo.

II.
*Luc. 1,27.
*Deu.24,1.
d Decēdiēte de &c.
e No hagas dificultad de &c.
f Ot. de tomar à &c.
por tu muger.
*Luc. 1,38.
g Saluador, o salud.
*Act. 4,11.
h G. fue hecho.
*Isa.7,14.
i Entretanto q̃ estuuo preñada de &c. ni por esso se sigue de aqui que des pues la conociess, porq̃ no sa pretende aqui prouar mas sino q̃ Christo fue cō cebido sin obra de varon.demas q̃ es phrasi de la Escr. hastā &c. por jamas.
Isa.22,14.

a

Biblia del Oso
Translated by Casiodoro de Reina 1569
(first complete Spanish Bible)

Gutenberg Bible (in Latin, 1455)

5

THE BIBLE AND CHRISTIAN AFFECTIONS

Burning Hearts

On the road to Emmaus, two disciples were joined by the risen Lord, though he hid his identity from them as they talked together. Later, when they knew it was Jesus who had visited them, they reflected and said, 'Did not our heart burn within us while he talked with us on the road, and while he opened the Scriptures to us?' (Lk. 24.32) Hearing the Scriptures should lead to burning hearts.

As we stated earlier, Christians read the Bible for a variety of reasons, including the following:

Doctrine – learning what to believe,
Discernment – learning how to respond to the times,
Discipleship – growing in faith, character, and holiness,
Deeper Relationship to God – growing in love for God,
Development in Ministry – becoming more effective servants.

The categories of 'Discipleship' and 'Deeper Relationship to God' involve the formation of Christian affections. Affections are related to the emotions, and affections are often manifested through the emotions. However, the affections are more permanent than emotions. Affections are the deepest desires of the heart, the most intrinsic and basic motivations—such as love, joy, hope, courage, and gratitude. These Christian affections are formed and strengthened, in part, by our encounters with God in his Word (1

Pet. 2.2). Through reading and studying God's Word, we are transformed into God's image (2 Cor. 3.14-18).

The Sanctifying Effect of Scripture

This transformation can be called 'sanctification' (Jn 17.17). Although we often associate sanctification and holiness with outward behavior, genuine sanctification is the transformation of the desires and affections that takes place in the heart. In conversion, God gives us a 'new heart' (Ezek. 36.26); and the heart must be continually purified by the blood of Christ, by the Word of God, and through the Holy Spirit. It is from a sanctified heart that we do the will of God (Eph. 6.6).

The study of Scripture has a sanctifying effect upon us, because 'the word of God is living and powerful, … and is a discerner of the thoughts and intents of the heart' (Heb. 4.12). As we read the Bible, the Bible reads us. Moreover, while reading us, the Bible also changes us.

The Christian Affections

It might be argued that the affective dimension is too 'subjective' to be included in academic study. Expecting objections to the affective approach, Daniel C. Mcguire remarks, 'It is not for nothing that the rationalist is upset by the inclusion of affectivity … Affectivity imports mystery and depth. We can feel more than we can see or say.'[45] For this reason, biblical scholarship has given little attention to this affective dimension of the Bible. Yet I would argue that the function of Scripture is to evoke (and provoke) the passions and to form the affections. The study of the Bible, therefore, can benefit from a perspective that appreciates the affective dimensions of the text and that takes full advantage of the passions that are brought to the text by the interpreter.

It is well known that the affections played a significant role in the spirituality of Jonathan Edwards and John Wesley. Deep affective currents have been observed also in the Eastern Orthodox

---

[45] Daniel C. Maguire, '*Ratio Practica* and the Intellectualistic Fallacy', *Journal of Religious Ethics* 10.1 (1982), pp. 22-39 (23).

tradition, a tradition that influenced both Edwards and Wesley. Dale Coulter has expounded upon the affective dimension in Catherine of Siena,[46] Bernard of Clairvaux, Richard of St. Victor, Catherine of Genoa, and Martin Luther, concluding that their common theology of 'encounter centers upon affectivity as the point of contact between the divine and human.'[47] These studies, among many others, have shown that the concern for the formation of the affections is present in a wide variety of traditions.

The affections, not to be confused with transitory feelings or emotions, are the abiding dispositions and passions of the heart that characterize a person's deepest desires.[48] The Scriptures, therefore, teach us not only what to think (orthodoxy) and what to do (orthopraxy) but also what to desire (orthopathy).

The process of affective interpretation requires at least four cooperative moves on the part of the hearer. First, the hearer of the psalm must identify and acknowledge the affective dimensions of the text, an acknowledgement that is by no means automatic or common for scholars, who tend to concentrate their attention upon historical critical concerns. Every passage of Scripture includes an affective dimension, which may involve hope or despair, love or hate, trust or fear, admiration or scorn, pride or shame, joy or despondency, to mention but a few examples.

Second, the hearer of the Bible must acknowledge his or her own passions that are brought to the interpretive process. It is important that the hearer of the text recognize when his or her affections correspond to the affections present in the text and when they do not correspond, because the passions of the hearer can dramatically impact the resulting interpretation.

Third, the hearer of the psalm must be open to the emotive impact of the text. Before the hearer can experience the affective dimension of the text, he or she may be required to enter the world

---

[46] Catherine of Siena, *The Dialogue* 13 (trans. and intro. Suzanne Noffke, OP; New York, NY: Paulist Press, 1980), p. 48; cited in Dale Coulter, 'Pentecostals and Monasticism: A Common Spirituality?', *Assemblies of God Heritage* 30 (2010), pp. 43-49 (45).

[47] Dale M. Coulter, 'The Spirit and the Bride Revisited: Pentecostalism, Renewal, and the Sense of History', *Journal of Pentecostal Theology* 21.2 (2012), forthcoming.

[48] Land, *Pentecostal Spirituality*, p. 34. The affections, of course, play a key role in the creation of feelings and emotions.

of the biblical text and to enter the emotive flow of the textual stream. Robert O. Baker argues that the reading of the biblical text involves both the mind and the affections of the reader. He insists that 'reading the Bible is not just a cognitive experience, but an affective one as well'.[49]

Fourth, the hearer must allow himself or herself to be transformed by the affective experiencing of the Bible. As the hearer engages the biblical text, his or her affections are shaped by that engagement. Thus, through the hearing of the text the desires of the heart are transformed and redirected toward God so that the affections of gratitude, trust, and love (affections that foster worship) are generated and nourished.

Every biblical text includes an affective dimension, but the level of affective content varies from one text to another, depending upon the genre of the text in question. The highest concentration of affective language will be found in the poetic literature such as that found in the Psalms, the prophets, and the apocalyptic literature. The message of psalmic or prophetic poetry cannot be described by examination of the logical argument alone; in fact, there are times that poetry contains no logical argument.

Like the Psalms, prophetic speech also depends heavily upon affective language. Abraham Heschel observes, 'The prophet's words are outbursts of violent emotions'.[50] Similarly, Walter Brueggemann insists that prophetic speech uses 'language that is passionate, dangerous, and imaginative'.[51]

Wisdom literature also contains a high concentration of affective language, though the subject matter is different from that of the Psalms and the prophets. The fact that the Proverbs are initially addressed to 'my son (1.8) is an affective device. Furthermore, individual proverbs often appeal to affective language in order to influence the behaviour of the hearers. In chapter one alone, we find reference to those who are 'greedy for gain (v. 19). We read that

---

[49] Robert O. Baker, 'Pentecostal Bible Reading: Toward a Model of Reading for the Formation of the Affections', *Journal of Pentecostal Theology* 7 (1995), pp. 34-48 (46).

[50] Abraham J. Heschel, *The Prophets* (2 vols.; New York: Harper & Row, 1962), I, p. 4).

[51] Walter Brueggemann, *Hopeful Imagination: Prophetic Voices in Exile* (Philadelphia: Fortress Press, 1986), p. 15.

'fools hate knowledge' (vv. 22, 29), and they 'depise' wisdom's rebuke (v. 30). We learn that wisdom will 'laugh at' and 'mock' the foolish when their calamity comes (v. 26).

The New Testament epistles often contain high concentrations of affective language, but those concentrations vary from one epistle to another. The Apostle Paul frequently evokes affections such as love, pity, fear, shame, and hope. I would argue further that the familial and affectionate tone of Paul's epistle to the Philippians must be contrasted to the more formal tone of Romans, the accusatory tone of Galatians, and the corrective tone of first Corinthians.

The lowest concentration of affective language will be found in the narrative texts, but even the simplest narrative creates a certain tone to which the reader responds unconsciously. Regarding the language of Genesis 22, for example, in which Abraham and Isaac address one another as father and son (vv. 7-8), carry on an intimate conversation, then proceed 'the two of them together (vv. 6, 8), the pathos could scarcely be greater.

Because the level of affective content varies from one text to another, the importance of examining the affective dimension also varies. When interpreting the Psalms, the prophets, and other highly emotive texts, an investigation of the affective language and tone is crucial. These texts simply cannot be understood if the affective dimension is overlooked.

The process of identifying the affective content of a text begins with locating any words or phrases whose content is explicitly affective. Words that signify 'love', 'hate', 'anger', 'desire', 'fear', 'hope', and 'gratitude' are affective by definition and are easily located. In addition to naming the explicitly affective terminology, the passage should be examined for more subtle indicators of affective tone. Even without explicitly affective terminology, the literary shaping of the text creates an affective dimension that can be evaluated (though with more difficulty). For example, an examination of the Samuel, Saul, and David stories reveals that Samuel is presented in such a way that the reader develops confidence in Samuel's integrity and authority. The reader, therefore, does not question Samuel's actions in regard to the deposing of Saul and the choosing of David. Furthermore, Saul is presented in ways that make the reader distrustful of him. Finally, David enters the story as a humble, faithful, and brave youth who is the ideal leader. However, when David commits adultery and murder and when David fails to protect his daughter Tamar, the reader is confronted with a depiction of David that is dark and troubling.

Case Studies

Any number of biblical passages might be used as case studies for the significance of affective language. Let us look very briefly at three examples:

Jonah

In an article devoted to the puzzling final verse of the book of Jonah, Rickie Moore calls attention to the passionate language found in the book.[52] The message of the book of Jonah emerges in part from those elements that are hidden in the first half of the book but which rise to the surface in the second half. Jonah's motive for fleeing, which is hidden in the beginning, becomes clear in the second part of the book. Jonah's feelings, his passions, are subdued in the first half of the book, but they burst forth in the second half. At the beginning of Jonah's story, he is dispassionate, apathetic, and indifferent to his own fate.

In the second half of the book, Yahweh relents on his threat to destroy the Ninevites, and Jonah explodes in anger. He is so angry that he prays to die. Apparently, he no longer desires to live in a world where his enemies are offered a reprieve and where evil is so quickly pardoned. The passions of Jonah are further explored in the dialogues between Yahweh and Jonah in chapter four. Is it possible that by highlighting the animosity of Jonah towards the Ninevites, the story may provoke the reader to examine his or her own hostilities towards the 'other'?

---

[52] R.D. Moore, '"And also much cattle": Prophetic Passions and the End of Jonah', *Journal of Pentecostal Theology* 11 (1997), pp. 35-48.

Judges 10

In an earlier article, I proposed that the book Judges includes significant affective content.[53] For example, in response to his unfaithful people, Yahweh becomes angry; he is so angry that he refuses to save his covenant people from oppression. 'I have saved you seven times', declares Yahweh, 'but I will not save you again' (v. 13). Yes, God is angry; he is so angry that he becomes sarcastic: 'Go and cry out to the gods that you have chosen. They will save you' (v. 14). He is so angry that when the Israelites repent for the second time, he remains silent. However, the anger of Yahweh, though genuine and intense, is not enduring.

Yahweh can be angry, but he also can be moved with intense compassion; he is grieved by Israel's suffering; he suffers with them. The narrator tells us that 'Yahweh is grieved by Israel's suffering' (v. 16). The words of verse sixteen indicate a draining, depleting, diminishing, exhausting compassion. Yahweh appears to be torn in two directions. Yahweh will not be manipulated and exploited, but he suffers when his people suffer.

Psalm 1

The common interpretation of Psalm 1 as a call for obedience does not quite capture the emphasis of the text.[54] Specifically, the psalm affirms the person who 'delights' in God's instruction (1.2), thus pointing to the affections rather than to behaviour as the key element of the righteous person. The agenda of Psalm 1 is to persuade the reader to delight in and meditate upon the Torah. Overstating the demand for obedience ignores the important affective dimension of the psalm. The word 'delight' has reference to the affections. It denotes 'the direction of one's heart or passion'.[55]

Instead of calling for obedience to the Torah, Psalm 1 evokes affection for the Torah. Psalm 1.2 suggests that delight in the Torah 'is the determining and effective disposition of the truly happy

---

[53] Lee Roy Martin, 'God At Risk: Divine Vulnerability in Judges 10.6-16', *Old Testament Essays* 18.3 (2005), pp. 722-40.

[54] See Lee Roy Martin, 'Delight in the Torah: The Affective Dimension of Psalm 1', *Old Testament Essays* 23.3 (2010), pp. 708-27.

[55] W. Van Gemeren, *New International Dictionary of Old Testament Theology and Exegesis* (5 vols.; Grand Rapids, MI: Zondervan 1997), V, p. 231.

life'.[56] The entire Psalm includes no commands or injunctions, and it includes no language that falls within the semantic range of 'obey'. The language is that of affirmation ('Blessed is the man'), which evokes a desire for righteousness by means of the indirect and subtle effect of the poem's inviting and hopeful mood. The hearer of Psalm 1 is told that the person who delights in the Torah will flourish like a well-watered tree. Therefore, the emphasis of Psalm 1 is not upon deeds but delight, not on duty but desire, not on obedience but on affections that are rightly oriented towards God.

Once the affective content of the biblical text has been identified, it should be interpreted with the same care that is afforded to propositional or rational content. The goal is to determine how the tone may contribute to shaping the reader's perceptions of the text, and to determine how the reader's character might be transformed by the affective dimensions of the text. As we study the Bible, we must allow our affections to be transformed by the Holy Spirit—to be sanctified by the Word.

For Review and Study

1. Explain the sanctifying effect of the Word of God.
2. Define the nature of the Christian affections and how they differ from emotions.
3. Discuss the four cooperative moves required for affective interpretation.
4. What do we mean by 'affective language'?
5. What are some ways that the story of Jonah might affect the hearer of the story?
6. What are some ways that Judges 10 might affect the hearer of the story?
7. What are some ways that Psalm 1 might affect the hearer of the story?

---

[56] H.-J. Kraus, *Psalms: A Commentary* (Minneapolis, MN: Augsburg Pub. House, 1988), p. 117.

6

INTERPRETING FIGURES OF SPEECH

Literal meaning and figurative language

The Bible uses figurative language

Although the Bible is a special book, we should read it naturally and we should interpret its words as we would in ordinary daily use. As we discussed in Chapter 2, we call this the 'literal meaning.' God did not intend that the Bible should be a puzzle or a secret message. The Bible is written in normal human language, using words, grammar, and literary standards in their straightforward meanings. Much of the Bible utilizes figurative, symbolic language. In order to become better interpreters of Scripture, it is important that we learn how to recognize and interpret figurative language.

What is figurative language?

Figurative language is the symbolic use of words to convey a meaning that is different from the literal meaning. Our everyday use of language is saturated with figurative, symbolic language. Similarly, the Bible is filled with figurative language. Ps. 23.1 tells us, 'The Lord is my shepherd.' However, we are not literally 'sheep,' and God is not literally a 'shepherd.' The symbol of the Lord as our shepherd communicates to us that he is our provider, our guide and our protector.

Why does the Bible use figurative language?

E.W. Bullinger has written a book entitled *Figures of Speech Used in the Bible*. He names over two hundred different kinds of figures of speech in the Bible, and he lists over eight thousand examples from the Bible.[57] Why does the Bible use so many figures of speech?

Figures of speech are expressive and exciting

John the Baptist, when he sees Jesus coming toward the Jordan River, says, 'Behold! The Lamb of God who takes away the sin of the world!' (Jn 1.29). John's naming of Jesus as the 'lamb of God' is a colorful expression that brings to mind the passover lambs that have been slain for the sins of Israel. It captures the innocence of Jesus, his suffering and death. It brings to mind the prophecy in Isa. 53.7, which says, 'He was oppressed and he was afflicted, Yet he opened not his mouth; he was led as a lamb to the slaughter, And as a sheep before its shearers is silent, So he opened not his mouth.'

Figures of speech add emphasis

When Jesus was warned to beware of king Herod, he responded, 'Go, tell that fox, 'Behold, I cast out demons and perform cures today and tomorrow, and the third *day* I shall be perfected.' (Lk. 13.32). In calling Herod a 'fox,' Jesus added emphasis to his answer.

Figures of speech add depth and clarity

The psalmist tells us, 'The LORD is my rock and my fortress and my deliverer; My God, my strength, in whom I will trust; My shield and the horn of my salvation, my stronghold' (Ps. 18.2). The figurative language here is powerful, and it describes God in concrete ways that are visual and experiential.

d. Figures of speech are brief but full of meaning

James warns us us to be careful in what we say to each other. Rather than giving us a lengthy exposition, he says, 'And the tongue *is* a fire' (Jas 3.6). This very brief statement is filled with meaning. The word 'tongue' represents our speech, our communications with each other. The word 'fire' represents the destructive power of speech. To say that the 'the tongue is a fire' means that when we speak, we can cause great harm. Our speech has the power to bless or to offend, to help or to hurt. Our words can burn other people, harming them irreparably.

---

[57] E.W. Bullinger, *Figures of Speech Used in the Bible* (Grand Rapids, MI: Baker, 2003), originally published in 1898.

e. Figures of speech are easy to remember

One of my favorite verses says, 'Your word *is* a lamp to my feet and a light to my path' (Ps. 119.105). The symbolic language of 'lamp' and 'light' makes a permanent impression upon the mind and makes the verse very easy to remember.

f. Figures of speech cause the reader to ponder the meaning of the Scripture

Figurative language pulls the reader into the world of the text and requires the reader to use his or her imagination. For example, Peter warns us saying, 'Be sober, be vigilant; because your adversary the devil walks about like a roaring lion, seeking whom he may devour' (1 Pet. 5.8). This representation of the devil as a 'roaring lion' who desires to devour me causes me to think deeply about my spiritual life. It makes me aware that the devil is my enemy. It reminds me of the fact that I need God's protection against the evil one.

g. Figurative language speaks to the heart

As human beings, we are complex people who have not only minds but also hearts. Figures of speech often speak to the heart, that is, to our affective dimension. For example, the prophet Isaiah says, 'But those who wait on the LORD Shall renew *their* strength; They shall mount up with wings like eagles, They shall run and not be weary, They shall walk and not faint' (Isa. 40.31). Isaiah's promise brings great joy to my heart. He says that God will cause me to fly like an eagle. This verse ministers not only to my mind but also to my emotions. We will say more about the affective dimension of Scripture in the chapter on interpretation of the Psalms, which are written in the form of poetry and use many figures of speech.

The most important figures of speech

Metaphor
One of the most common figures of speech in the Bible is the metaphor. The metaphor compares one thing to another by using the verb 'ser.'

Metaphors of Jesus

In the Gospel of John, Jesus uses a series of metaphors to describe himself in his relationship to us. He declares, 'I am the bread of life' (Jn 6.35). The metaphor of Jesus as 'bread' emphasizes the lifegiving and sustaining power of Jesus. He says also, 'As long as I am in the world, I am the light of the world' (Jn 9.5). The metaphor of 'light' suggests that Jesus brings truth, knowledge, and guidance to his followers. Jesus adds another metaphor, saying, 'I am the door. If anyone enters by Me, he will be saved' (Jn 10.9). He is the door, meaning that we must come through him to enter into eternal life. The fact that Jesus cares for his sheep is evident in the following statement: 'I am the good shepherd' (Jn 10.11). The good shepherd gives his life for the sheep. Lastly, Jesus says, 'I am the vine, you *are* the branches' (Jn 15.5). As the vine, Jesus is our source of life, sustenance, and growth. We are the branches, and we must remain connected to the vine (Jesus) if we hope to remain alive and bear fruit.

Other metaphors

In his sermon on the mount, Jesus says, 'You are the light of the world. A city that is set on a hill cannot be hidden' (Mt. 5.14). The word 'light' is a metaphor that symbolizes our witness in the world. Other examples of the metaphor include the following.

'The LORD is my rock and my fortress' (2 Sam. 22.2)
'The LORD is my shepherd' (Ps. 23.1)
'But I am a worm, and no man' (Ps. 22.6)
'Their throat is an open tomb' (Ps. 5.9)
'He is a shield to all who trust in him' (Ps. 18.30)
'You are the salt of the earth' (Mt. 5.13)

Metonymy

The metonymy identifies something by means of something else that is closely related.

The 'tongue' as a figure of speech

For example, Prov. 12.18 says, 'But the tongue of the wise promotes health.' The metonymy here is the 'tongue,' which symbolizes 'words.' That is, it is not the tongue itself that brings healing; rather, it is the words that come off the tongue that bring healing.

'Hyssop' as a symbol of the 'blood'

An important metonymy occurs in the book of Psalms when the psalmist repents to God and asks, 'Purge me with hyssop, and I shall be clean' (Ps. 51.7). Hyssop is a small bushy plant, an herb, which was used in the first passover and in Old Testament purification rituals. The hyssop was dipped into the blood of the sacrificial animal, and in the case of the passover, the blood was then spread upon the door. In the case of other ceremonies the blood was sprinkled upon the altar and the people (Exod. 24.6-8). Therefore, it is not the hyssop itself that purifies; it is the blood which is upon the hyssop that purifies.

Other metonymies

In Gen. 42.38, Jacob in his grief speaks to his sons and says, 'you would bring down my gray hair with sorrow to the grave.' It is not only Jacob's gray hair that will go down to Sheol, but it is also his entire body. Gray hair is a characteristic of old age; therefore, his mention of gray hair symbolizes his entire aged body. Another example is found in Lk. 16.29. Abraham says, 'They have Moses and the prophets; let them hear them.' In fact, they do not have Moses and the prophets because Moses and the prophets are dead, but they have the words of Moses and the words of the prophets as they stand recorded in the Old Testament. Therefore, 'Moses' here represents the words of Moses, and 'the prophets' represents the words of the prophets. Finally, the Apostle Paul declares, 'For many walk, of whom I have told you often, and now tell you even weeping, that they are the enemies of the cross of Christ' (Phil. 3.18). The metonymy here is in the words 'the cross of Christ.' Paul is not speaking of the literal cross that is made of wood; he is speaking of the cross as a symbol of the death of Jesus and the message of the Gospel that issues from the cross. The word 'cross,' therefore, symbolizes the message of the sacrificial death of Jesus Christ.

Hypocatastasis

The hypocatastasis is similar to the metaphor. We said earlier that the metaphor compares one thing to another by using the verb 'to be.' Similarly, the hypocatastasis compares one thing to another, but it does NOT use the verb 'to be.'

In the Psalms

Hypocatastasis is very common in the book of Psalms. In the following example, the word 'dogs' is a hypocatastasis: 'For dogs have surrounded Me; The congregation of the wicked has enclosed Me. They pierced My hands and My feet' (Ps. 22.16). The word 'dogs' is a figure of speech that symbolizes the angry, violent people who are surrounding the speaker. Another hypocatastasis that symbolizes evil people is Ps. 59.7, which says, 'Swords are in their lips; For they say, "Who hears?"' The word 'swords' is a symbol for harmful words that cut and destroy.

Symbols of God's people

Hypocatastasis is often used to represent God's people. For example, the psalmist calls Israel a 'vine.' He writes, 'You have brought a vine out of Egypt; You have cast out the nations, and planted it' (Ps. 80.8). This is a beautiful picture of God's care for his people. God took Israel out of Egypt and made a place for them in the promised land of Canaan. In the New Testament, Jesus refers to his people as a flock of sheep. He says, 'Do not fear, little flock' (Lk. 12.32). Just as a flock of sheep need have no fear when their shepherd is nearby, so we need not fear because Jesus is our shepherd, and he will protect us.

Symbols of God

Not only is hypocatastasis used to symbolize God's people, but it is also used to symbolize God himself. As we mentioned earlier, John the Baptist refers to Jesus as a 'lamb.' When Jesus approaches the Jordan River, where John was preaching and baptising, John proclaims, 'Behold! The Lamb of God who takes away the sin of the world' (Jn 1.29). This hypocatastasis uses the word 'lamb' to symbolize Jesus as a sacrificial animal. The symbolism points to the passover ceremony, in which an unblemished lamb was slaughtered to save the people from death. The blood of the lamb was applied to the door, and the household was saved (Exod. 12.23). Our final example of hypocatastasis comes from the prophet Jeremiah. Speaking through Jeremiah, the Lord says, 'For My people have committed two evils: They have forsaken Me, the fountain of living waters, And hewn themselves cisterns—broken cisterns that can hold no water' (Jer. 2.13). In this figure of speech, God is revealed as fresh, life-giving water. But the Israelites have forsaken God, who is the 'fountain of living water,' and they have created their own source of water, 'broken cisterns.' Just as the 'fountain' represents their lifegiving covenant with God, the 'cisterns' represent substitutes and counterfeits of their own devising.

Hyperbole

We mentioned above that figures of speech add emphasis and get our attention. The hyperbole is a good example of this emphatic nature of figurative language. The hyperbole is an intentional and obvious exaggeration for the sake of emphasis. I heard someone say, 'I am so hungry that I could eat a horse.' Of course we know that it would be impossible for one person to eat a horse; therefore, we understand the statement to be symbolic. It really means, 'I am very, very hungry.'

Exaggerated heights

The Bible often uses hyperbole to get our attention. For example, the cities of Canaan are described in the following way: 'the cities *are* great and fortified up to heaven' (Deuteronomy 1.28). To say that the walls reach up to heaven is obviously an exaggeration, but it is very effective as a symbolic description of the very high walls. Similarly, the psalmist describes the mariners on the sea when their ship rides the stormy waves: 'They mount up to the heavens, They go down again to the depths' (Ps. 107.26). The words 'heaven' and 'depths' are symbols of the rise and fall of the gigantic waves as they lift the ship and then cause it to descend into the trough.

Exaggerated troubles

Because of his troubles, the psalmist often speaks of his grief and his weeping in terms of hyperbole. His weeping is so profuse that he uses the symbolism of the 'flood' and the 'river.' For example, he writes, 'All night I make my bed swim; I drench my couch with my tears' (Ps. 6.6). Also, he says, 'Rivers of water run down from my eyes, Because men do not keep Your law' Ps. 119.136).

The teachings of Jesus

Jesus was very serious about his teachings. He rarely used humor, but he often used hyperbole in order to make his lesson more memorable and emphatic. Two examples should be sufficient here. In

Mt. 5.30, Jesus is pressing upon his hearers the urgency and seriousness of obedience. He says, 'And if your right hand causes you to sin, cut it off and cast it from you.' This statement is an intentional and obvious exaggeration that is intended to shock the hearers and get their attention. Jesus does not want us to mutilate our bodies, but he does want us to realize the gravity and the eternal consequences of sin. Jesus knows that cutting off the hand would not prevent sin because sin comes from the heart (Mt. 5.28). In another hyperbole, Jesus says, 'If anyone comes to Me and does not hate his father and mother, wife and children, brothers and sisters, yes, and his own life also, he cannot be My disciple' (Lk. 14.26). This statement is obviously a hyperbole that is used to emphasis the deep level of commitment necessary to be a follower of Jesus. Nowhere in the Bible are we told to hate anyone; in fact we are everywhere told to love one another, to love our neighbor, to love our father and mother, and even to love our enemies. Nevertheless, our love for Jesus must supersede all other loves, and our dedication to God must be greater than any other commitments in life. We must love God even more than we love ourselves.

Simile

What is a simile?

The simile is another comparison. The simile compares one thing symbolically to another thing by using the words 'like' or 'as.' For example, Peter declares that humans are 'like grass' and their glory is 'like the flower.' He says, 'All flesh is as grass, and all the glory of man as the flower of the grass. The grass withers, and its flower falls away' (1 Pet. 1.24). How are we like grass? Is it because we are the color green? No, it is because we are temporal and mortal—like the grass, we die.

Old Testament examples

One of the most significant similes in the Bible is found in the book of Genesis. God says to Abraham, 'Blessing I will bless you, and multiplying I will multiply your descendants as the stars of the heaven and as the sand which is on the seashore; and your descendants shall possess the gate of their enemies' (Gen. 22.17). In this important prophetic passage, God promises to Abraham that his children will be as numerous as the 'stars of heaven' and as the 'sand of the seashore.' The stars and the sand represent an innumerable multitude. This figurative language makes God's promise vivid and inspiring.

Many similes are found in the Psalms. The psalmist announces that the evil nations who have rebelled against the Lord will be smashed to pieces. He says that the Lord will easily break them 'like a potter's vessel' (Ps. 2.9).

In Psalm 10, the writer lists several characteristics of the wicked person: (1) he is full of pride; (2) he will not seek God; (3) he is profane and dishonest; and (4) 'He lies in wait secretly, as a lion in his den; he lies in wait to catch the poor; he catches the poor when he draws him into his net' (Ps. 10.9). The words 'like a lion' form a simile. The symbolism characterizes the wicked person as one who attacks those who are weaker, particularly the poor, and devours them for his own enjoyment.

The process for the purification of silver is used as a simile when the psalmist writes, 'The words of the LORD are pure words, Like silver tried in a furnace of earth, purified seven times' (Ps. 12.6). In order to remove any foreign elements, silver is melted and filtered. Silver that has been purified seven times is very, very pure. Similarly, the words of the Lord are very, very pure. There is nothing foreign or unclean in God's words.

New Testament examples

New Testament examples of the simile are also abundant. Jesus compares himself to a mother hen when he says, 'O Jerusalem, Jerusalem, the one who kills the prophets and stones those who are sent to her! How often I wanted to gather your children together, as a hen gathers her chicks under her wings, but you were not willing!' (Mt. 23.37) The symbolism here compares Jesus to the hen and the people of Jerusalem to her baby chicks. When danger is near, the chicks run and gather beneath the wings of their mother hen. Similarly, Jesus wants to gather his people and protect them from whatever dangers are approaching.

In another simile that signifies danger, Jesus says to his disciples, 'Go your way; behold, I send you out as lambs among wolves' (Lk. 10.3). This simile describes the mission of the Church. We carry the Gospel of love and peace into a world of hatred and violence.

Lambs are harmless and helpless, but wolves are powerful enough to kill. The lambs, however, are always protected by the good shepherd, who watches over them night and day. Therefore, when we go into the world, we do not depend upon our own strength and cleverness; instead we depend upon the care and protection of our shepherd, Jesus.

The book of Revelation is one of the most symbolic books in the Bible. In chapter one, Jesus appears in a vision to John, and John writes this description of Jesus: 'His head and hair were white like wool, as white as snow, and his eyes like a flame of fire' (Rev. 1.14). This description includes three similes: 'like wool,' 'like snow,' and like 'a flame of fire.' The first two similes are easy to understand—Jesus' hair was pure white, like wool and like snow. The third one, however, is more difficult to interpret. When John says that Jesus' eyes were 'like flames of fire,' is he referring to the colors of fire? No, I believe he is telling us that the eyes of Jesus were bright and glowing like a flame in the darkness.

Personification

What is personification?

The figure of speech that we call personification is used often in poetry because of its colorful and dramatic effect. Personification is the attributing of personal, human qualities to impersonal, non-human things. In the prophecy of restoration, for example, Isaiah declares, 'The wilderness and the wasteland shall be glad for them, and the desert shall rejoice' (Isa. 35.1). The wilderness, of course, cannot be 'glad,' nor can the desert 'rejoice'; but in order to portray the wonders of the work of God, Isaiah uses this symbolic language.

Personification in scenes of worship

Personification is often used in scenes where God is being praised. For example, the psalmist declares, 'Let the heavens rejoice, and let the earth be glad; Let the sea roar, and all its fullness' (Ps. 96.11). The heavens and the sea are not literally capable of glorifying God, but the psalmist calls upon them to rejoice and to be glad. Another example of worship is found in Isa. 55.12, where the prophet proclaims, 'For you shall go out with joy, And be led out with peace; The mountains and the hills Shall break forth into singing before you, And all the trees of the field shall clap their hands.' As before, we know that the mountains and hills cannot sing, and the trees cannot clap their hands. For one thing, they have no hands. Furthermore, they are not human and do not possess the capacity for worship. The prophet, however, wants to offer a vision of the world in which everything contributes to the praise and glory of God. We could add here John's prophecy from Revelation:

> And every creature which is in heaven and on the earth and under the earth and such as are in the sea, and all that are in them, I heard saying: 'Blessing and honor and glory and power be to him who sits on the throne, and to the Lamb, forever and ever' (Rev. 5.13).

The personification of wisdom

In the book of Proverbs, we find a lengthy personification in which wisdom is personified in the form of a woman. The Scripture says, 'Wisdom calls aloud outside; She raises her voice in the open squares... Turn at my rebuke; Surely I will pour out my spirit on you; I will make my words known to you' (Prov. 1.20-23). Here wisdom is like a woman who is calling out to the people who pass by, inviting them to come and be blessed. Wisdom offers the Spirit and knowledge to all who will turn away from the paths of foolishness.

Anthropomorphism

Giving human form to God

Anthropomorphism is the attributing of human form to God. As we know, God is a spirit (Jn 2.24) and does not possess a physical body. Describing the attributes of God can be difficult because God is a spirit; therefore, the biblical writers sometimes use anthropomorphism as a means of illustrating God's characteristics. One of the most common anthropomorphisms is the use of the word 'hand' to signify the power of God. For example, Moses tells the Israelites, 'for with a strong hand the LORD has brought you out of Egypt' (Exod. 13.9).

Anthropomorphisms in prayers

Anthropomorphisms are often found in the prayers of the Bible. For example, David prays, 'Bow down Your ear to me, Deliver me speedily' (Ps. 31.2). Through symbolism David is asking for the Lord to hear his prayer. He is asking God to listen and to respond with the answer. In a similar fashion, the psalmist prays, 'According to the greatness of Your power Preserve those who are appointed to die' (Ps. 79.11). The greatness of the Lord's 'arm' represents his power and might. The Lord has the power to save us from death.

Anthropomorphisms can represent God's actions

We know that God does not literally have a mouth, but still the following Scripture is quite profound: 'man shall not live by bread alone; but man lives by every word that proceeds from the mouth of the LORD' (Deut. 8.3). This anthropomorphism represents the action of God in speaking to us. It helps us to picture in our minds that God is speaking his Word to us personally. His words are coming forth out of his mouth. Another kind of action is captured in the following verse of Scripture: 'For the eyes of the LORD run to and fro throughout the whole earth, to show himself strong on behalf of those whose heart is loyal to him' (2 Chron. 16.9). The 'eyes' of the Lord represent his ability to perceive and to know everything that is happening upon the earth. It is both a comfort and a warning for us to know that God is at all times watching our lives and our behavior. If we are faithful to God, he is watching over us to protect us and to bless us.

Other figures of speech

As we stated earlier, there are over two hundred different figures of speech in the Bible. We have described only the most common and useful of these figures. Other figures of speech that you will encounter in Scripture include the following.

Zoopomorphism

Zoopomorphism is the attributing of animal forms to God. For example, the psalmist speaks of God as if he has wings and feathers. He says, 'He shall cover you with his feathers, And under his wings you shall take refuge' (Ps. 91.4). The wings of God represent his protective covering which he spreads over his people.

Euphemism

A euphemism is the use of a less offensive term for a harsh one. For example, God said to Abraham, 'You shall go to your fathers in peace' (Gen. 15.15) The words 'go to your fathers in peace' is a euphemistic way of saying, 'you will die.'

Synecdoche

Synecdoche is a figure of speech in which the part stands for the whole or the whole for the part. The phrase, 'He who has clean hands and a pure heart' (Ps. 24.4) mentions only the hands and the heart, but the righteousness of these two parts represents the righteousness of the whole person.

Litotes

Litotes is a deliberate understatement, the opposite of hyperbole, which we discussed earlier. Abraham speaks disparagingly of himself when he says, 'Indeed now, I who am but dust and ashes have taken it upon myself to speak to the Lord' (Gen. 18.27). When the twelve Israelite spies returned from Canaan, they compared themselves to the Canaanites saying, 'There we saw the giants (the descendants of Anak came from the giants); and we were like grasshoppers in our own sight, and so we were in their sight' (Num. 13.33).

How to understand figures of speech

In order to make sense of figurative language we must understand the meaning of the figures and how they relate to reality. For example, before we can understand the meaning of the metaphor 'the Lord is my shepherd,' we must know the role of a shepherd. What is a shepherd? What does a shepherd do? Why do sheep need a shepherd? In order to interpret figures of speech we must understand the customs, the culture, and the history of the biblical world.

For Review and Study

1. What is figurative language?
2. Give an example where figurative language adds emphasis.
3. Why do you think that figurative language is easy to remember?

4. Figurative language pulls the reader into the world of the text and requires the reader to use his or her imagination. How does 1 Pet. 5.8 cause you to use your imagination?
5. Figures of speech often speak to the heart, that is, to our affective dimension. How do you feel when you read Isa. 40.31?
6. Define 'metaphor.'
7. What does John mean when he calls Jesus 'the lamb of God'?
8. Enumerate three examples of hyperbole in the Bible.
9. The simile compares one thing symbolically to another thing by using the words 'like' or 'as.' Explain the simile in Mt. 23.37.
10. Define 'personification.'
11. Explain the meaning of the 'wings' of God in Ps. 91.4.12.
12. Explain the meaning of 'euphemism' and give one example.
13. Explain the meaning of the synecdoche in Ps. 24.4.
14. How we can better understand the figurative language of the Bible.

7

INTERPRETING THE PROVERB, RIDDLE, AND FABLE

In the previous chapter we discussed several important figures of speech that are used in the Bible. We focused upon the figures of speech that are often limited to a word or phrase. We will now expand our view of figurative language by looking at the literary forms that we call the proverb, the riddle, the fable, the type, the symbol, the allegory, and the parable. These literary forms are extended figures of speech. That is, they are more lengthy sayings that are expressed through symbolic language.

Words of wisdom

Proverbs, riddles, and fables are considered a part of the wisdom literature of the Bible. The wisdom books are Proverbs, Job, and Ecclesiastes. In addition to these books of wisdom, several of the Psalms can be categorized as wisdom literature (Psalms 1, 32, 37, 49, 73, 78, 112, 119, 127, 128, 133, and 145).

The proverbs, riddles, and fables in the Bible should be interpreted from the perspective of the wisdom literature. How do we define the wisdom literature of the Bible? The wisdom writings are characterized by the following series of emphases.

Human experience
The wisdom writings emphasize common sense human experience whereas the rest of the Old Testament emphasizes divine

revelation. The wisdom tradition flows out of human investigation, particularly the investigation of human experience. Experience is the normal everyday patterns of life.

Creation and nature
The wisdom literature emphasizes creation and nature whereas other parts of the Old Testament emphasize history. Most of the Old Testament focuses more on the history of the people of Israel and the intervention of God in history, such as the exodus and the exile. The wisdom tradition, however, focuses upon the natural order of things in nature as we observe them.

Universal principles
The wisdom writings emphasize the universal application of truth whereas other parts of the Old Testament are written with particular reference to Israel, Zion, and particular people. Except for its reference to its authors, the proverbs do not name names or give dates. The proverbs fit all of life universally; they do not give details and particulars.

The individual
The wisdom literature emphasizes the individual whereas other parts of the Bible emphasize the community. In Deuteronomy, for example, we hear God speaking to all of Israel when he says, 'Hear, O Israel' (Deuteronomy 6.4). The book of Proverbs, however, is a teaching addressed to the individual, particulary to 'my son' (Prov. 1.8, 10, 15). The proverbs speak about individual behavior and character.

The Proverb

What is a proverb?
I remember from my childhood that my mother would say, 'Don't cry over spilt milk' or, she might say, 'One in the hand is worth two in the bush' or 'Beggars can't be choosers' or 'Don't count your chickens before they hatch.' All of us can easily identify these as proverbs. But just what is a proverb? A Spanish writer, Miguel de Cervantes, spoke of proverbs as 'short sentences drawn from long experience.' A proverb captures in a memorable phrase or two some aspect of daily life that everyone has experienced.

Definition of the proverb

The proverb is a saying, usually two lines, that cleverly captures in words some aspect of universal human experience. Proverbs are found in all cultures, and they seem to be a natural result of human experience. Proverbs encapsulate our habits and our patterns of life.

Proverbs are not absolute laws.

Proverbs are not laws, but they are accurate expressions of the way things happen as a rule. Proverbs are not absolutes, but they express a pattern. There may be exceptions, but the proverb still represents the rule of thumb. Proverbs are not promises; they are observations about the way the world works. The proverb expresses a pattern that consistently and predictably represents the way we experience the world.

Kinds of proverbs

Most of the Old Testament proverbs consist of two lines that express either a contrast, a restatement, cause and effect, or a comparison. The following list describes the most common types of proverbs.

Proverbs of contrast

In a proverb employing contrast, the first line makes a statement and the second says something in opposition, contrast, or seeming contradiction to the first. But when read together, the two lines reflect different dimensions of the same truth. Contrasting proverbs predominate in Proverbs 10–15.

Some examples of proverbs of contrast are.

'A wise son makes a father glad, but a foolish son is a grief to his mother' (Prov. 10.1).

'The Lord is far from the wicked, but he hears the prayer of the righteous' (Prov. 15.29).

Proverbs of restatement

This kind of proverb states the same thing in two different ways so as to reinforce and sometimes to bring out an additional aspect of the main problem or main idea. Proverbs of restatement occur most frequently in chapters 16-20.

Some examples of restatement are:

'Pride goes before destruction, and a haughty spirit before stumbling' (Prov. 16.18).
'He who begets a fool does so to his sorrow, and the father of the fool has no joy' (Prov. 17.21).

Proverbs that show cause and effect

In many of the proverbs, the second line tells the effect or result of the first line. In such cases, the second line completes or enlarges on the meaning of the first line. Cause and effect proverbs appear frequently in chapters 17, 20, and 21. The following are some examples of cause and effect.

'He who returns evil for good, evil will not depart from his house' (Prov. 17.13).
'The sluggard does not plow after the autumn, so he begs during the harvest and has nothing' (Prov. 20.4).

Proverbs of comparison

Some proverbs make their point by using a comparison, usually in the form of a simile, a literary device that we discussed in Chapter 4. Comparisons occur especially in the second collection of Solomon's proverbs beginning at chapter 25. The following are some examples of comparison:

'Like vinegar to the teeth and smoke to the eyes, so is the lazy one to those who send him' (Prov. 10.26).
'Like apples of gold in settings of silver is a word spoken in right circumstances' (Prov. 25.11).
'Like a dog that returns to its vomit is a fool who repeats his folly' (Prov. 26.11).

Extended proverbs

Extended proverbs are longer than the usual two lines. Such extended proverbs occur mostly in the 'words of the wise' (Proverbs 22–24) and in the observations of Agur (chapter 30) and King Lemuel (chapter 31). A few such extended proverbs also appear in the Proverbs of Solomon that the men of Hezekiah transcribed (Proverbs 25–29). The following are some examples of extended proverbs:

An exhortation to hear the words of the wise (Prov. 22.17-21)
A warning against strong drink (Prov. 23.29-35)

A description of the sluggard's field (Prov. 24.30-34)

The numerical saying

There are other wisdom forms such as numerical sayings. Proverbs chapter 30 has several good examples of numerical sayings. For example,

> There are three things that will not be satisfied,
>   Four that will not say, 'Enough':
> Sheol and the barren womb,
>   Earth that is never satisfied with water,
>   And fire that never says, 'Enough.'
> The eye that mocks a father and scorns a mother,
>   the ravens of the valley will pick it out,
>   and the young eagles will eat it (Prov. 30.15-17).

The prophet Amos also uses this kind of symbolism in chapters one and two when he is talking about the judgment that is coming to the nations (including Israel and Judah). Amos says,

> Thus says the Lord,
> 'For three transgressions of Judah and for four
> I will not revoke its punishment,
>   because they rejected the law of the Lord
>   and have not kept his statutes;
> their lies also have led them astray,
>   those after which their fathers walked.
> So I will send fire upon Judah
>   and it will consume the citadels of Jerusalem' (Amos 2.4-5).

The use of the term 'three and for four' is a symbolic way of emphasizing the seriousness and the severity of the saying.

The autobiographical saying

An autobiographical saying is a statement in which the author says something like, 'I searched for wisdom and this is what I learned.' You can find some of these in the book of Ecclesiastes. For example, Solomon says, 'I set my mind to know wisdom and to know madness and folly; I realized that this also is striving after wind' (Eccl. 1.17). Other autobiographical sayings are found in the early chapters of the book of Proverbs, where the writer talks about experiencing the seductions of the harlot, who is trying to seduce him into the path of death.

Imagined speech

Imagined speech represents a kind of event that could take place. For example, Proverbs chapter 7 reports the speech of a prostitute as she attempts to seduce a young man. What the prostitute says is an imagined representative and dramatized speech. Her speech represents the temptation to abandon wisdom and to pursue folly.

Interpreting the proverb

As we stated above, the proverb should be interpreted as a part of the larger genre of wisdom literature. The proverb, therefore, should be placed in its literary and theological context. In addition, there are other characteristics of biblical proverbs that impact their interpretation.

Beginning with the fear of the Lord

The Bible incorporates the wisdom tradition by starting with the fear of the Lord. The fear of the Lord is the beginning of wisdom. Notice the following examples:

> The fear of the Lord is the beginning of knowledge (Prov. 1.7).
> The fear of the Lord is the beginning of wisdom (Prov. 9.10).
> Behold the fear of the Lord, that is wisdom (Job 28.28).
> The conclusion, when all has been heard, is: fear God and keep his commandments, because this applies to every person (Eccl. 12.13).

The wisdom tradition is common throughout the ancient near east, but Israel brought wisdom under the terms of the covenant. Israel gave wisdom a starting point in the fear of the Lord. The people of Israel learned the fear of the Lord at Mount Sinai. So for Israel that Sinai experience was the beginning of their wisdom. Moses said that when Israel came to the mountain, that is when they learned wisdom. He declared, 'So keep and do [the commandments], for that is your wisdom and your understanding in the sight of the peoples who will hear these statutes and say, 'Surely this great nation is a wise and understanding people" (Deut. 4.6).

Recognizing wisdom's limits

Another way that wisdom is incorporated into the Bible is by recognizing wisdom's limits. This is a motif that can be found scattered throughout the book of Proverbs. Human wisdom and study has its limits, and when we have reached the end of our limitations, we need God's help. For example, we read.

A man's heart plans his way,
  But the LORD directs his steps (Prov. 16.9).
The horse is prepared for the day of battle,
  But deliverance is of the LORD (Prov. 21.31).
Houses and riches are an inheritance from fathers,
  But a prudent wife is from the LORD (Prov. 19.14).

All of these proverbs bear the theme that human wisdom and human achievement are limited. There is a gap that can only be filled by the grace and by the revelation of God. Ultimately, life cannot be found apart from God reaching out to us.

Another limitation of wisdom is that wisdom tends to make us proud. Wisdom and knowledge make us proud, but the fear of the Lord makes us humble. The fear of the Lord then is the beginning of wisdom. These proverbs that recognize the limits of wisdom keep insisting upon the mystery. We may be able to master wisdom, but we can never master the mystery of God.

Presenting wisdom in covenantal terms

Not only does the Bible incorporate the wisdom tradition by starting with the fear of the Lord, but also wisdom in the Bible is covenantal. That is, the wisdom literature does not exist apart from God's whole revelation in the Bible. The whole revelation of God includes the teaching of Moses and the word of the prophets. The human investigation found in the wisdom literature by itself is not sufficient. We require also the prophetic revelation and the Torah revelation, the other parts of Scripture, to give us a full and complete revelation of the Lord and to bring us to our final place with God. Proverbs is linked textually with the rest of Scripture in Proverbs chapter 30. Here Agur combines the wisdom tradition with the rest of the Scripture, showing the necessity of all parts of Scripture.

Proverbs is also linked to the Torah and the Prophets theologically. The Proverbs, the Torah, and the prophets have a strong emphasis upon retribution theology. That is, you reap what you have sown. You can see this all the way from Deuteronomy forward into the prophets. In Deuteronomy, if you obey, you be blessed and if you disobey, you will be cursed. Proverbs has that same retribution theology. The primary way that the proverb puts it is that if you are wise you will prosper and succeed and live a long life. But if you pursue folly, if you forsake wisdom, you will be unsuccessful and die early. Both Proverbs and the prophets say that if you are faithful to God and faithful to the covenant you will find life, and if you are unfaithful you will find death. Both Proverbs and the prophets share this theology of retribution.

Proverbs in the New Testament
Although most of the Proverbs in the Bible are found in the Old Testament, Jesus and the other New Testament writers sometimes used proverbs in their teaching and preaching. For example, Jesus described the state of judgment that would exist in the last days by saying, 'Wherever the corpse is, there the vultures will gather' (Mt. 24.28). On another occasion, Jesus diagnosed the attitude of the people of Nazareth when he said to them, 'You will surely say this proverb to me, 'Physician, heal yourself'' (Lk. 4.23). Other proverbs of Jesus include the following.

> A city on a hill cannot be hidden (Mt. 5.14).
> No one can serve two masters (Mt. 6.24).
> It is not the healthy who need a doctor, but the sick (Mt. 9.12).
> If a blind man leads a blind man, both will fall into a pit (Mt. 15.14).
> No servant is greater than his master (Jn 13.16).

The apostle Paul used proverbs on several occasions. He warned about the corrupting influence of evil by saying, 'A little leaven leavens the whole lump' (1Cor. 5.6; Gal. 5.9).

The Riddle

Definition of the riddle
A riddle is a question or statement intentionally worded in a puzzling manner, often containing paradox, and propounded in order that it be guessed or answered. For example, 'What has a mouth but cannot eat; what moves but has no legs?' The answer is 'a river.' Also, 'The more you take, the more you leave behind,' and the answer is, 'steps.' The riddle involves a matching of wits; the challenger offers a riddle with a concealed meaning which the opponent must discover.

Purpose of the riddle

The riddle was a test of wisdom.

Today, riddles are regarded as a form of amusement, a game. In biblical times, however, a riddle was a more serious matter than in modern times. In the Bible, the ability to tell riddles and solve riddles was considered a sign of great wisdom. As a test of wisdom, the riddle concealed valuable information from the unworthy while divulging important facts to those deserving them. The introduction to the book of Proverbs concludes the goal of instruction with these words: 'to understand a proverb and a figure, the words of the wise and their riddles' (Prov. 1.6). One of the wisdom psalms declares.

> Hear this, all peoples; Give ear, all inhabitants of the world ... My mouth shall speak wisdom, And the meditation of my heart shall give understanding. I will incline my ear to a proverb; I will disclose my riddle on the harp. (Ps. 49.1-4)

Many riddles were handed down from generation to generation. Again, we look to a wisdom psalm, which says, 'Give ear, O my people, to my law; Incline your ears to the words of my mouth. I will open my mouth in a parable; I will utter ancient riddles, Which we have heard and known, And our fathers have told us' (Ps. 78.1-3).

Riddles play a prominent role in the account of King Solomon, Israel's wisest man. We read, 'Now when the queen of Sheba heard of the fame of Solomon, she came to test him with riddles ... So Solomon answered all her questions; there was nothing so difficult for the king that he could not explain it to her' (1 Kgs 10.1-3; see also 2 Chron. 9.1-4). Solomon's wisdom made such a great impression upon the Queen that she was 'left breathless' (1 Kgs 10.5).

Riddles can also be used for evil purposes. According to Dan. 8.23, the fierce ruler that many believe to be the Antichrist will have the ability to 'understand riddles' (Dan. 8.19, 23). This ability is a sign of his great intelligence.

The riddle could be told as a wager.

In the Bible, riddles sometimes were told as a wager. Samson's riddle to the Philistines (Judg. 14.14) was of this kind. Samson was so infatuated with a Philistine woman of Timnah that he married her despite the objections of his parents. The wedding feast, like that celebrated in certain parts of the East today, was a seven-day banquet, at which various kinds of entertainment were offered. Samson, equal to the demands of the occasion, proposed a riddle for his thirty companions. If they could not guess the answer, they would be required to give Samson thirty changes of clothing. The riddle said, 'Out of the eater came something to eat, And out of the strong came something sweet' (Judg. 14.14). When the men were still unable to guess the riddle after three days, they threatened Samson's bride and forced her to get the answer from him. Because of the urgent and tearful implorings of his bride, he tells her the solution; and she betrays it to the thirty young men. On the seventh day of the wedding feast, the men gave Samson the answer—'What is sweeter than honey? And what is stronger than a lion?' Because he lost the wager, Samson slew thirty Philistines and took their clothing. Then, in anger, he left the house of his bride and returned home.

Samson's offer of the riddle was a way for him to gain acceptance and entry into the world of his Philistine bride. The Philistines, however, were unwilling to allow Samson to enter their world, so they won the bet through dishonesty—they cheated.

The riddle was a part of prophetic revelation.
According to Num. 12.6-8, the Lord communicated with prophets by means of visions, dreams, or riddles. The Lord said, 'If there is a prophet among you, I, the LORD, make myself known to him in a vision; I speak to him in a dream. Not so with my servant Moses ... I speak with him face to face, even plainly, and not in riddles.' This Scripture implies that the riddle belonged to the essence of prophecy. It was said that Daniel had 'an excellent spirit, knowledge, and understanding to interpret dreams, explain riddles, and solve problems' (Dan. 5.12). The prophet Amos saw a vision of an ordinary basket of summer fruit, but the vision was a riddle. In the Middle East, summer fruit is fully ripe and will soon be rotten. The overripe fruit represented the nation of Israel who had turned away from God and who would soon be destroyed. Israel was ripe for judgment. Ezekiel 17.1-10 is a symbolic riddle in which the king of

Babylon is compared to an eagle who takes in his beak the king of Judah, who is symbolized by the highest branch of a cedar tree.

The fable

Definition of the fable

The fable is a short symbolic story in which animals, plants, and other inanimate objects speak and act like human beings. The fable, like the allegory and the parable, makes a moral point through the telling of a story. In 1 Kgs 4.32-34, we read that Solomon spoke three thousand proverbs and one thousand five songs. We are also told,

> Also he spoke of trees, from the cedar tree of Lebanon even to the hyssop that springs out of the wall; he spoke also of animals, of birds, of creeping things, and of fish. And men of all nations, from all the kings of the earth who had heard of his wisdom, came to hear the wisdom of Solomon.

The statement that Solomon spoke about the plants and animals may mean that he was gifted in the telling of fables.

Examples of the fable

The Old Testament contains two excellent examples of the fable. The first one is spoken to the lords of Shechem by Jotham, the brother of Abimelech.

Jotham's fable of the thorn king

In Judges chapter 9, Abimelech murdered all of his seventy brothers except Jotham, who escaped. Then the lords of Shechem illegitimately crowned Abimelech as king. When Jotham heard that Abimelech had been made king, he went and stood on top of Mount Gerizim, and called out to the lords of Shechem, 'Listen to me, you men of Shechem, That God may listen to you! The trees once went forth to anoint a king over them. And they said to the worthy olive tree, 'Reign over us!" (Judg. 9.7, 8). But the olive tree, content to produce oil, did not desire to be king. The trees then went to the productive fig tree and vine, but neither of them wanted to be king either. Finally, the trees asked the worthless thorn bush to be king, and the thorn agreed to rule; but he promised tyranny, saying to the trees, 'If in truth you anoint me as king over you, Then come and take shelter in my shade; but if not, let fire come out of the thorn bush and devour the cedars of Lebanon!' (Judg. 9.15). Jothan then revealed the meaning of the fable, saying,

> You have risen up against my father's house this day, and killed his seventy sons on one stone, and made Abimelech, the son of his female servant, king over the men of Shechem, because he is your brother—if then you have acted in truth and sincerity with Jerubbaal and with his house this day, then rejoice in Abimelech, and let him also rejoice in you. But if not, let fire come from Abimelech and devour the men of Shechem and Beth Millo; and let fire come from the men of Shechem and from Beth Millo and devour Abimelech! (Judg. 9.18-20)

Jotham then fled and hid until Abimelech's rule had ended. Jotham's fable of the thorn king proved to be a prophetic word. After three years of Abimelech's rule, animosity developed between him and the people of Shechem. In the ensuing battle between Abimelech and Shechem, the city of Shechem was destroyed and Abimelech was killed.

Jehoash's fable of the proud briar

The second fable is an insult spoken by Jehoash the king of Israel and is addressed to Amaziah the king of Judah. At the age of twenty-five Amaziah becomes king of Judah, and he attacks and defeats the neighboring Edomites. In his new-found confidence he sets his eyes upon reclaiming the northern kingdom of Israel. To this end he sends a message to Jehoash king of Israel, inviting him to go to war. He writes, 'Come, let us face one another in battle' (2 Kgs 14.8). Jehoash replies with a condescending and mocking fable. He replies saying,

> The briar bush that was in Lebanon sent to the cedar that was in Lebanon, saying, 'Give your daughter to my son as wife'; and a wild beast that was in Lebanon passed by and trampled the briar. You have indeed defeated Edom, and your heart has lifted you up. Glory in that, and stay at home; for why should you meddle with trouble so that you fall—you and Judah with you? (2 Kgs 14.9-10)

In the parable, a briar bush, which is a worthless plant filled with thorns, asks the magnificent cedar tree to give his daughter to the briar's son as bride. A wild beast happened to pass by and trampled the brier bush. Jehoash warns that Amaziah will be similarly trampled. Amaziah, however, was lifted up with pride, and he would not heed the warning of Jehoash. As the fable predicted, Amaziah was defeated in battle and Jerusalem was looted.

Other sayings that are similar to the fable

Throughout the wisdom literature and the prophetic literature, we find numerous poetic passages that include talking plants and animals. These passages do not represent complete fables, but they carry similar symbolism in which the plants and animals represent the actions and attitudes of people. One example from the Proverbs says, 'The leech has two daughters, 'Give!' and 'Give!' (Prov. 30.15). The insatiable demand of the leech's daughters represents the greed of people who are never satisfied.

For Review and Study

1. Where in the Bible do we find wisdom literature?
2. Enumerate four major emphases of the wisdom literature.
3. What do we mean when we say that the wisdom literature emphasizes 'human experience'?
4. What is the difference between an emphasis upon 'creation' and an emphasis upon 'history'?
5. Explain how the wisdom literature emphasizes the 'individual' instead of the 'community.'
6. What is the definition of the proverb?
7. Note some reasons why the proverbs are not absolute laws.
8. List the eight kinds of proverbs.
9. Which kind of proverb normally includes a 'simile'?
10. Where do we find examples of the 'extended proverbs'?
11. What is an 'autobiographical saying'?
12. What kind of speech is found in Proverbs 7?
13. In the biblical view of wisdom, where does wisdom begin?
14. Explain 'wisdom's limits.'
15. We said that biblical wisdom is presented 'in covenantal terms.' What does that mean?

16. Give two examples of proverbs that are found in the New Testament.
17. What is a riddle?
18. Explain the three purposes of the riddle.
19. What is the definition of the fable?
20. Name two biblical examples of the fable.

8

INTERPRETING PARABLES

In this chapter we will study the parable, the allegory, and the type. In their use of figurative language these literary forms bear resemblance to the proverb, the riddle, and the fable, which we examined in Chapter 5.[58]

Definition of the parable

The definition of the parable is not fully agreed upon by biblical scholars, and therefore the lists of Jesus' parables vary considerably. Most scholars agree that Jesus told at least thirty parables. We may define the parable as a story that illustrates a spiritual truth. The parable is true to life, something which can be observed in human experience.

Unlike the proverb, which is written in poetic form, the parable is narrative in form but figurative in meaning. Parables use both similes and metaphors to make their comparisons, and parables are told in the Bible to inform, convince, or persuade their audiences. Jesus utilized parables to motivate his hearers to make wise choices in life. To Jesus' original audiences the parables both revealed and concealed new truths regarding God's kingdom program. Those who responded rightly were called disciples, and to them it was

---

[58] This chapter draws from the following sources: Vernon D. Doerksen, 'The Interpretation of Parables,' *Grace Theological Journal* 11.2 (1970), pp. 3-20; and Mark L. Bailey, 'The Kingdom in the Parables of Matthew 13,' *Bibliotheca Sacra* 155, no. 617 (1998), pp. 29-38.

granted to understand the mysteries of the kingdom. The same truth was concealed from those who were unreceptive to the message of Jesus.

Parables in the Old Testament

Parables were a popular form of wisdom instruction, but they do not occur frequently in the Old Testament. Short parables, however, are found in the wisdom books and in the prophets. For example, we read, 'Without having any chief, officer, or ruler, the ant prepares her food in summer and gathers her sustenance in harvest' (Prov. 6.7-8). This very short narrative is spoken in order to teach us that we must take the initiative to work hard even if we have no leader to give us instructions.

In another parable, Solomon tells the following story.

> There was a little city with few men in it; and a great king came against it, besieged it, and built great snares around it. Now there was found in it a poor wise man, and he by his wisdom delivered the city. Yet no one remembered that same poor man (Eccl. 9.14-15).

The meaning of the parable is given in the following verse: 'Then I said: Wisdom is better than strength. Nevertheless the poor man's wisdom is despised, and his words are not heard' (Eccl. 9.16).

Some scholars classify Isa. 28.24-29 as a parable; it reads.

> Does the plowman keep plowing all day to sow? Does he keep turning his soil and breaking the clods? When he has leveled its surface, does he not sow the black cumin and scatter the cumin, plant the wheat in rows, the barley in the appointed place, and the spelt in its place? For he instructs him in right judgment, his God teaches him. For the black cumin is not threshed with a threshing sledge, nor is a cartwheel rolled over the cumin; but the black cumin is beaten out with a stick, and the cumin with a rod. Wheat must be ground; therefore he does not thresh it forever, break it with his cartwheel, or crush it with his horsemen. This also comes from the LORD of hosts, Who is wonderful in counsel and excellent in guidance.

The farmer knows not only how and when to plow but he knows also when to sow the various seed. He knows that he must harvest cumin in a different fashion from the way that he harvests wheat. The parable teaches us that God knows how to disciple his people at every season in their experience. God knows when he should chastise us and when he should encourage us.

Parables in the New Testament

The only parables that we find in the New Testament are those which are told by Jesus. Parables make up approximately one third of the teaching of Jesus in the Gospels. Jesus told so many parables that Mark comments, 'without a parable he did not speak unto them' (Mk 4.34). The great number of parables demonstrates the importance of them in the teaching ministry of Jesus. Although his parables are often simple, they are memorable; and they remain well-known throughout history and around the world.

The function of parables in the Gospels

It is generally agreed that Jesus was the master teacher, and his skillful use of parables is a significant part of his teaching method. I suggest three functions of the parables in the Gospels: (1) The parables clarified the teachings of Jesus for his disciples. (2) The parables obscured the teachings of Jesus from his opponents. (3) The parables applied the teachings of Jesus to life.

The parables clarified the teachings of Jesus for his disciples

Because the parables are stories, they are easily understood and remembered, and they hold the attention of the audience. Mark 4.1, 2 demonstrates this fact. On one occasion, a great multitude had gathered, and he taught them by parables. The group stayed all day; finally in the evening they were sent away. It appears that the parabolic method was a good way of keeping their attention (Mk 4.1-2, 33-35). The story-telling method is a powerful means of imparting truth, and Jesus made effective use of it.

Even unbelievers were able to understand many of the parables. On one occasion when Jesus taught that we should love our neighbor, a man challenged Jesus by asking the question, 'Who is my neighbor?' Jesus responded by telling the parable of the Good

Samaritan (Lk. 10.30-36). The parable illustrates the meaning of 'neighbor.' This parable was understood clearly by the unbelieving lawyer who had asked the question. Jesus then told the man, 'Go and do likewise' (Lk. 10.37).

At another time, while eating at the home of Simon the Pharisee, Jesus told the parable of the two debtors:

> There was a certain creditor who had two debtors. One owed five hundred denarii, and the other fifty. And when they had nothing with which to repay, he freely forgave them both. Tell Me, therefore, which of them will love him more? Simon answered and said, I suppose the one whom he forgave more. And he said to him, You have rightly judged.

Simon, to whom Jesus addressed this parable, was apparently an unbeliever, but he was able to understand the meaning and respond to the question posed by Jesus. Jesus said to him, 'You have rightly judges.' The parable was effective for illustrating the teaching of Jesus.

The parables obscured the teachings of Jesus from his opponents

When Jesus was asked why he spoke in parables he responded, 'Because it is given unto you to know the mysteries of the kingdom of heaven, but to them it is not given' (Mt. 13.11; cf. Lk. 8.10; Mk 4.11, 12). In many settings, particularly after his rejection by the nation of Israel was becoming clear, Jesus saw the need to speak in a manner understood by his true followers but not understood by the mere curious or those who were hostile to his ministry. Mt. 12 is a turning point in the ministry of Jesus, and the leaders of Israel have shown clear opposition to his ministry. In the next chapter, Matthew 13, Jesus expounded the parables of the kingdom. At the close of the first parable, we are introduced to the purpose of the parabolic method. The disciples asked Jesus, 'Why do you speak in parables?' (Mt. 13.10), and Jesus replied,

> Because it has been given to you to know the mysteries of the kingdom of heaven, but to them it has not been given ... Therefore I speak to them in parables, because seeing they do not see, and hearing they do not hear, nor do they understand. And in them the prophecy of Isaiah is fulfilled, which says: Hearing you

will hear and shall not understand, And seeing you will see and not perceive; For the hearts of this people have grown dull. Their ears are hard of hearing, And their eyes they have closed, Lest they should see with their eyes and hear with their ears, Lest they should understand with their hearts and turn, So that I should heal them. But blessed are your eyes for they see, and your ears for they hear; for assuredly, I say to you that many prophets and righteous men desired to see what you see, and did not see it, and to hear what you hear, and did not hear it (Mt. 13.11-17).

Through his use of parables, Jesus revealed the truth to his followers, while at the same time he concealed the truth to those who were not receptive.

The parables applied the teachings of Jesus to real life

Whenever Jesus told a parable, it was not to entertain his listeners or even to impart information alone. The parables required the hearers to apply the teachings of Jesus to their own lives in concrete ways. The parables called for a response on the part of the hearers. As we mentioned above, when Jesus told the parable of the Good Samaritan, he concluded with the words, 'Go and do likewise' (Lk. 10.37).

Types of parables in the Gospels

The parables of Jesus can be classified into three groups based upon their function within the ministry of Jesus: (1) the teaching parables, such as the parables of the Sower, the Tares, and the Mustard Seed, which relate in a general way to teachings concerning the Kingdom of God; (2) the evangelic parables, such as the parables of the Lost Sheep, the Lost Son, and the Great Supper, which deal with Christ's love for the sinner; and (3) the prophetic or judicial parables, such as the parables of the Ten Virgins and the parable of the Wicked Vinegrower.

The parables can also be classified based upon their subject matter. Many of the parables have a common subject or theme, such as the 'seed' parables, or a common character, such as the 'servant parables.' All seven parables in Matthew 13 relate to the kingdom of God. The parables of Jesus can be listed according to the following subjects.

Seed parables
1. The Sower (Mt. 13.3-8)
2. The Weeds (Mt. 13.24-30)
3. The Mustard Seed (Mt. 13.31-32)
4. Yeast (Mt. 13.33)
5. The Seed Growing Secretly (Mk 4.26-29)

Nature parables
1-5. All the seed parables listed above
6. The Two Houses—on rock and sand (Mt. 7.24-27)
7. The New Cloth and New Wineskins (Mt. 9.16-17)
8. The Hidden Treasures—in a field (Mt. 13.44)
9. The Pearl of Great Price (Mt. 13.45-46)
10. The Fishing Net (Mt. 13.47-50)
11. The Workers in the Vineyard (Mt. 20.1-16)
12. The Wicked Vinegrowers (Mt. 21.33-46)
13. The Barren Fig Tree (Lk. 13.6-9)
14. The Lost Sheep (Lk. 15.4-7)

Servant parables
These are parables in which the master departs, leaving the servants on their own. When he returns, the good servants are rewarded and/or the bad ones are punished.
1. The Two Servants (Mt. 24.45-51)
2. The Talents (Mt. 25.14-30)
3. The Doorkeeper (Mk 13.34.37)
4. The Pounds—or Minas (Lk. 19.11-27)

The servant departs or is away and then returns to report to his master. The reckoning received is unexpected.
1. The Unforgiving Servant (Mt. 18.23-35)
2. The Workers in the Vineyard (Mt. 20.1-16)
3. The Wicked Vinegrowers (Mt. 21.33-46)
4. The Shrewd Manager (Lk. 16.1-9)
5. The Servant's Reward (Lk. 17.7-10)

Father parables
1. The Two Sons (Mt. 21.28-32)
2. The Wicked Vinegrowers (Mt. 21.33-46)
3. The Wedding Banquet (Mt. 22.1-14)
4. The Prodigal Son (Lk. 15.11-32)

King parables
1. The Unforgiving Servant (Mt. 18.23-35)
2. The Wedding Banquet (Mt. 22.1-14)
3. The King's Rash War (Lk. 14.31-33)
4. The Pounds—or Minas (Lk. 19.11-27)

Money (or treasure) parables
1. The Hidden Treasure (Mt. 13.44)
2. The Pearl of Great Price (Mt. 13.45-46)
3. The Unforgiving Servant (Mt. 18.23-35)
4. The Workers in the Vineyard (Mt. 20.1-16)
5. The Talents (Mt. 25.14-30)
6. The Two Debtors (Lk. 7.41-43)
7. The Good Samaritan (Lk. 10.25-37)
8. The Rich Fool (Lk. 12.16-21)
9. The Shrewd Manager (Lk. 16.1-9)
10. The Pharisee and the Tax Collector (Lk. 18.9-14)
11. The Pounds—or Minas (Lk. 19.11-27)

Harvest parables
1. The Weeds (Mt. 13.24-30; see vv. 30, 39)
2. The Wicked Vinegrowers (Mt. 21.33-46; see v. 41)
3. The Talents (Mt. 25.14-30; see vv. 24, 26)
4. The Seed Growing Secretly (Mk 4.26-29)

Women parables
1. The Yeast (Mt. 13.33)
2. The Virgins (Mt. 25.1-13)
3. The Lost Coin (Lk. 15.8-10)
4. The Unjust Judge (Lk. 18.1-8)

Social or domestic parables
1. The Wedding Banquet (Mt. 22.1-14)
2. The Ten Virgins (Mt. 25.1-13)
3. The Doorkeeper (Mk 13.34-37)
4. The Rude Children (Lk. 7.31-35)
5. The Good Samaritan (Lk. 10.25-37)
6. The Friend at Midnight (Lk. 11.5-8)
7. The Great Banquet (Lk. 14.15-24)
8. The Lost Coin (Lk. 15.8-10)
9. The Prodigal Son (Lk. 15.11-32)

10. The Servant's Reward (Lk. 17.7-10)
11. The Unjust Judge (Lk. 18.1-8)
12. The Pharisee and the Tax Collector (Lk. 18.9-14)

Compassion parables
1. The Good Samaritan (Lk. 10.25-37; see v. 33)
2. The Great Banquet (Lk. 14.15-24; see v. 21)
3. The Lost Sheep (Lk. 15.4-7; see v. 4)
4. The Prodigal Son (Lk. 15.11-32; see v. 20)

Rejoicing parables
1. The Hidden Treasure (Mt. 13.44)
2. The Lost Sheep (Lk. 15.4-7)
3. The Lost Coin (Lk. 15.8-10)
4. The Prodigal Son (Lk. 15.11-32)

Feast parables
1. The Wedding Banquet (Mt. 22.1-14)
2. The Ten Virgins (Mt. 25.1-13)
3. The Great Banquet (Lk. 14.15-24)
4. The Prodigal Son (Lk. 15.11-32)

Refusal parables
1. The Unforgiving Servant (Mt. 18.23-35).
The servant whose debts were canceled refused to cancel a debt someone owed him; therefore, the king put him in jail and refused to cancel his debt after all.
2. The Wicked Vinegrowers (Mt. 21.33-46).
The tenants refused to treat the landowner's servants and his son kindly; therefore, the landowner refused to leave his vineyard in those tenants' hands.
3. The Wedding Banquet (Mt. 22.1-14).
Those invited to the wedding banquet refused to come; therefore, the king refused to let them live.
4. The Talents (Mt. 25.14-30).
The man with one talent refused to invest it; therefore, the master refused to let him keep even the one talent.
5. The Rich Fool (Lk. 12.16-21).
The rich fool refused to honor God; therefore, God refused to allow him to live.
6. The Barren Fig Tree (Lk. 13.6-9).

The owner of a fig tree refused to let it grow.
7. The Great Banquet (Lk. 14.15-24).
Those invited to the banquet made excuses for not attending and refused to come.[59]

The parables of the Kingdom
Many of Jesus' parables are related to the kingdom of God. The parables were used to illustrate some of the great truths concerning the kingdom. Matthew 13 includes seven parables that teach the 'mysteries of the kingdom of heaven' (Mt. 13.11). For these parables Jesus uses the introductory formula, 'The kingdom of heaven is like ...' The reason for the centrality of the kingdom in the parables is the priority it held in Jesus' entire ministry. The kingdom of God was the central message of John (Mt. 3.2), Jesus (Mt. 4.17), and the disciples (Mt. 10.5–7). While many of the parables state directly that they are about the kingdom, still other parables have an indirect connection to the kingdom message. Interpretation of the parables must be based upon Jesus' understanding of the kingdom of God. We must recognize the two-fold nature of the kingdom. In one sense it is a present kingdom (Matthew 13), and in another sense it is a coming kingdom (the Ten Virgins, the Talents). The following parables relate to the kingdom of God.

Progress in the kingdom
    The Weeds
    The Mustard Seed
    The Yeast
    The Seed Growing Secretly
Conflict between Jesus' concept of the kingdom and that of the Pharisees
    The New Cloth and New Wineskins
    The Rude Children
Grace and sinners in the kingdom
    The Hidden Treasure
    The Pearl of Great Price
    The Workers in the Vineyard
    The Two Sons
    The Rude Children

---

[59] This list is according to Roy B. Zuck, *Basic Bible Interpretation* (Wheaton, IL: Victor Books, 1991), pp. 205-208.

The Two Debtors
The Barren Fig Tree
The Great Banquet
The Lost Sheep
The Lost Coin
The Prodigal Son
The Pharisee and the Tax Collector

Characteristics of those in the kingdom
- Compassion: The Good Samaritan
- Humility: The Servant's Reward
- Faithfulness: The Two Servants
  - The Talents
  - The Pounds or Minas
- Persistent prayer: The Friend at Midnight
  - The Unjust Judge
- Wealth: The Rich Fool
  - The Shrewd Manager
- Forgiveness: The Unforgiving Servant
- Sacrifice: The Unfinished Tower
  - The King's Rash War

Rejection of the King and his kingdom
- The Sower
- The Two Sons
- The Wicked Vinegrowers
- The Wedding Banquet
- The Rude Children
- The Great Banquet
- The Pounds-or Minas

Judgment on those who reject the King and/or reward for those who accept him
- The Two Houses
- The Weeds
- The Fishing Net
- The Worker in the Vineyard
- The Wicked Vinegrowers
- The Wedding Banquet
- The Two Servants
- The 10 Virgins
- The Talents

The Doorkeeper
 The Two Debtors
 The Barren Fig Tree
 The Great Banquet
 The Pounds—or Minas

Alertness at and preparedness for the King's coming
 The 10 Virgins
 The Doorkeeper

Parables of the Kingdom in Matthew 13
 1. The Sower (13.13-23), which teaches that the good news of the Gospel will be rejected by most people.
 2. The Wheat and the Weeds (13.24-30, 36-43), which teaches that people with genuine faith and people with a false profession of faith will exist together between Christ's two advents.
 3. The Mustard Seed (13.31-32), which teaches that the kingdom will grow rapidly from a small beginning.
 4. The Yeast (13.33-35), which teaches that people who profess to belong to God will grow in numbers without being stopped.
 5. The Hidden Treasure (13.44), which teaches that Christ came to purchase (redeem) Israel, God's treasured possession.
 6. The Pearl (13.45-46), which teaches that Christ gave his life to provide redemption for the church.
 7. The Net (13.47-52), which teaches that Angels will separate the wicked from the righteous when Christ comes.

Four Important Guidelines

Four specific guidelines will help us to understand the meaning of Jesus' parables: (1) Study the historical and cultural background of the parable. (2) Observe the occasion of the parable. (3) Analyze the characters and events within the parable. (4) Search for an interpretation of the parable in the surrounding biblical text, either before or after the parable.

Study the background

Illustrations from daily life

Perhaps even more than any other literature type in the Bible, understanding the historical and cultural setting of parables is crucial. Jesus used illustrations from everyday life that people back then would have immediately understood. If we do not understand their historical background, then we cannot fully grasp the meanings of the parables. Jesus made reference to a fishing net, a vineyard, a wedding banquet, oil lamps, and a fig tree. We must understand these references in their historical and cultural settings before we can comprehend the meaning of the parables.

Life in Jesus' day

An understanding of life in Palestine is essential to an understanding of many of the parables. The value of the 'talent' and the 'pence' must be known to appreciate the lesson of forgiveness taught by the parable of the Unmerciful Servant (Mt. 18.23-34). The common practice of sowing grain should be familiar to understand the parable of the Sower (Mt. 13.3-8). Understanding the cultural background is essential for interpreting the parables properly.

Observe the occasion

Sometimes the meaning of the parable is revealed by observing the occasion surrounding the telling of the parable. Jesus often told parables to answer a question, meet a challenge, or invite the hearers to change their thinking. Discovering the need that prompted the parable is a significant step toward unlocking its meaning within its original context. The need may be seen in the material that introduces the parable or it may be revealed after the parable is told.

We could point to six kinds of occasions or purposes that led to Jesus' parables: parables in answer to questions, parables in answer to requests, parables in answer to criticism, parables given with a stated purpose, parables following an exhortation or principle, and parables with the purpose implied but not stated.[60]

---

[60] See Zuck, pp. 211-15.

Parables in answer to a question

In Mt. 9.14 the disciples of John ask Jesus, 'Why do we and the Pharisees fast often, but your disciples do not fast?' Jesus does not answer their question directly, but in answer to their question, Jesus gives the Parable of the Bridegroom. The parable teaches that fasting is not necessary while Jesus is on earth with his disciples. He also gives the parables of the Old Garment and New Wineskins to show that he has introduced a new era in God's plan.

On another occasion, Jesus taught that we should love our neighbor, but an expert in the Law asked the question, 'Who is my neighbor?' In answer to the question, Jesus told the parable of the Good Samaritan (Lk. 10.25-37).

At a different time Peter asked the question, 'Lord, how many times shall I forgive my brother when he sins against me? Up to seven times?' (Matthew18.21). Peter's question prompted Jesus to give the Parable of the Unforgiving Servant.

Parables in answer to requests

A young man approached Jesus and requested the following: 'Teacher, tell my brother to divide the inheritance with me.' Jesus responded to his request by telling a parable.

> The ground of a certain rich man yielded plentifully. And he thought within himself, saying, 'What shall I do, since I have no room to store my crops?' So he said, 'I will do this: I will pull down my barns and build greater, and there I will store all my crops and my goods. And I will say to my soul, 'Soul, you have many goods laid up for many years; take your ease; eat, drink, and be merry." But God said to him, 'Fool! This night your soul will be required of you; then whose will those things be which you have provided?' So is he who lays up treasure for himself, and is not rich toward God (Lk. 12.16-21).

Parables in answer to criticism

The Pharisees and the teachers of the Law criticized Jesus saying, 'This Man welcomes sinners and eats with them' (Lk. 15.2). In response to their criticism against him, Jesus told the Parables of the Lost Sheep, the Lost Coin, and the Lost Son. The first of these, the Lost Sheep, reads,

> What man of you, having a hundred sheep, if he loses one of them, does not leave the ninety-nine in the wilderness, and go after the one which is lost until he finds it? And when he has found it, he lays it on his shoulders, rejoicing. And when he comes home, he calls together his friends and neighbors, saying to them, 'Rejoice with me, for I have found my sheep which was lost!' I say to you that likewise there will be more joy in heaven over one sinner who repents than over ninety-nine just persons who need no repentance (Lk. 15.4-7).

These parables teach the love of God for lost sinners. They show that Jesus ate with sinners because he is the savior who finds the lost sinner. When Jesus was criticized for associating with a sinful woman, he gave the Parable of the Two Debtors (Lk. 7.40–43).

Parables given with a stated purpose

Jesus told the parable of the Unjust Judge in order to teach his disciples that they should always pray and never give up. Luke writes,

> Then he spoke a parable to them, that men always ought to pray and not lose heart, saying: 'There was in a certain city a judge who did not fear God nor regard man. Now there was a widow in that city; and she came to him, saying, 'Get justice for me from my adversary.' And he would not for a while; but afterward he said within himself, 'Though I do not fear God nor regard man, yet because this widow troubles me I will avenge her, lest by her continual coming she weary me." Then the Lord said, 'Hear what the unjust judge said. And shall God not avenge his own elect who cry out day and night to him, though he bears long with them? I tell you that he will avenge them speedily' (Lk. 18.1-8)

Parables following an exhortation

Several times Jesus gave an exhortation and then followed it with a parable to illustrate his point. Jesus speaks of his return in Mark 13, and he warns his disciples in Mark 13 saying, 'But of that day and hour no one knows, not even the angels in heaven, nor the Son, but only the Father. Take heed, watch and pray; for you do not know when the time is.' Then he gave the following parable.

> It is like a man going to a far country, who left his house and gave authority to his servants, and to each his work, and

commanded the doorkeeper to watch. Watch therefore, for you do not know when the master of the house is coming—in the evening, at midnight, at the crowing of the rooster, or in the morning—lest, coming suddenly, he find you sleeping. And what I say to you, I say to all: 'Watch!' (Mk 13.34-37)

In Mt. 7.21, Jesus taught that not everyone who professes to be a Christian will enter heaven. He said, 'Not everyone who says to Me, 'Lord, Lord,' shall enter the kingdom of heaven, but he who does the will of My Father in heaven.' This stern warning is following by a parable that illustrates the teaching.

> Therefore whoever hears these sayings of Mine, and does them, I will liken him to a wise man who built his house on the rock: and the rain descended, the floods came, and the winds blew and beat on that house; and it did not fall, for it was founded on the rock. But everyone who hears these sayings of Mine, and does not do them, will be like a foolish man who built his house on the sand: and the rain descended, the floods came, and the winds blew and beat on that house; and it fell. And great was its fall (Mt. 7.24-27).

According to the parable, only those persons who hear and obey the teachings of Jesus will enter the kingdom of God.

Parables with the purpose implied but not stated
The parable of The Talents (Mt. 25.14-30) does not have a purpose statement, nor is it preceded or followed by an exhortation or principle. It does not occur in response to a question, request, or criticism. The parable does, however, seem to point up what is expected of Jesus' followers while he is away. That is, he expects his followers to serve him faithfully while he is absent. This meaning can be determined because the parable is placed immediately after the parable of the Wise and Foolish Virgins and just before Jesus tells about the last judgment. The parable of the Virgins describes the second coming of Jesus and his teaching on the last judgment tells us that we must give an accounting of all that God has put in our hands to do. Therefore, the parable of the Talents means that we must use our talents (one, two, or five) and that we will be rewarded accordingly at the coming of Jesus.

Analyze the characters and events

Sometimes the meaning of the parable is clearly evident from the occasion in which Jesus tells the parable. However, we often must analyze the parable itself in order to make connections to the teachings of Jesus. Parables are stories that teach spiritual truths, and stories consist of characters and their actions. Therefore, the truth is contained in the form of a comparison between either the characters or their actions.

Analyze the characters

In Luke 15, the outcasts and the sinners were coming near to Jesus, and he was teaching them. This angered the Scribes and Pharisees who said, 'This Man receives sinners and eats with them' (Lk. 15.2). In response to their complaint, Jesus tells three parables: the Lost Sheep, the Lost Coin, and the Lost Son. In each of the three parables there are three types of characters: those who are safe, those who are lost, and the person who rejoices when the lost are found. In the first parable there are ninety-nine sheep who are safe, one sheep who is lost, and the shepherd who rejoices when he finds the lost sheep. In the second parable there are nine coins that are safe, one coin that is lost, and the woman who rejoices when she finds the lost coin. In the third parable there is one son who is safe, one son who is lost, and the father who rejoices when the lost son returns. The characters who are safe represent the righteous; the characters who are lost represent the sinner; and the person who seeks the lost represents Jesus and/or the heavenly Father. The story is built around the contrast between those who are lost and those who are saved. The teaching of all three parables is that there is joy in heaven over one sinner who repents. The lesson is made even more profound in the final parable, the parable of the Lost Son, because the son who remains with his father does not rejoice when the lost son returns home. This final contrast is between the joy of the father and the jealousy of the brother. The jealousy of the safe son is a warning to the righteous that we must always open our arms to the sinner.

As in the parables described above, many other parables include a contrast, comparison, or conflict between two or more characters in the story. For example, the five wise virgins are contrasted to the five foolish virgins (Mt. 25.1-13). The five wise virgins have oil for their lamps and are prepared when the bridegroom comes; but the five foolish virgins do not have oil for their lamps, which means that they are unprepared when the bridegroom calls.

In the parable of the Good Samaritan, the priest and the Levite are contrasted to the Samaritan. The priest and Levite are unwilling to help the wounded man who lies in the ditch, but the Samaritan comes to the man and treats his wounds. Then he takes him to an inn and pays for his extended care. The irony here is that the Samaritan is considered by the Jews to be an outcast, yet he is more compassionate that the religious leaders, the priest, and Levite.

Analyze the events of the parable
Every story includes both characters and their actions. In many parables, it is not the characters themselves that carry the message of the parable, but it is their actions that hold the key to the message. For example, in the parable of the Two Sons, it is their actions that speak louder than words. After Jesus' triumphal entry into Jerusalem, the chief priests and scribes confronted him about his authority. Jesus replied to them by telling this parable.

> But what do you think? A man had two sons, and he came to the first and said, 'Son, go, work today in my vineyard.' He answered and said, 'I will not,' but afterward he regretted it and went. Then he came to the second and said likewise. And he answered and said, 'I go, sir,' but he did not go. Which of the two did the will of his father? They said to him, 'The first.' Jesus said to them, 'Assuredly, I say to you that tax collectors and harlots enter the kingdom of God before you' (Mt. 21.28-31).

In this parable, the actions of the two sons are contrasted. One son went into the vineyard, and the other did not go.

In another example, the parable of the Persistent Friend, the story centers upon the actions of the characters. The parable says,

> Which of you shall have a friend, and go to him at midnight and say to him, 'Friend, lend me three loaves; for a friend of mine has come to me on his journey, and I have nothing to set before him'; and he will answer from within and say, 'Do not trouble me; the door is now shut, and my children are with me in bed; I cannot rise and give to you'? I say to you, though he will not rise

and give to him because he is his friend, yet because of his persistence he will rise and give him as many as he needs (Lk. 11.5-8).

The message of the parable is that we must be persistent in our prayers. This message emerges from the friend's actions of asking with persistence.

Discover the most important elements in the parable

The message of the parable will unfold from the most important characters and actions in the story. Some parts of the parable are crucial to the point of the parable and other parts are unimportant. For example, in the parable of the Good Samaritan the priest, the Levite, and the Samaritan all have significance for the meaning of the parable; but the road, the innkeeper, and the two denarii function as supporting details and do not have any spiritual meaning.

The following questions can help to help identify the main point of the parables.

1. What characters appear in the parable? Which are the least important? Which are the two most important characters?
2. What is the main contrast found in the parable?
3. What are the major actions or events within the parable?
4. What concepts are repeated in the parable? Which are not?
5. Upon what does the parable dwell, that is, to what or to whom does the parable devote the most space?
6. What comes at the end of the parable?[61]

Search the surrounding passage

The meaning of the parable is often revealed by Jesus or by the Gospel writer. When Jesus told the parable of the Marriage Feast, he concluded by revealing its meaning: 'Many are called, but few are chosen' (Mt. 22.14). He also explained the meaning of the parable of the Ten Virgins. After telling the parable, he said, 'Watch therefore, for you know neither the day nor the hour in which the Son of Man is coming' (Mt. 25.13). In Mt. 13.3-9 Jesus gave the Parable

---

[61] See Robert H. Stein, *An Introduction to the Parables of Jesus* (Philadelphia: Westminster, 1981), p. 56.

of the Sower and then gave his explanation of the parable in 13.18-23. Likewise, in Mt. 13.24-30, Jesus told the Parable of the Wheat and Tares and then explained the parable in 13.36-43. The parable of the Workers in the Vineyard (Mt. 20.1-15) is followed by the explanation, 'So the last will be first, and the first will be last' (20.16).

The Gospel writer often supplies the interpretation of the parable either before or after Jesus finishes speaking. For example, Luke introduces the parable of the Woman and the Judge by informing us, 'Then he spoke a parable to them, that men always ought to pray and not lose heart' (Lk. 18.1). In another example, the parable of the pharisee and the publican who pray at the temple is introduced with these words: 'Also he spoke this parable to some who trusted in themselves that they were righteous, and despised others' (Lk. 18.9).

Conclusion

A parable reveals an analogy between the story and the intended spiritual lesson. The central truth of the parable can be identified by understanding what question, occasion, problem, or need is portrayed in the historical setting. This question or problem will usually relate to Jesus' disciples or to his opponents; therefore, it is related to the revealing and concealing purposes of the parables.

The careful approach that we use for interpreting parables is helpful when we are interpreting other Scriptures, whether they be prophecies, Gospels, or Epistles. Our interpretation of every Scripture should include studying the background, observing the occasion, analyzing the characters and events, and searching the surrounding passage for clues that will help in our interpretation.

For Review and Study

1. The parable is a story that illustrates a spiritual truth. Why are parables told in the Bible?
2. Enumerate the three functions of the parables in the Gospels.
3. Why did Jesus want to obscure his teachings from his opponents?

4. The parables of Jesus can be classified into three groups based upon their function within the ministry of Jesus. Name these three types of parables.
5. We must recognize the two-fold nature of the kingdom of God. Name five of the Kingdom parables.
6. Why is it important to study the historical and cultural background of the parables?
7. Enumerate the seven kinds of occasions or purposes that led to Jesus' parables.
8. When interpreting parables we must analyze the characters and events within the parable. Explain the three types of characters in the three parables from Luke 15.
9. Give an example of a Gospel writer supplying the interpretation of the parable either before or after Jesus finishes speaking.
10. How can the guidelines for interpreting parables be used for the study of other categories of biblical passages?

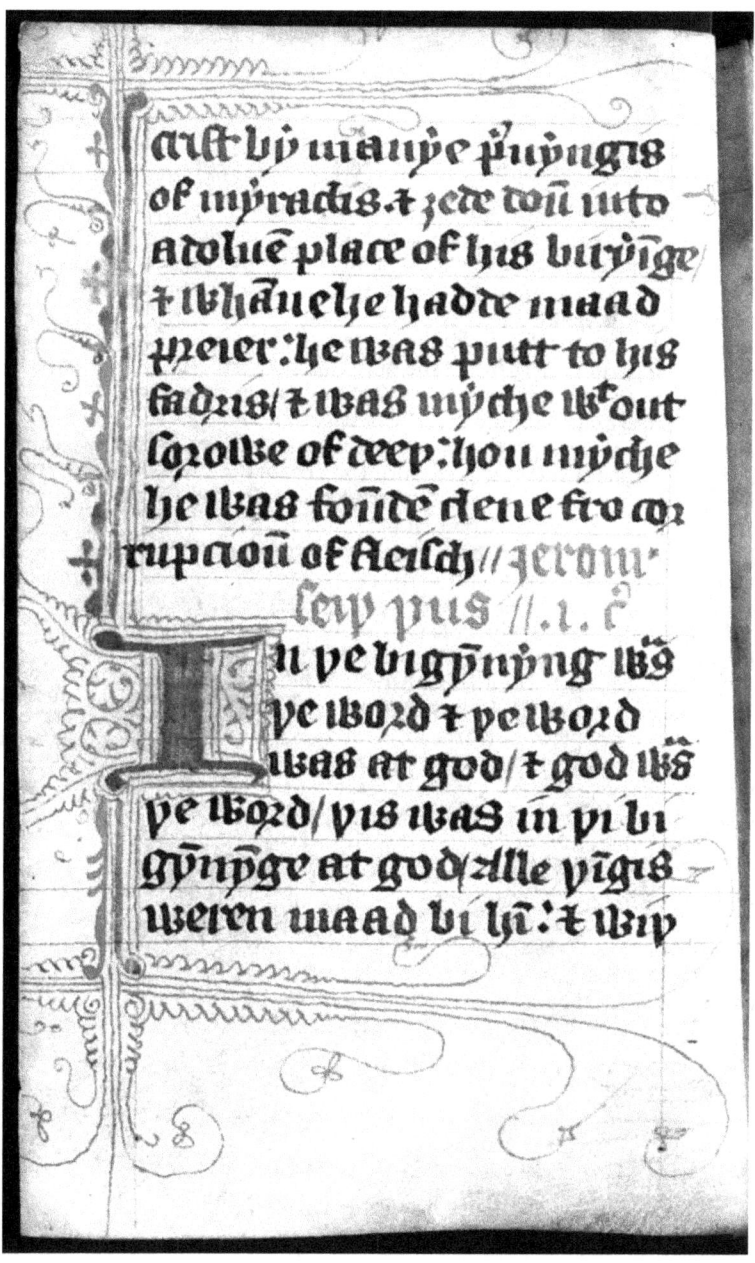

John Wycliffe Bible (1382)

S. Mathew. Fo. iij.

The Seconde Chapter.

When Jesus was borne in bethlehem a toune of iury/in the time of kynge Herode/beholde/there cam* wyse mē frō the este to Jerusalem sayinge: where is he that is borne kynge of the iewes? we have sene his starre in the este/and are come to worshippe hym.

¶ Herode the kynge/after he hadde herde this/was troubled/and all Jerusalē with hym/and he sent for all the chefe preestes and scrybes of the people/and demaunded of them where Christ shulde be borne. They sayde vnto him: in bethlehem a toune of iury. For thus is it wrytte by the prophet:
v And thou bethlehem in the lōde of *iury/shalt not be the leest as perteynynge to the pryncs of iuda. For out of the shall come a captayne/whych shall govern my people israhel.

¶ Then Herod prevely called the wyse men/and dyligently enquyred of them/the tyme of the starre that appered. And sent them to bethlehem sayinge: when ye be come thyder searche diligently for the chylde. And when ye haue founde hym brīge me worde/that y maye come and worshippe hym also. Whē they had herde the kynge/they departed/and lo the starre whych they sawe in the este went before them/vntyll it cā and stode over the place where the chylde was. Whē they sawe the starre/they were marveylously gladde. And entred in to the house/and fōd the childe with Mary hys mother/and kneled doune and worshipped hym/and opened there treasurs/and offred vnto him gyftes/gold/franckynsence/and myr. And after they were warned in their slepe/that they shulde not go a geyne to Herod/they returned into there awne countre another waye.

¶ After that they were departed/lo the angell of the lorde apered to Joseph in his slepe sayinge: aryse and take the chylde and his mother/and flye in to egipte/and abyde there tyll y brynge the worde. For Herod wyll seke the chylde to destroye:

C iij

knew her after / warde/but hit is the maner of the scripture so to speake/as gē. viij. c. the ravin cam not againe till the water was broke vp pe and the erth drye/the scripture meaneth nott /he cam agayne after warde : evyn soo here/hit foloweth not that ioseph ke we oure lady afs ter warde.

* wyse men. Of mathew they ar callid Magi, z in certeyne coūtreis i the est/philosophers conyn ge in naturall causes z effectes/and also the prestes/ were so callyd.

*Jury is the londe. Juda is that trybe or kynred that dwelt there in.

William Tyndale Bible 1525
First English Bible to be Printed on a Printing Press

9

INTERPRETING ALLEGORIES AND TYPES

In this chapter we will study the allegory and the type. The rules for interpreting the allegory are similar to those for interpreting the parable. However, interpreting the type is quite a different task.

The allegory

Like the parable, the allegory is a story that has a spiritual meaning. The main difference between the parable and the allegory is that the elements of the allegory represent specific persons and events, but the elements of the parable represent only general categories and spiritual lessons. For example, in the allegory of the Good Shepherd (Jn 10.1-16) the door represents Christ, the Shepherd also represents Christ, and the sheep represent those for whom Christ laid down his life. The hireling who flees represents religious leaders who are working only for their own interests. In contrast, the parable of the Good Samaritan does not symbolize any specific person or event. It represents the principle of loving one's neighbor, and the Samaritan in the story symbolizes a good neighbor. The Priest and the Levite who pass by do not symbolize anyone in particular; rather they represent any religious person who fails to love his neighbor.

Allegory in the Old Testament

A list of Old Testament allegories

Allegories appear in both the Old and New Testaments. The following list enumerates some of the most well-known allegories in the Old Testament.

Scripture	The Allegory and Its Meaning
2 Samuel 12.1-13	The Stolen Lamb King David was guilty of stealing the wife of Uriah the Hittite.
Psalm 23	The Lord is My Shepherd The Lord takes care of every believer.
Psalm 80.8-15	The Vine from Egypt Israel was brought out of Egypt and transplanted in Canaan.
Proverbs 5.15-18	Drinking from Your Own Cistern Every man should be faithful to his own wife.
Proverbs 9.1-6	Wisdom's House Wisdom is a woman who prepares a place of feasting for those who hunger for knowledge.
Isaiah 5.1-7	The Lord's Vineyard Israel is a vineyard that has been well tended but which bears worthless fruit.
Ezekiel 13.8-16	The Plastered Wall The words of the false prophets will fail.
Ezekiel 16	The Rescued Infant Israel is an abandoned baby that is cared for by God but grows up and becomes unfaithful.
Ezekiel 17	The Eagles and the Vine Babylon and Egypt are powerful, but they will be destroyed.
Ezekiel 23	Two Unfaithful Sisters Israel and Judah are unfaithful to God and will be punished.
Daniel 4	Nebuchadnezzar was a tree that was cut down and humbled.

The allegory of the stolen lamb

One of the most powerful allegories in the Old Testament is the allegory of the Stolen Lamb, which was told to King David by the prophet Nathan (2 Sam. 12.1-13). After David had committed adultery with Bathsheba and had murdered her husband, God directed Nathan to deliver a prophetic word in the form of a story. Nathan related the story as if it were a historical event, therefore David was unaware that the story was directed toward him. Nathan said to David,

> There were two men in one city, one rich and the other poor. The rich *man* had exceedingly many flocks and herds. But the poor *man* had nothing, except one little ewe lamb which he had bought and nourished ... And a traveler came to the rich man, who refused to take from his own flock and from his own herd to prepare one for the wayfaring man who had come to him; but he took the poor man's lamb and prepared it for the man who had come to him.

Upon hearing the story, David became very angry and threatened to execute the rich man who had stolen the lamb. Nathan then pointed to David and said, 'You are that man!' In this allegory, the rich man with many sheep represents David who had many wives. The poor man with only one sheep symbolizes Uriah who had but one wife. The rich man's act of stealing the sheep and slaughtering it stands for David's act of adultery with Bathsheba.

Allegory in the New Testament

A list of New Testament allegories

Allegories also appear in the New Testament. The following chart enumerates several prominent allegories.

Scripture	*The Allegory and Its Meaning*
John 10.1-16	The Good Shepherd Jesus loves his disciples enough to sacrifice his life on their behalf.
John 15.1-6	The True Vine Jesus is the source of the believer's life and strength.

1 Corinthians 3.10-15	The Builders Christian teachers are like builders. Each person has a different responsibility within the process of construction.
Galatians 4.21-31	Sarah and Hagar Abraham's wives, Sarah and Hagar, represent the two covenants, the New and the Old.
Ephesians 6.11-17	The Armor of God The various pieces of armor represent Christian virtues and attributes.

Sarah and Hagar

Paul's allegory of Sarah and Hagar is of a different type from other allegories in the Bible. Paul takes the historical narrative of Hagar and Sarah, along with their sons Ishmael and Isaac, as historical facts that also have allegorical significance. Hagar as the slave woman represents the Old Covenant. Sarah as the free woman represents the New Covenant. The child of Hagar was born according to the flesh. Isaac in contrast is a child of promise. The persecution between the two sons of Abraham represents the conflict between legalistic Judaism (Christian or anti-Christian forms) and Christianity with its stress on salvation by grace. The separation of Hagar and her child from Sarah and her child symbolizes the break which must be made between Judaism and Christianity. This type of argument shows Paul making use of the allegorical method to heighten the contrast for his readers between bondage (Galatians 4.24-25) and freedom (Galatians 4.26-31). Paul uses this kind of allegorical interpretation as an illustration, but it was not his usual method for interpreting the Old Testament.

Guidelines for interpreting allegories

Examine the context of the allegory

By examining carefully the context, the interpreter can often determine (1) who were the original hearers of the allegory, (2) the reason the original speaker (writer) used the allegory, (3) the meaning he assigned to each of the basic points of comparison, and finally, (4) the role of the allegory in developing the total thought being presented. If the interpreter does not consider carefully the context, it is almost impossible to avoid bringing his own ideas into the allegorical imagery.

Study the content of the allegory

As we saw in our discussion of the parable, the content of the story will contain clues to its spiritual meaning.

For example, in the allegory of the True Vine (Jn 15.1-10) there are three main points of comparison: (1) The vine symbolizes Jesus (15.1, 5). (2) The vinegrower represents God the Father (15.1). (3) The branches symbolize disciples, believers in Jesus (15.5).

First, the main point of the allegory is the life-giving role of the vine (Jesus). As long as the branch is attached to the vine, it will bear fruit. Therefore, Jesus declares, 'Apart from me you can do nothing' (15.5).

Second, the role of the Heavenly Father is represented by the actions of the vinegrower. He cuts off every branch that does not bear fruit, and he trims (prunes) the branches that bear fruit so that they may bear more fruit (15.2). He takes decisive action to eliminate fruitless branches and to bring to maximum production the branches that are attached to the vine.

Third, the action of the branches (disciples) themselves is considered. In this allegory, the branches are able to act, to make choices. The disciples are told to 'abide (remain) in me' (15.4). Action is also made clear by direct comparison: 'As the branch is not able to bear fruit by itself except it constantly abides in the vine, so neither can you except you constantly abide in me' (15.4). Jesus warns of the outcome if the disciple does not remain in the vine: 'If anyone does not abide in me, he is thrown away as the branch, and it withers and they gather them and cast them into the fire and they are burned' (Jn 15.6). A vital relationship demands a constant obedience, and answers to prayer depend on this vital, active relationship (15.7). Fruitbearing, as a sign of this vital relationship, brings glory to God and shows that the one so producing will be Christ's disciple in the future as well as in the present (15.8). In conclusion, obeying Christ's commandments is pictured as evidence that the disciple is abiding in Christ's love (15.9-10). This allegory dynamically portrays to the reader why he must maintain a fresh, living relationship to Jesus Christ and his Father. This is what discipleship means.

Conclusion

When attempting to interpret an allegory, we should include the following process.

1. Identify the original hearers or readers and their spiritual condition.
2. If possible, note why the allegory was told in the first place.
3. Search out the basic points of comparison stressed in the allegory. The content usually makes these clear by the emphasis put upon particular elements in the story. To find out what these stand for, look for explicit identification ('I am the true vine and my father is the vinegrower,' Jn 15.1) or implicit identification from things said in the context (materials built upon the foundation; see 1 Cor. 3.1-2, 4-5, 6-8, 9, 12-14).
4. After listing the basic points of comparison and the things for which they stand, state in as simple a manner as possible why these truths were essential for the original hearers or readers and why they are essential for us today.[62]

The Type

Definition of the type

In the Bible, a type is a person, an object, or an event that serves as a pattern for something that comes after it. For example, Noah's passage through the waters of the flood is said to be typical of water baptism (1 Pet. 3.20-21). The deliverance experienced by Noah corresponds to the deliverance that is experienced in Christian conversion and baptism.

The proverb, parable, and allegory each symbolize spiritual truth, but they may not refer to a real event. A type, however, is a pattern for a real person or event. While most symbolic language can refer to the past, the present, or the future, a type is always looking forward to a time in the future. Most of the types in the Bible are found in the Old Testament, and they typify people and events that come to pass in the New Testament.

---

[62] A. Berkeley Mickelsen, *Interpreting the Bible* (Grand Rapids, MI: Eerdmans, 1963), pp. 229-35.

Biblical types can be identified by the following criteria: (1) There must be a significant point of resemblance between the type and its later counterpart (which we call the 'antitype'). (2) There must be Scriptural evidence for the appropriateness of the type. We are not free to look for types unless the Scripture has given us some indication of their genuineness. (3) A type always prefigures something future.[63]

A list of biblical types

Biblical types can be classified according to the following categories: (1) persons whose lives and experiences illustrate a later person or truth, (2) historical events and places that foreshadow future events and truths, (3) rituals and institutions that typify future things or truths. The following chart lists the most important types in the Bible.

Type	*Symbolism (Antitype)*
Adam	Jesus Christ represents redeemed humanity, replacing Adam who represents sinful humanity (Rom. 5.14)
Melchizedek	The eternal priesthood of Jesus (Heb. 7.3-17)
Aaron	The priestly ministry of Jesus (Heb. 5.4-5)
Jonah's 3 Days in the Fish	Jesus' 3 days in the grave (Mt. 12.40)
Passover	The sacrificial death of Jesus (1 Cor. 5.7)
Feast of Unleavened Bread	The holy life of believers (1 Cor. 5.7-8)
Feast of Firstfruits	The Resurrection of Jesus and the believers (1 Cor. 15.20-30)
Feast of Pentecost	The Baptism in the Holy Spirit (Joel 2.28; Acts 2.1-47)
The Sabbath	The Spiritual rest that believers find in Jesus Christ (Colossians 2.17; Heb. 4.3-11)

---

[63] Louis Berkhof, *Principles of Biblical Interpretation* (Grand Rapids, MI: Baker, 1950), p. 145.

The Tabernacle	Access to God through Jesus Christ (Heb. 8.5; 9.23-24)
Whole Burnt Offering	The sacrificial death of Jesus (Heb. 10.5-7; Eph. 5.2)
Rock that gave water in the wilderness	Spiritual life that comes through Christ (1 Cor. 10.1-12)

For Review and Study

1. Explain the definition of 'allegory.'
2. List four allegories from the Old Testament.
4. List three allegories from the New Testament.
5. What four things can we learn by examining the context of the allegory?
6. Explain the three comparisons found in the allegory of the True Vine (John 15).
7. In conclusion, what three things should we include in our process of interpreting allegory?
8. Give the definition of the 'type.'
9. List the three criteria for identifying types.
10. Name three Old Testament characters and their typological significance.
11. List three Old Testament feasts and their typological symbolism.

10

INTERPRETING BIBLICAL POETRY

The Nature of poetry

The widespread use of poetry

Poetry appears in the literature of every culture throughout history, and each culture develops its own forms and styles of poetry. Most of us can easily identify poetry that is written in our native language, but we may find it difficult to recognize poetry that comes from another culture. Therefore, some guidance is necessary to help us in identifying and interpreting the poetry of the Bible, which originates from the ancient Hebrew culture.

2. Definition of poetry

Poetry may be defined as a written composition that intensively expresses feelings and ideas through its choice of exalted language and its patterned arrangement of words and phrases. This means that although poetry may appear in a variety of forms, it can be distinguished from ordinary writing by its (a) content, (b) sound, (c) structure, and (d) purpose.

Poetic content

In its content, poetry includes a high concentration of figurative language and word play. The poetry of the Bible takes full advantage of the figures of speech that we discussed in Chapter 4, including metaphor, simile, personification, and hyperbole. For example, the prophet Isaiah uses the simile when he declares, 'Though your sins are like scarlet, they shall be white as snow' (Isa. 1.18).

Word play in the Bible is often based upon the use of similar root words. For example, Micah uses play on words when he says, 'In Beth Aphrah, roll yourself in the dust' (Mic. 1.10). The name 'Aphrah' comes from the same Hebrew word as 'dust,' so that the literal translation might be 'In the House of Dust, roll yourself in the dust.'

Poetic sounds

In its sound, poetry exhibits intentional combinations of word sounds. Common poetic devices based upon sound include assonance, alliteration, consonance, and rhyme. Assonance is the repetition of vowel sounds, such as the repetition of the 'e' sound in the phrase, 'Hear the mellow wedding bells.'[64] Alliteration is the repetition of consonant sounds at the beginning of words, such as the repetition of the letter 's' in the phrase, 'the sweet smell of success.' Consonance is the repetition of final consonant sounds, such as the repetition of the 'st' sound in the saying, 'First and last,' the 'ds' in 'odds and ends,' and the 't' in 'short and sweet.' Rhyme is the repetition of one or more syllables, such as the repetition of the final sound in the first three lines of the following verse.

> Yes we'll walk with a walk that is measured and slow,
> And we'll go where the chalk-white arrows go,
> For the children, they mark, and the children, they know
> The place where the sidewalk ends.[65]

Biblical poetry commonly uses assonance, alliteration, and consonance, but rhyme is uncommon.

Poetic structure

In its structure, poetry utilizes some sort of verse structure that may include meter or rhythm. In the older Bible versions the verse structure of poetry was not evident, but in newer translations, the poetic portions of Scripture are visible in their proper form. A good example would be Gen. 9.26-27, which appears in older versions as prose but appears in newer versions as poetry.

> And he said,
> Blessed *be* the LORD,

---

[64] Edgar Allen Poe, 'The Bells.'
[65] From the poem, 'Where the Sidewalk Ends', by Shel Silverstein.

> The God of Shem,
> > And may Canaan be his servant.
> May God enlarge Japheth,
> > And may he dwell in the tents of Shem;
> > And may Canaan be his servant.'

The verse structure of Hebrew poetry is based upon parallelism of lines. A poetic verse may consist of one, two, or three lines, but most often it will be two lines, with the second line related in some fashion to the first line. The second line may restate the thought of the first line (synonymous parallelism); it may state the antithesis of the first line (antithetical parallelism); or it may complete the thought of the first line (synthetic parallelism).

Note the following examples:

Synonymous parallelism
> *The heavens declare the glory of God;*
> > *the skies proclaim the work of his hands* (Ps. 19.1-2)

The second line repeats the same general idea using different terminology. 'Heavens' and 'skies' are synonyms, and 'declare' and 'proclaim' are synonyms.

> *Do not fret because of evildoers,*
> > *Nor be envious of the workers of iniquity* (Ps. 37.1)

In this case, 'fret' is synonymous with 'be envious,' and 'evildoers' is synonymous with 'workers of iniquity,'

Antithetical parallelism
> *The Lord knows the way of the righteous,*
> > *but the way of the ungodly shall perish* (Ps. 1.6)

The second line states a truth that is the counterpart to the first line. In this instance, 'the righteous' are opposite to 'the ungodly'; and the actions of the Lord in the first line are opposite to his actions in the second line.

> *For evildoers shall be cut off;*
> > *But those who wait on the* LORD *shall inherit the earth*
> (Ps. 37.9)

Here we see that evildoers have a different end from those who wait upon the Lord.

Synthetic parallelism

Synthetic parallelism is simply a term that is used to designate all the other kinds of connections that can be made between the first line and the second line of a Hebrew poetic verse. The second line may relate to the first line in the following ways.

The second line may provide the **reason** for the first line.
> *Blessed be the* LORD!
>> *because he has heard the voice of my supplications*
> (Ps. 28.6)

The second line may ask a **question** based upon the first line.
> *For in death there is no remembrance of you;*
>> *in Sheol who can give you praise?* (Ps. 6.5)

The second line my give the **answer** to the first line.
> *How can a young man keep his way pure?*
>> *By guarding it according to thy word* (Ps. 119.9)

The second line may be a **quotation** that was introduced in the first line.
> *I had said in my alarm,*
>> *'I am driven far from your sight'* (Ps. 31.22)

The first line may be something that is **'better'** than what is in the second line.
> *Better is a little that the righteous has*
>> *than the abundance of many wicked* (Ps. 37.16)

The first line may be a **simile** with the meaning of the simile found in the second line.
> *As a father pities his children,*
>> *so the* LORD *pities those who fear him* (Ps. 103.13)

Although parallelism of lines is the most distinctive mark of Hebrew poetry, another structural technique is the acrostic poem (e.g. Psalms 25, 34, 111, 112, 119, and 145). An acrostic is a poem in which each verse begins with successive letters of the Hebrew alphabet. Psalm 119 is unique in that it consists of 22 sections, one for each letter of the Hebrew alphabet, and every verse within a section begins with the same letter. Outside the book of Psalms, acrostics appear in Prov. 31.10-31 and Lamentations chapters 1, 2, and 4. In biblical times, the average believer did not possess a copy of the Scriptures. Therefore, it was important that people be able to memorize as much of the Bible as possible. Poetry was an aid to memorization, and acrostic poetry was even more easily remembered than standard poetry.

d. Poetic purpose

In its purpose, poetry intends not so much to inform the mind as to affect and move the heart. A significant attraction of biblical poetry is its ability to draw the reader into the poetic world through visual imagery, imaginative symbols, and appeals to the reader's emotions. This affective dimension of poetry speaks to the heart and to the passions with a fervent freshness and honesty. With deep anger the prophet Amos predicts doom for Israel.

I hate, I despise your feast days,
  And I do not savor your sacred assemblies.
Though you offer Me burnt offerings and your grain offerings,
  I will not accept them,
  Nor will I regard your fattened peace offerings.
Take away from Me the noise of your songs,
  For I will not hear the melody of your stringed instruments.
But let justice run down like water,
  And righteousness like a mighty stream (Amos 5.21-24).

Later, however, the prophet Zephaniah offers joyful words of comfort. After God sends judgment he will return with mercy.

In that day it shall be said to Jerusalem:
Do not fear; Zion,
  let not your hands be weak.
The LORD *your God in your midst,*
  The Mighty One, will save;
He will rejoice over you with gladness,
  He will quiet you with his love,
  He will rejoice over you with singing (Zeph. 3.16-17).

Thus, the poetry of the Bible gives witness to both the greatest joys of life and to its greatest agonies. For example, the emotions of the psalmist range from despair ('My heart is in anguish within me, the terrors of death have fallen upon me' Ps. 55.4) to elation

('Bless the Lord, O my soul: and all that is within me, bless his holy name' Ps. 103.1) and every feeling between those extremes.

Poetry in the Bible

Poetry in the Old Testament

Poetical and prophetical books

Approximately one third of the Old Testament is written in poetic form. The books of Psalms, Song of Solomon, Lamentations, Ecclesiastes, Proverbs, and Job consist almost entirely of poetry. In addition to these so-called 'poetical books.' the prophetical books of Isaiah through Malachi are composed mostly of poetry. We discussed in Chapter 5 the interpretation of the wisdom books (Proverbs, Ecclesiastes, and Job). This chapter will focus upon the poetry of Psalms, but let us first take a look at poetry throughout the Bible.

Poetry in the narrative books

Poetry can be found throughout the Old Testament. What follows is a partial list of poetic sections that are found in the narrative books.

Gen. 4.23-24	Lamech's Song
Gen. 49.2-27	Jacob's Blessing
Exod. 15.1-21	Victory Song at the Red Sea
Num. 21.14-31	Three Little Songs
Num. 23.7-10	First Oracle of Balaam
Num. 23.18-24	Second Oracle of Balaam
Num. 24.3-9	Third Oracle of Balaam
Num. 24.15-24	Fourth Oracle of Balaam
Deut. 32.1-43	Song of Moses
Deut. 33.2-29	Blessing of Moses
Judg. 5	Victory Song of Deborah
1 Sam. 2.1-10	Song of Hannah
2 Sam. 1.17-27	David's Lament over Saul and Jonathan
2 Sam. 22.2-51	David's Hymn
2 Sam. 23.1-7	David's Last Words
1 Chron. 16.8-36	A Song of Thanksgiving

Poetry in the New Testament

Although most of the Bible's poetry is found in the Old Testament, poetry can also be found in the New Testament. Most of the poetry in the New Testament is composed of quotations from the Old Testament or short poetic sayings. In addition to the quotations and short sayings, there are a number of passages that consist of longer sections of poetry. They include the following.

Mt. 5.3-10	The Beatitudes (also Lk. 6.20-26)
Mt. 11.17	Jesus' Defense
Luke 1.46-55	Mary's Song
Luke 1.67-79	Zecharias' Prophecy
Luke 2.29-32	The Blessing of Simeon
Rom. 8.31-37	The Love of Christ
1 Cor. 13	Celebration of Love
2 Cor. 4.8-9	Paul's Testimony
Phil. 2.5-11	Hymn of the Incarnation
1 Tim. 3.16	The Mystery of Godliness
2 Tim. 2.11-13	A Faithful Saying
Rev. 7.15-17	John's Vision of the Redeemed

When interpreting the poetic sections of the New Testament, we should keep in mind the characteristics of poetry. That is, the poetic sections will use figurative language, they may include poetic sounds, they will exhibit a poetic structure, and they will be intended to move the heart and the affections.

The Poetry of the Psalms

The Psalms are lyric poetry and exhibit all of the features of poetry. The 150 Psalms were written by a variety of Hebrew authors over the span of several hundred years. The Psalms include several types of songs that vary considerably in style, content, and form. The Psalms are cited often in the New Testament, where many of them are associated with the life of Jesus the Messiah. The importance of the Psalms is illustrated further by their continued use throughout history both in public liturgy and in private devotions.

The Psalms and worship

Songs of Israel

The book of Psalms is sometimes referred to as the songbook of Israel. Christians have consistently witnessed to the power of the Psalms to give voice to their prayers and their expressions of worship. The Psalms have this power because, unlike other parts of Scripture, they are not God's words directed towards Israel. The Psalms are Israel's words directed to God in worshipful and prayerful response to his presence and actions among them. As long as Christians continue to acknowledge God's presence and activity in the Church, the Psalms will serve as a meaningful expression of the Christian response to God in worship and prayer. The Psalms provide examples of prayer and worship, and they have much to say about our worship today.

Songs of worship

The Psalms tell us that worship is deep, intense, and passionate, and that prayer is honest and fervent. In fact, the Psalms' honesty and fervency may at times seem harsh, especially on those occasions when the psalmist prayed for the violent destruction of enemies and their children (e.g. Ps. 3.7). These imprecatory psalms are difficult to reconcile with Christ's command to love our enemies. It should be remembered, however, that these psalms are cries for help, emerging from situations of deep suffering and oppression, and that the New Testament allows for God's intervention as vindicator of his people (Rom. 12.19; 1 Thess. 1.8; 2 Tim. 4.14; Heb. 10.30-31; Jude 14-15; Rev. 6.10).

Songs of faith

The diversity of experiences that we find in the Psalms testifies to a dynamic life of faith. At first glance, we may view the Psalms as songs of praise only, but we find other types of songs as well. In the Psalms we find passionate prayers—what scholars call the laments. We also find exalted praises—the hymns. The lament and the hymn are opposite poles of Christian experience. The prayers of lament speak to our times of great pain, and the hymns teach us to rejoice in times of great joy. The Psalms teach us that life is always moving, always changing, always developing. The Psalms demonstrate how to worship God even in the midst of these changes and movements.

Songs of instruction

Not only do the Psalms offer a model of worship, but they also instruct us in many other ways. The prayers for deliverance teach us about God's ability and willingness to save his people. God's acts of deliverance are mentioned in the thanksgiving Psalms and in the hymns. God's saving work includes his providential care, his forgiveness of sin, his healing of sickness, and his giving of his Spirit (Ps. 51.10-11). God is also portrayed powerfully as creator and sovereign of the universe. As king, God is enthroned in heaven, active on earth, and coming to reign over the world (Ps. 96). Therefore, we should worship him!

Songs of prophecy

The writers of the New Testament found in the Psalms many testimonies to Jesus Christ. Christians have viewed the Psalms as predictive of the birth, life, death, and teachings of Jesus. Jesus himself quoted from the Psalms many times, and in the entire New Testament we find over one hundred quotations from the Psalms. The following list give examples of the Messianic citations from the Psalms.

Psalm 2.1-2	Opposition to the Messiah
Psalm 2.7	The divinity of Jesus
Psalm 2.9	The rule of Jesus
Psalm 16.8-11	The resurrection of Jesus
Psalm 22	The crucifixion
Psalm 31.5	The death of Jesus
Psalm 34.20	Jesus' bones not broken
Psalm 40.6-8	The faithfulness of Jesus
Psalm 41.9	Betrayed by a friend
Psalm 69.4	The rejection of Jesus
Psalm 69.9	Jesus cleanses the temple
Psalm 78.2	Predicts Jesus' use of parables
Psalm 110.1	The divinity of Jesus
Psalm 110.4	The eternal priesthood of Jesus
Psalm 118.22-23	Jesus as the cornerstone
Psalm 118.26	Refers to Jesus' triumphal entry

Authorship of the Psalms

Interpretations of the Psalms often focus on their relationship to the psalmist David. However, when interpreting the Psalms, we should keep in mind that David did not compose all of them. David is credited with 73, which is less than half of the 150. The remaining 77 are attributed to a variety of authors, including Moses (Psalm 90), Solomon (Psalms 72 and 127), Heman (Psalm 88), and Ethan (Psalm 89). A number of Psalms are attributed to musical guilds known as the Sons of Korah (Psalms 42, 44-49, 84-85, 87-88) and the Sons of Asaph (Psalms 73-83), while still other psalms are of anonymous origin. Psalm 137 was written after the Babylonian captivity. Some psalms are grouped by usage—the Pilgrimage songs, or Songs of Ascent (Psalms 120-134) and the Hallel, or Praise Songs (Psalms 113-118, 146-150).

Superscriptions to the Psalms

Of the 150 psalms, 116 have headings (often called 'superscriptions') containing one or more of the following: the author's name, the traditional setting of the psalm, typological designation, musical accompaniment, and other musical instructions. For example, the heading of the third Psalm reads, 'A Psalm of David, when he fled from Absalom his son.' Most scholars maintain that these headings are not a part of the original composition. However, the presence of the headings in both the Septuagint and in the Qumran scrolls suggests that they are very ancient. Furthermore, the fact that headings are found on the psalms that begin at 2 Sam. 23.1 and Hab. 3.1 may show that the practice of attaching a heading was a normal part of composition.

Psalm types

By employing a variety of psalm types, the Hebrew psalmists were able to respond in worship to the many different situations in their lives. Biblical scholars have identified five basic genres of psalms: the individual lament, the communal lament, the communal hymn, individual thanksgiving psalms, and royal psalms. Other scholars would also include wisdom psalms, psalms of Zion, historical psalms, and psalms of trust. These genres do not exhibit strict, ironclad structures, nor do they explain the nature of every song in the entire collection; but they are helpful guides to the basic forms of biblical psalmic expression. We will examine four of the most common types of psalms.

Songs of Instruction (wisdom psalms)

The book of Psalms is a book of prayers and praises, but it begins with a Psalm of instruction. Psalm 1 includes neither prayer nor praise; it is a wisdom psalm. The wisdom psalms include several of the key themes that may be found in the wisdom literature of Proverbs, Job, and Ecclesiastes. These characteristic themes are the family, God's law, justice, life's choices, life's inconsistencies, the trust or fear of God, and the contrast between the wicked person and the righteous person. The following chart shows the presence of these themes in Psalms 1, 73, and 128.

	Psalm 1	Psalm 73	Psalm 128
The wicked and the righteous	1-3, 4-6		
God's retribution	3, 6	18, 19, 27	2, 5
God's law	2		
Trust/fear of God		21-24	1, 4
Inconsistencies of life		1-20	
Family			3, 6

Other psalms of instruction are Psalms 32, 37, 49, 78, 112, 119, 127, 133, and 145.

The presence of these wisdom psalms within Israel's song book suggests the importance of instruction as a part of worship. Some churches today have abandoned Christian education. They have eliminated Sunday School and other education classes.[66] However, the biblical example of worship includes the teaching component. The book of Psalms begins with teaching and includes teaching throughout the book. We will learn in other psalms that prayer and praise are valuable aspects of worship, but the very first psalm emphasizes worship as a learning experience, and the curriculum for learning is the 'law of the Lord' (Ps. 1.2). We read in the New Testament that when the early Christians gathered together for worship they combined teaching, fellowship, eating, praying, and praise.

---

[66] See Wilfredo Calderón, *Pedagogía Práctica para la iglesia que cumple su misión educativa* (Miami, FL: Gospel Press, 2007), p. 5.

they continued steadfastly in the teaching of the apostles and in fellowship, in the breaking of bread, and in prayers ... with one accord in the temple, and breaking bread from house to house ... praising God (Acts 2.42-47).

Songs of Prayer (lament psalms)

The most common genre in the book of Psalms is the Song of Prayer, which Bible scholars call 'the lament.' The lament is the worshiper's cry to God for deliverance from distress. The sufferer's trouble may take the form of sickness (Psalm 6), personal or corporate sin (Psalm 51), oppression (Psalm 10), or an accusation (Psalm 17). The lament usually begins with an address to God, followed by the specific complaint or need. The worshiper may then confess trust in God and offer up a petition to God. The lament may include a declaration of assurance that God has heard the prayer and conclude with a promise to praise God with a thanksgiving offering. Note the following example of the lament (Psalm 54).

1. Address to God
   O God, save me (v. 1)
2. Complaint (reason for the prayer)
   strangers have risen up against me and oppressors have sought after my life (v. 3)
3. Confession of trust in God
   Behold, God is my helper (v. 4)
4. Petition for help
   Vindicate me ... Hear my prayer (vv. 1-2)
5. Assurance of being heard
   he has delivered me out of all trouble (v. 7)
6. Vow of praise offering
   I will freely sacrifice unto you; I will praise your name, O Lord (v. 6).

This psalms of lament teach us the importance of being open and honest with God. We have learned in our religious circles to mask our true feelings. When it comes to our relationship with God, the psalms teach us that we can be totally open and honest with God. The psalms of lament teach us that we should make a place for prayer in our worship services. Many churches have turned worship into nothing but celebration, and they have relegated prayer to the back rooms. Biblical worship provides a time and place for passionate prayer, for crying out to God. The New Testament instructs us to include times of prayer for people in the congregation (Jas 5.13-18). We are to 'be anxious for nothing, but in everything by prayer and supplication, let [our] requests be made known unto God (Phil. 4.6). Peter says, 'casting all your care upon him, because he cares for you' (1 Pet. 5.7). The early church prayed together in times of need (Acts 1.14; 2.42; 3.1; 4.31; 6.4, 6; 8.15; 12.5; 13.1-3; 14.23; 16.13, 25; 20.36).

The lament psalms include Psalms 3-7, 9-14, 16, 17, 22, 25-28, 31, 35, 36, 38-40, 42-44, 51-64, 69-71, 74, 77, 79, 80, 83, 85, 86, 88, 90, 94, 102, 106, 108, 109, 120, 123, 126, 130, 137, and 140-143.

Songs of Testimony (thanksgiving psalms)

The Song of Testimony, or Thanksgiving Psalm, is a public celebration of answered prayer. It is a testimonial to all who are present. The thanksgiving psalm is based upon the final element of the lament. At the end of the lament, the petitioner promises that when the prayer has been answered, he or she will offer a thanksgiving sacrifice. After God has answered the prayer and brought deliverance, the psalmist comes with his or her family and friends to the temple. At the temple, an offering or sacrifice is made in thanks to God. A Song of Testimony is sung to commemorate the occasion in praise to God. The Song of Testimony normally includes three basic parts, as seen in Psalm 30:

1. The reason for praising God
   I will extol you, O God, for you have lifted me up (v. 1)
2. The narration of the specific deliverance being celebrated
   I cried unto you and you healed me ... you kept me alive that I should not go down to the grave (vv. 2-3)
3. A renewed vow to praise God
   O Lord my God, I will give thanks to you forever (v. 12)

The Song of Testimony teaches us the value of public thanksgiving. This psalm of thankful testimony is meant to encourage the congregation who hear the song. Our deliverance is not complete until we give witness to it. God's purposes in bringing deliverance are incomplete without our testimony. The Song of Testimony teaches us the value of sharing our personal experiences with others. Our children need to hear that God has answered our prayers. Our friends and family need to hear what God has done in our lives. Some churches have become very impersonal, in which the members of the congregation no longer share their lives with each other. These psalms demonstrate the value of telling our story to one another in the context of worship.

The Songs of Testimony include Psalms 30, 34, 41, 66, 84, 87, 91, 92, 103, 111, 116, 118, 121, 122, 131, 138, 139, and 146.

Songs of Praise (hymns)

On the one hand, the Song of Testimony, which we discussed above, offers praises to God because of a specific event in the life of the worshiper. On the other hand, the hymn offers praises to God because of his eternal attributes. It is a psalm that is uttered in praise of God's more comprehensive virtues (e.g., 'Praise him for his mighty acts,' Ps. 150.2). The hymns emphasize both God's majesty and his love. His majesty is expressed through affirmations of his sovereignty and his rule over creation. His love is expressed through statements about his works of salvation and provision. The Songs of Praise (Hymns) normally begin with an invitation to worship, followed by the reason for praise, and conclude with a concluding invitation to worship. Note the following example.

1. Call to Worship
   Praise the Lord; Praise the name of the Lord
   Praise him, O you servants of the Lord (Ps. 135.1)
2. Motive for Worship
   A. God's Majesty
      (1) God's majesty in creation
         Whatever the Lord pleases, he does,
         In heaven and in earth,
         In the seas and in all the deep places (Ps. 135.6)
      (2) God's majesty in his sovereignty
         For I know that the Lord is great,
         And our Lord is above all gods (Ps. 135.5)
   B. God's Love
      (1) God's love in salvation (especially the exodus)

>   *He destroyed the firstborn of Egypt*
>   *Both of man and beast.*
>   *He sent signs and wonders* (Ps. 135.8-9)
>
>   (2) God's love in provision and care
>   *He raises the poor out of the dust,*
>   *And lifts the needy out of the ash heap* (Ps. 113.7)
>
> 3. Concluding Call to Worship
>   *Blessed be the LORD out of Zion,*
>   *Who dwells in Jerusalem!*
>   *Praise the LORD!* (Ps. 135.21)

While the Songs of Testimony teach us to praise God for specific acts of deliverance, the Hymns teach us to praise God for his unchangeable attributes. He is the God who is majestic and exalted, the King of kings, the Lord of lords, the God of gods. So let us praise him! He created the heaven, the earth, the angels, and all of humanity. So let us praise him! As creator, God has the power to rule and reign over the earth and over all earthly kingdoms. Let us praise him! Not only is God majestic in his holiness, but he is also loving, kind, and compassionate. Let us praise him! He saved Israel from the bondage of Egypt. Let us praise him! He gave them the land of Canaan, and he continues to provide for the needs of his people. Therefore, let us praise him. The Hymns teach us that the goal of worship is praise. When times are good we should praise God, and when times are bad we should praise God.

The Hymns include Psalms 24, 29, 33, 46, 48, 50, 67, 68, 75, 76, 81, 82, 90, 100, 105, 107, 113, 114, 115, 117, 124, 125, 129, 134, 135, 136, 147, 149, and 150.

Other types of psalms

Other types of psalms are less prominent, such as the Royal Psalms (Psalm 2, 18, 20, 21, 45, 72, 101, 110, 132, 144), the Historical Psalms (Psalm 78, 136), the Enthronement Psalms (Psalm 47, 93, 95-99), Songs of Creation (Psalm 8, 19, 65, 104, 148), and the Songs of Zion (Psalm 122).

Significance of the Psalm types

The different kinds of Psalms teach us different aspects of worship. The presence of the Wisdom Psalms within Israel's song book suggests the importance of instruction as a part of worship. The Songs of Prayer demonstrate that biblical worship should provide a time and place for passionate prayer, for crying out to God. The Songs of Testimony demonstrate the value of telling our story to one another in the context of worship, praising God for specific acts of deliverance. The Hymns teach us to praise God for his unchangeable attributes. They show us that the goal of worship is absolute praise.

Steps for interpreting the poetry

In order to interpret poetry effectively we must give attention to its unique characteristics. That is, we must consider its (1) content, (2) sounds, (3) structure, and (4) purpose. In its content, poetry includes a high concentration of figurative language and word play. In its sound, poetry exhibits intentional combinations of word sounds. In its structure, biblical poetry utilizes verse structure that is based upon parallelism. In its purpose, poetry intends not so much to inform the mind as to affect and move the heart.

The following steps can be helpful in reading poetry and interpreting its message.

1. Outline the structure
What is the structure or the apparent divisions and subdivisions of the psalm? What distinguishes these parts? What holds them together? Is there a progression, development, climax, or focal point? Who is the speaker? To whom is the psalm addressed? Note the types of parallelism. Observe any movements between speakers, addressees, topics, and verb tenses. What type of psalm is this (wisdom, prayer, testimony, hymn)? What does that tell you about its purpose? Make a list of prominent themes and concepts that are repeated.

2. Examine the figures of speech
Analyze the metaphors, similes, hyperboles, and other figures of speech. How do they impact the hearer and help to form the message? What are the prominent contrasts, comparisons, and symbolisms? How do they function in the passage?

3. Observe contextual connections

How does the psalm reflect, respond, or relate to the surrounding psalms? To the book of Psalms as a whole? To the surrounding historical and sociological situations in ancient Israel and in the life of the psalmist? If the psalm has a superscription that suggests a context in the life of the psalmist, how does that context impact the meaning of the psalm? How does this psalm relate to the themes, patterns, and traditions found elsewhere in the Old Testament and in the ancient world?

4. Identify the affective mood

Poetry draws the reader into the poetic world through visual imagery, imaginative symbols, and appeals to the readers emotions. This affective dimension of poetry speaks to the heart and to the passions with a fervent freshness and honesty. What is the mood of the psalm? Is it joyful, hopeful, light, heavy, encouraging, convicting, mournful, sad, prayerful, thankful? Is there movement from one mood to another, such as from sadness to joy? How should we feel after studying this psalm? What parts of the psalm are particularly moving?

5. Apply the psalm to your own life and church

The psalms emerge from Israel's life with God and express the struggles and joys of living in covenant with God. The psalms express our greatest fears, our deepest longings, and our fondest hopes. We may want to ask the following questions: What does this psalm teach us about God and how he relates to his people? What does it teach us about how we should relate to God and communicate with him? In light of our study, how is life informed, formed, or transformed by this psalm? What response is being called for? How might this passage be speaking beyond its own day even unto our own? How does this psalm inform us about our worship?

For Review and Study

1. Explain the definition of 'poetry.'
2. The structure of biblical poetry is based upon parallelism of lines. What is parallelism?
3. Define synonymous parallelism and give an example.
4. Define antithetical parallelism and give an example.

5. Define synthetic parallelism and give an example.
6. What is an acrostic poem?
7. How is the purpose of poetry different from the purpose of prose?
8. Enumerate three examples of poetry in the New Testament.
9. Who were the authors of the Psalms?
10. What information is included in the superscriptions?
11. List nine types of psalms.
12. What do the psalms of lament teach us about our relationship to God?
13. The Song of Testimony is a public celebration of answered prayer. What do we learn from this type of psalm?
14. How is the Song of Praise (hymn) different from the Song of Testimony?
15. What are some important elements to consider when outlining the structure of a psalm?
16. What are some important elements to consider when identifying the affective component of a psalm?

Codex Vaticanus (handwritten Greek, AD 350)

Modern Scribe Copying the Hebrew Bible
On Parchment Using a Goose Quill Pen

11

INTERPRETING BIBLICAL NARRATIVE

Narrative in the Bible

The Bible is filled with stories, and those many stories combine to form one grand story—the story of God in relation to his people. The Old Testament narrates the story of God and his people Israel, while the New Testament narrates the story of Jesus and his Church. We observed earlier that a large portion of the Bible is written in the form of poetry, and we looked also at the genre of literature that we call 'wisdom.' A still larger part of the Bible is written in the form of stories—what scholars call 'narrative literature.' Old Testament books that consist mostly of narrative include Genesis, Exodus, Numbers, Deuteronomy, Joshua, Judges, Ruth, 1 & 2 Samuel, 1 & 2 Kings, 1 & 2 Chronicles, Ezra, Nehemiah, Esther. In the New Testament, the narrative books are Matthew, Mark, Luke, John, and Acts.

The elements of narrative

In order to interpret these narrative books, it is important that we understand the elements that come together in the telling of a story. Biblical narrative literature is composed of five basic elements: (1) the narrator, (2) the plot, (3) the characters, (4) the point of view, and (5) the setting. The *narrator* is the author of the book, the person who tells the story. The *plot* is the sequence of events that makes up the story. The *characters* are the participants in the story, and they may be human, divine, or even animals (e.g., the serpent in Genesis 3 and the donkey in Numbers 22). *Point of view* is the perspective from which the story is told. The *setting* is the time and location in which the story takes place. These five basic elements that come together to create narrative would suggest the following guidelines for our interpretations.

1. Listen to the words of the narrator.

Identity of the narrator

The first element of narrative, the narrator, is the person who tells the story. The identity of the biblical narrator is sometimes known and sometimes unknown. Tradition tells us that Moses is the narrator of Genesis-Deuteronomy, and that Ezra is the narrator of 1 & 2 Chronicles, Ezra, and Nehemiah, but we we do not know the narrators of Joshua-Kings. In the New Testament, we know that Matthew, Mark, Luke, and John are narrated by the same men after whom the books are named. We also know that Luke is the narrator of the book of Acts.

Function of the narrator

The narrator sets the stage, relates events, describes characters, and allows characters to speak for themselves. In the Bible, the narrator claims a prophetic voice, so that the voice of the narrator is equivalent in authority to the voice of God. Other characters in the story may not always be truthful. For example, in the book of Exodus, we should not automatically accept the words of Pharaoh as truth. However, we can believe as truth everything that is said by the narrator. For example, we read in Genesis 22 the story of Abraham's intended sacrifice of Isaac. Scholars and commentators have discussed the meaning of the story, and they hold different opinions. However, if we listen to the narrator, we will know the meaning of the passage. The narrator tells us in Gen. 22.1 that 'God tested Abraham.' The narrator's words are very appropriate, given the fact that the story of Genesis 22 is the final event in Abraham's life. For 10 chapters in Genesis, we have read about Abraham's good qualities and his bad qualities. At times he was faithful, and at other times he seemed to be unfaithful. At times he believed God, and at other times he seemed to doubt God. Genesis 22 is the culmination of Abraham's life; it is his final test. With this final and greatest test

Abraham is proven to be worthy of the title 'the father of the faithful.'

2. Follow the events of the plot.
The second element of narrative, the plot, is the sequential arrangement of actions (events) that make up the story. Within the plot, we expect to see order, cause and effect, conflict, rising tension, climax, and dénouement.

Plot includes an ordered arrangement of events.

The events in a plot are not random; they occur in a particular *order*. For example, the events in the story of Noah are placed in a particular order, with his drunkenness coming at the end of the story. Can you imagine how different the story would read if he had gotten drunk at the beginning of the story instead of at the end? Also, scholars have observed that the four Gospels do not follow the identical chronology of events. That is because each Gospel has its own unique emphasis. The events are arranged in such a way to emphasize the theological point that the Gospel writer wants to stress. In order to understand the Gospels properly, we should interpret each Gospel according to its own chronology.

Events in the plot show evidence of cause and effect.

The events are not disconnected; they are joined by *cause and effect*. For example, Samson's unfaithfulness, expressed through his pursuit of women, is the cause of his eventual downfall at the hands of Delilah (Judges 13-16).

Events will include rising tension.

Normally, the events in the plot will involve *conflict* between characters that provokes *rising tension* in the story. This conflict grows more intense throughout the story. The tension continues to intensify until it reaches a *climax*, which is then followed by a *dénouement*, a resolution of the lines in the plot. For example, the story of King Saul involves a number of conflicts. His disobedience and pride generate conflict between Saul and the prophet Samuel. Also, Saul's loss of the Holy Spirit, coupled with young David's great success against the giant Goliath, produces a growing conflict between Saul and David (1 Samuel 16-31). The tension between Saul and David is resolved only when Saul is killed in battle. Saul's death is the climax of the plot. The *dénouement* consists of David's grieving over Saul and Jonathan and of his memorial song in their honor (2 Samuel 1).

Plots may be complex.

A plot may include crucial turning points and more than one climax; and the climax may lead to tragedy rather than resolution. For example, the turning point in the Gospel of John is Chapter 11, in which Jesus raises Lazarus from the dead. The raising of Lazarus lifts Jesus to such a popular status that the chief priests and Pharisees decide to have Jesus put to death (Jn 11.43). The climax of the Gospel of John at first appears to be the crucifixion, but then we learn that the true climax is the resurrection.

Often, a story may consist of a weaving together of multiple plots, which may be called sub-plots. In biblical narrative, individual stories with their own plot may be joined together in a larger story to form an overall plot for the book. The book of Judges, for example, consists of numerous individual stories that we might call 'episodes.' However, the entire book has an overall plot that follows the Israelites from a time of unity, faithfulness, and victory in Chapter 1 to a time of disunity, idolatry, and chaos in Chapter 21. This is also true of the Gospels, where the individual stories in the life of Jesus carry their own message, and the stories come together to form the larger story of the Gospel.

3. Pay attention to the descriptions of the characters.

Descriptions of characters

The third element of narrative, the characters, are the participants in the story. The description of the characters may be a key element in the story. For example, the judge Ehud is described as left-handed, a fact that becomes very important later in the story. The characters may be described directly (by the narrator or by other characters) or indirectly (by their actions, by their thoughts, by their words, and by comparisons with other characters). The characters vary in the amount of information that is given about them. One of the most complete descriptions of a character in the Bible is found in the introduction to Job. Job's moral character is affirmed by the statement that he is 'perfect and upright, fearing God and shunning evil.' His standing in the community is also mentioned by way of the statement that Job was rich. His righteousness is also affirmed through his actions. We are told that Job offered sacrifices daily for his children. This description of Job provides the background for the entire story, in which Job's righteous character is put to the ultimate test.

Interaction of characters

It is also important to observe how characters within the story interact with each other and how they change and develop as the story unfolds. As the story progresses, characters will often be contrasted to each other. The first example of contrasting characters is found in the story of Cain and Abel. We read,

> Now Abel was a keeper of sheep, but Cain was a tiller of the ground. And in the process of time it came to pass that Cain brought an offering of the fruit of the ground to the LORD. Abel also brought of the firstborn of his flock and of their fat. And the LORD respected Abel and his offering, but he did not respect Cain and his offering. And Cain was very angry ... and it came to pass, when they were in the field, that Cain rose up against Abel his brother and killed him (Gen. 4.2-8).

Another example of the way characters are contrasted is found in the story of Jacob and Esau. We are told that 'Esau was a skillful hunter, a man of the field; but Jacob was a mild man, dwelling in tents. And Isaac [their father] loved Esau because he ate *of his* game, but Rebekah [their mother] loved Jacob' (Gen. 25.27-28). These important contrasts between Jacob and Esau form the basis for much of the story that follows in Genesis 25-32.

4. Examine the point of view.

The fourth element of narrative, the point of view, is the perspective from which a story is told. There are three points of view in any narrative: the view from the narrator, the view from the characters, and the view from the reader. The narrator controls what the reader knows about the story and its characters. For example, in the story of Job, the readers know more than the characters within the story. Job and his friends do not know that Satan is the instigator of the attacks against Job, but the readers know it all along (an example of dramatic irony, which we will discuss below). Therefore, as we read the story, we should try to put ourselves in Job's place and imagine how he must have felt. In other words we should give attention to the point of view of the characters as well as that of the narrator.

5. Consider the setting of the story.

Geographical setting

The fifth element of narrative, the setting, includes the location of the story in space and time. We should notice the location, how the location changes, and why the location might change. For example, it seems important that in Gen. 35.1 God instructs Jacob to return to Bethel, the place of his earliest encounter with God. Another Old Testament example is Judg. 2.1, where we read that 'the angel of the Lord went up from Gilgal to Bochim,' where he delivered a stinging rebuke from the Lord to Israel. Gilgal was the headquarters of the Israelites during their campaigns of conquest in the book of Joshua. Therefore, its mention recalls a time of victory and blessing for Israel. The angel, however, has left Gilgal and has taken up a position at Bochim, which means 'weepers,' and his message recounts Israel's recent defeats and pronounces judgment upon their disobedience.

Temporal setting

The temporal setting relates to the time when the story takes place. It is important to remember that the Bible is not a book of history as much as it is a book of theology; therefore, its stories may or may not relate events in chronological order. For example, the book of Judges does not present the different judges in chronological order; rather it presents them in geographical order from south to north. Furthermore, although the final chapters serve as a fitting conclusion to the message of Judges, the events of these chapters actually occurred near the beginning of the era of the judges, as can be seen from the mention of the priest Phinehas (Judg. 20.28), who was high priest soon after Joshua died (Josh. 24.33). As stated earlier, the Gospels follow a common chronology of Jesus' birth, life, death, and resurrection; but within that common chronology we find many variations. These variations should not be considered 'contradictions' because the writers of that day did not follow modern rules for the writing of history. The Gospels are primarily theological narratives, and a certain amount of variation in arrangement of material is allowed.

References to time (or the lack of such references) have a bearing upon the message of the book. The prophet Ezekiel, on the one hand, is very careful to supply precise dates for his prophecies. Jonah, on the other hand, seems to intentionally avoid any specific information that might reveal the time of its events. This intentional omission of temporal setting moves our attention away from a specific historical setting and causes us to think of the book in more symbolic terms.

Dates and times can be important indicators of themes and motifs within a book. The book of Judges includes significant references to time. We are told the numbers of years that Israel suffered under oppression, the numbers of years that each judge ruled, and the numbers of years between episodes of oppression. It is significant that the early judges (Othniel, Ehud, Deborah, and Gideon) were able to maintain peace for at least 40 years (one generation). However, the later judges (Jephthah and Samson) were unable to maintain the peace for more than 20 years. This decline in effectiveness is part of the overall motif of spiritual and moral decline that we see in the book of Judges.

Common literary devices

In addition to the basic elements of narrative (listed above), you should be alert for other common literary devices that may appear in the story. The following six literary devices occur throughout the Bible.

1. Imagery
Imagery is the presentation of verbal pictures. For example, in Isaiah 6, the prophet sees the king of the universe, seated on his throne, with the train of his robe stretching through the temple. Smoke fills the temple, and seraphim fly back and forth above the throne of God, crying, 'Holy, holy, holy is the Lord of hosts. The whole earth is full of his glory!' (v. 3). This is powerful imagery.

2. Tone

Tone is the particular feeling or mood that is expressed in the story. At the beginning of 1 Samuel chapter 1, we are introduced to a young woman named Hannah who is unable to have children. Hannah is tormented because of her inability to have children. Her husband tries to console her, but Hannah still weeps and cries. She goes to the tabernacle and pours out her heart in prayer. The tone of this passage is very touching and gets the reader involved emotionally in Hannah's story. The tone creates sympathy for Hannah. The tone then shifts from sorrow to joy when Hannah gives birth to her son, Samuel. The joy is expressed in Hannah's song of rejoicing (1 Samuel 2).

3. Poetic justice

Poetic justice is found when a character in the story experiences a fitting retribution. Poetic justice means that the good person is eventually blessed, and it means that the evil person is finally punished. For example, Joseph suffers many injustices, but in the end he is exalted and saves his entire family (Genesis 37-50). Another example is found in the book of Esther, when Haman plots to kill Mordecai, but it is Haman who is finally killed. He is hanged on the very gallows he built for Mordecai. That is poetic justice.

4. Paradox

Paradox is the simultaneous presentation of events, statements, or ideas that seem to contradict one another. Paradox is quite common in all types of biblical literature. For example, in Exodus 5-15, Pharaoh's heart becomes increasingly hardened. At times it seems that Pharaoh hardens his own heart, but at other times it seems that God hardens Pharaoh's heart. Does Pharaoh harden his own heart, or does God harden Pharaoh's heart? The book of Exodus would seem to say that both are true. We might ask the question, 'Do we have free will or is God sovereign?' The answer is that both are true. It is a paradox, requiring us to hold together two ideas that seem to be in tension.

5. Dramatic irony

Dramatic irony is a literary device that allows the reader to know something the characters in the story do not know. For example, in Luke 24, the disciples are mourning over the death of Jesus, but the readers already know that Jesus is risen. Dramatic irony contributes to the building of suspense in the story.

6. Allusions to other Scriptures
An allusion is an expression designed to call to mind another Scripture without mentioning it explicitly. For example, when Joshua and Israel pass through the waters of Jordan, we are reminded of Moses and Israel passing through the Red Sea. We find another allusion to the Red Sea in Isa. 43.2, which says, 'When you pass through the waters, I will be with you; and through the rivers, they shall not overflow you.'

Narrative Theology

Biblical narrative is theological in focus.
A large portion of the Bible is given to us in the form of story (narrative literature). Story is Israel's preferred method for writing their theology. They did not have what we call systematic theology. Systematic theology was invented later and was based upon categories of Greek philosophy.

The Old Testament narrative books are not books of *systematic* theology, but they are books of theology all the same. Therefore, they are more than 'history.' The books that we often call the 'Historical Books' are called in the Hebrew tradition 'Former Prophets.' All of the narrative books (Genesis-Nehemiah) are more than history; they are 'salvation history,' prophetic history. These books are theological testimony that offers an account of the Hebrew faith. Biblical narrative tells the story of the interaction between God and Israel in order to produce a response from their audience.

Biblical narrative presents a message for today.
The narrative books present a theological message to its original readers, and they also present a message for today's reader as well. As a prophetic word, these books challenge and inform all believers. Our goal as interpreters is to seek for the theological message of the text, to be confronted by it, and to then to be conformed to it. Thus, the biblical narrative is an authoritative word for today.

Practical application of biblical narrative

After we examine a story from the Bible, there still remains the task of applying the message to believers and the Church of today. In the book of Acts, we read that Paul and four other men made a vow and shaved their heads (Acts 21.23-26). Should we follow Paul's example? The early Christian women wore veils (1 Cor. 11.5). Does it follow that Christian women of today should wear veils? How are we to make application?

The principle of analogy

I would suggest that our interpretation should be modeled after the example of the New Testament writers when they interpret the Old Testament. In I Corinthians, Paul talks about the Israelites in the wilderness, and he says, 'Now all these things happened to them as examples, and they were written for our admonition, upon whom the ends of the ages have come' (1 Cor. 10.11). Therefore, the stories of the Old Testament (and the New Testament) were written as examples to us. There are times when we face the same challenges to faith that were experienced by believers in the Bible. I call this method the principle of analogy. An analogy is a correspondence or significant similarity between the biblical story and our story.

An example of interpretation by analogy

An excellent example of the principle of analogy is found in the book of Hebrews. The writer of Hebrews compares the situation of his readers to the similar situation faced by the Israelites in Numbers 13-14. There in the wilderness of Kadesh Barnea, God commanded Israel to enter the Promised Land and to conquer the evil Canaanites. However, when they learned of the Canaanite walled cities, the Israelites refused to go into the Promised Land. Because of their disobedience, God declared that all of the adults would die in the wilderness, never to see the good land. They subsequently wandered for 40 years until all of that generation had died. The story is recounted in the Psalms, where the psalmist declares, 'Today, if you will hear his voice, do not harden your hearts as in the rebellion, in the day of trial in the wilderness ... so I swore in my wrath, "They shall not enter into my rest"' (Ps. 95.7-11). The writer of Hebrews cites the psalm and reminds his readers of the Old

Testament story. He compares the situation of the Hebrew Christians to that of the Israelites. The Hebrew Christians were being persecuted for their faith in Jesus, and apparently they were considering going back to Judaism. In Christ they would enter into eternal rest; but if they disobeyed God and went back to Judaism, they would face God's wrath. To the Israelites and to the early Christians the question of obedience was a question of faith. Israel failed to believe God. The question remains, 'Will the Hebrew Christians believe God or not?' (Heb. 3.12, 19; 4.2, 3)

The biblical story and our story

Every biblical story includes points at which we can compare our own journey of faith to that of the biblical characters. Abraham is called to leave the comfort of his home and family. We may face a similar call from God. Joshua is commanded to march around the walls of Jericho and trust that God will bring victory. We also may be required to believe God for a great miracle. David chooses to risk his own life in order to battle the giant Goliath. We may encounter similar choices. In the New Testament, the Syrophoenician woman refuses to be silent as she cries out to Jesus. We also must cry out to God for his help in the time of need. Jesus' disciples pray expectantly and wait for the coming of the Holy Spirit. We also must pray and wait for the Holy Spirit's power to come into our lives. As we read the stories of the Bible, we should search for points of correspondence to our own story, points at which we might find encouragement (or rebuke) from the biblical narrative.

For Review and Study

1. Name the five New Testament narrative books.
2. List the five components of narrative literature.
3. Define the word 'plot.'
4. Discuss the ways that characters may be described.
5. Tell one example of a biblical story in which characters are contrasted to each other.
6. What is tone, and what is the tone of 1 Samuel 1-2?
7. Explain the meaning of poetic justice in the life of Joseph.
8. Define paradox? What is the primary paradox in Exodus 5-15?
9. What is dramatic irony? How does it function in Luke 24?
10. Discuss two allusions to Israel's passing through the Red Sea.

11. What is Israel's preferred method for writing theology?
12. How does biblical narrative present a message for today?
13. Explain the significance of 1 Cor. 10.11 for our interpretation of biblical narrative.
14. Describe an example of interpretation by analogy.
15. How do we relate the biblical story to our own story?

12

INTERPRETING PROPHECY

When we think about the subject of prophecy, we are faced with two common misconceptions. On the one hand, conservative Christians often think of the biblical prophets only as predictors of the future. On the other hand, many liberal theologians believe the prophets to be only social reformers. Both of these viewpoints contain a bit of truth, but neither view is sufficient to encompass the biblical portrayal of the biblical prophet. Certainly, the prophets predicted future events, and there is no doubt that they also intended their prophecies to produce radical social change. However, the ministry of the prophets was different from the work of the fortune teller or the social reformer.

Characteristics of Prophecy

The prophets were messengers of God.
When we look to the beginnings of prophecy in the Old Testament, we learn that the prophets were fundamentally messengers of God. They were ambassadors representing God before the nation of Israel. They delivered not their own message but Yahweh's message. The role of the prophets as messenger is demonstrated clearly by two factors: (1) their commission and (2) their use of the *messenger formula*.

The prophetic call and commission

At the time of their calling, the prophets received a commission from God. The commission of each prophet was unique; nevertheless, every prophet was appointed to be a spokesperson for God. God said to Moses, 'Now therefore, go, and I will be with your mouth and teach you what you shall say' (Exod. 4.12). To Jeremiah, he said, 'Behold, I have put My words in your mouth' (Jer. 1.9). God commissioned Ezekiel and said, 'Son of man, go to the house of Israel and speak with My words to them' (Ezek. 3.4).

Isaiah's call narrative, more than any other, shows most clearly that the prophet was commissioned as a court messenger of the divine King. The setting of Isaiah's call (Isaiah 6) is plainly one of a royal court complete with entourage and sovereign deliberations about sending a messenger. The Lord asks, 'Whom shall I send, and who will go for us?' The prophet answers, 'Here I am, send me.' Then the prophet is commissioned: 'Go and speak to his people.' Just as an ancient king would send a spokesperson to carry his message, God sends Isaiah to carry his message to Israel and to the nations. Therefore, the prophet's role as messenger is evident from the nature of the divine commission.

The prophets' use of the messenger formula

The messenger role is also demonstrated in the prophets' use of the *messenger formula*. In the ancient world, whenever a spokesperson would carry a message from the king, the spokesperson would introduce the message with the words, 'Thus says the king ...' For example, in the days when Hezekiah ruled over Judah, the Assyrians invaded the land and surrounded Jerusalem. The messenger of the Assyrian king sent word to Hezekiah, demanding that Jerusalem surrender. The Assyrian spokesman introduced his message with the words, 'Thus says the great king, the king of Assyria ...' (2 Kgs 18.19).

In similar fashion, the prophets introduced their messages with the messenger formula, 'Thus says the Lord ....' The first example is found in the book of Exodus, when Moses approaches Pharaoh and says, 'Thus says the LORD God of Israel: 'Let My people go" (Exod. 5.1). Altogether, the prophets of the Old Testament use the phrase, 'Thus says the Lord,' over 400 times.

The prophets were preachers of the Word of God.
In their role as messengers, the prophets proclaimed the message that had been given to them by the Lord. This message is known as 'the word of the Lord.' We read that the word of the Lord 'came' to the prophets (Isa. 38.4). We also read that the prophets called upon their audience to 'hear the word of the Lord' (Isa. 1.10).

The word of the Lord is the prophetic revelation. The prophets received the word of the Lord through dreams, visions, angelic visitations, and through the voice of the Holy Spirit. The prophets proclaimed the message that God gave to them through these means of revelation.

The prophets expressed the passions of God.
The prophetic experience of the word of the Lord was so dramatic, so intense, so transformative, that the prophets received a new view of reality. By the Holy Spirit, they were enabled to see the world from God's perspective. Whenever the word of the Lord came to the prophets, it caused them to see everything differently. Their nation, their society, their worship, and their own lives were brought under the light of God's revelation.

This transformation of the prophet's view of the world means that the prophet becomes more than a messenger of God's *words*; the prophet becomes the messenger of God's *heart*. The passions of God are formed in the heart of the prophet, and the prophet pours them forth unto the people. Thus, there are times when the prophet embodies God's anger at Israel's unfaithfulness, and streams of wrath gush from his mouth. For example, the Lord tells Israel, 'Your sacrifices sicken me … I hate your festivals …I will not hear your prayers; your hands are full of blood' (Isa. 1.13-15). At other times the prophet feels the divine compassion in all its immeasurable depth. At those times, words of comfort flow forth like healing oil. For example, Isaiah writes,

He will feed his flock like a shepherd;
He will gather the lambs with his arm,
And carry them in his bosom,
And gently lead those who are with young (Isa. 40.11).

The prophets predicted future events.
The message of the prophets sometimes includes threats of judgment or promises of blessing. In either case, the threats or promises

may entail predictions of future events. If the hearers refuse to repent, God will act to perform his judgments. Likewise, if the hearers will turn to God, he will act to perform salvation and blessing.

However, the message of the prophets does not center upon the future. Less than 5% of Old Testament prophecy relates to the new covenant age. Most of the Old Testament prophecies relate to the immediate future concerning Israel, Judah, and the other nations. The purpose of predictive prophecy is not to satisfy our curiosity about the future. Its purpose is to call us back to God by reminding us that God is in control of the future.

The prophets emphasized covenant faithfulness.
The prophets often predicted the future, but they did so as a way of encouraging faithfulness. The demands of the prophets centered upon the Mosaic covenant. For example, Jeremiah rebuked Israel for their failure to honor the Sabbath day (Jer. 17.19-27). Faithfulness to the covenant brings blessing, and disobedience brings judgment. The blessings include life, health, prosperity, agricultural abundance, respect and safety. Punishments include death, disease, drought, dearth, danger, disruption, defeat, deportation, destitution, and disgrace. The prophetic proclamation centered upon these categories of blessing and punishment.

Types of prophetic speech
The prophets' concern for covenant faithfulness resulted in two primary types of preaching: (1) the threat of judgment and (2) the promise of blessing. When reading the prophets, it is helpful to determine the type of prophetic speech that is found in each passage.

The judgment speech

The judgment speech is the basic form of the prophetic message. The judgment speech often contains two parts: (1) the specific accusations of unfaithfulness and (2) details of the type of judgment that will be imposed if the people do not repent. For example, Amos proclaims the following judgment.

For three transgressions of Judah, and for four,
I will not turn away its punishment,
Because they have despised the law of the LORD,
And have not kept his commandments.
Their lies lead them astray,

> *Lies which their fathers followed.*
> *But I will send a fire upon Judah,*
> *And it shall devour the palaces of Jerusalem* (Amos 2.4-5).

The accusations of unfaithfulness may include both social evils and spiritual transgressions. The social sins are seen as evidence of religious apostasy. The prophets recognized that sins against our neighbor are proof that we do not love God.

The salvation speech

The salvation speech is a promise of blessing or deliverance. The major emphasis in the salvation speech is upon divine mercy and grace. The prophets declare that salvation is due only to the merciful intervention of God himself. Sometimes the salvation speech predicts a deliverance that is near at hand, but sometimes it reaches far into the future. For example, Zechariah promises,

> Thus says the LORD of hosts:
> My cities shall again spread out through prosperity;
> > The LORD will again comfort Zion,
> > And will again choose Jerusalem (Zech. 1.17).

The woe oracle

The woe oracle is a particular type of judgment speech that contains the word 'woe' followed by details regarding the subject, the transgression, and the judgment. The word 'woe' signifies tragedy and imminent sorrow. It is a powerful device for announcing judgment and doom. For example, Isaiah declares,

> Woe to those who call evil good, and good evil ...
> > Woe to those who are wise in their own eyes,
> > And prudent in their own sight!
> Woe to men mighty at drinking wine,
> > Woe to men valiant for mixing intoxicating drink,
> Who justify the wicked for a bribe,
> > And take away justice from the righteous man!
> Therefore, as the fire devours the stubble,
> > And the flame consumes the chaff,
> So their root will be as rottenness,
> > And their blossom will ascend like dust;
> Because they have rejected the law of the LORD of hosts,

And despised the word of the Holy One of Israel.
(Isa. 5.20-24)

The prophets utilized poetic forms of speech.

As we mentioned in Chapter 9, the prophetical books of Isaiah through Malachi are composed mostly of poetry. The poetry of the prophets is highly symbolic, and it is the language of the heart. The goal of prophetic poetry is not simply to pass along information. The goal is to provoke and transform the imagination. Poetic symbolism and figurative language are well-suited for expressing the spiritual experiences and visions of the prophets. The straightforward language of prose is not sufficient to capture the awe and mystery of the powerful encounters between the prophets and the Lord of glory. Poetry alone is able to cut deeply to the heart of sinful rebellion, and only poetry can generate hopeful expectation for a future that appears to be unattainable through normal human means.

The prophets' use of poetry produces difficulties and uncertainties in interpretation. Poetry sparks the imagination, but its inherent ambiguity means that it supplies only parts of the picture, not the whole picture. For example, let us consider the following prophecy.

> When the Lord has washed away the filth of the daughters of Zion, and purged the blood of Jerusalem from her midst ... then the LORD will create above every dwelling place of Mount Zion, and above her assemblies, a cloud and smoke by day and the shining of a flaming fire by night (Isa. 4.4-5).

The promise of a cloud by day and a flaming fire by night is obviously an allusion to God's protection of Israel during the wilderness wanderings. Are we to understand that God will once again cover his people with the cloud and with the fire? Or is this promise to be understood as a symbol of divine presence and protection? I would suggest that it is poetic symbolism, not to be taken literally.

The prophets were uncompromising

The prophets were transformed by their encounter with God

As we mentioned earlier, the prophetic experience of the word of the Lord was so dramatic, so intense, so transformative, that the prophets received a new view of reality. By the Holy Spirit, they were enabled to see the world from God's perspective. This transformation caused the prophets to be uncompromising in their convictions and to appear abnormal to the rest of the world. They were often considered to be insane.

The prophets utilized extreme symbolic actions.

Along with their rigid attitude, the prophets exhibited other strange behavior. They sometimes engaged in unusual symbolic actions that drew attention to their prophecies. These could be called acting parables or object lessons for the observers. For example.

Hosea ...
- bought back his wife at the slave market (Hos. 3.1-4).
- He gave symbolic names to his children (Hos. 1.3-9).

Isaiah ...
- walked naked in Jerusalem three years (Isa. 20.1-3).
- He gave his children symbolic names (7.3; 8.1; 8.18).

Jeremiah ...
- wore a linen belt, buried it, then dug it up (Jer. 13.1-7).
- He lived a celibate lifestyle (16.1-3).
- He smashed a clay jar (19.1-11).
- He wore a yoke (27.1-12).

Ezekiel ...
- ate a scroll (Ezek. 2.8-3.3).
- He modeled the siege of Jerusalem on a clay tile (4.1-3).
- He lay on his left side 390 days and on his right 40 days (4.4-8).
- He rationed his food and cooked it over dried dung (4.9-17).
- He shaved his head and beard, disposing of it in four parts (5.1-17).
- He clapped his hands and stamped his feet (6.11-14).
- He dug through the wall carrying an exile's baggage (12.3-7).
- He ate his meals nervously (12.17-20).
- He clapped his hands and struck his sword three times (21.14-17).
- He did not mourn the death of his wife (24.15-24).
- He joined two sticks together (37.15-23).

The prophets gave their lives for God.

The prophets' stern and unbending approach often brought about persecution and even death. The prophets were willing to face death because they had already surrendered their lives to God. During their initial prophetic experience, God had claimed their lives for himself.

Historical context of the Old Testament prophets

In order to understand the prophets, we should study the context in which they ministered. We should place each of the prophets within the overall story of the people of Israel. The seventy years of exile (beginning 586 BC) is the event that is most consequential for understanding the prophets. The following time line may be helpful in placing the prophets in their historical contexts.

782 BC—*Israel Divided.*
The nation was split into two kingdoms (The northern kingdom called Israel, and the southern kingdom called Judah).
721 BC—*Israel Exiled.*
The northern kingdom, Israel, was conquered by the Assyrians, and the people went into exile.
605 BC—*Judah Conquered.*
The southern kingdom, Judah, was conquered by Babylon, and the nobility were exiled to Babylon (including Daniel).
597 BC—*Jerusalem Taken.*
Judah rebelled against Babylon, but Nebuchadnezzar again conquered Jerusalem, exiling King Jehoiachin.
586 BC—*Temple Destroyed.*
Jerusalem and the Temple were destroyed by Nebuchadnezzar of Babylon. All of the inhabitants were taken into exile in Babylon.
536 BC—*First Return.*
Cyrus, the Persian ruler who conquered Babylon, allowed the Jews to return to Jerusalem, led by Zerubbabel.
516 BC—*Second Temple.*
The Jews finished building the second Jerusalem temple.
457 BC—*Second Return.*
Ezra led a second return of Jews to Jerusalem.
445 BC—*Walls Rebuilt.*
Nehemiah rebuilt the walls of Jerusalem.

PROPHET	DATES	MAIN AUDIENCE	PROMINENT THEME
Jonah	780	Assyria	Call for repentance in Ninevah
Amos	760	Israel	Hypocrisy of Israel (N. Kingdom)
Hosea	750-725	Israel	God's love for Israel (N. Kingdom)
Isaiah	745-680	Judah	Judgment and salvation
Micah	735-700	Judah	Judgment
EXILE OF ISRAEL			
Zephaniah	639	Judah	Day of the lord
Jeremiah	627-580	Judah	Judah's last hour
Nahum	615	Assyria	Judgment of Ninevah
Obadiah	605	Edom	Judgment of Edom
Habakkuk	605	Judah	Live by faith
Daniel	605-530	Exiles	God's view of history
Joel	600	Judah	Day of the Lord
Ezekiel	593-570	Exiles	Future restoration
EXILE OF JUDAH			
Haggai	520	Jerusalem	Reconstruction of the temple
Zechariah	520-485	Jerusalem	Restoring hope & expectancy
TEMPLE REBUILT			
Malachi	450	Jerusalem	Appeal to faithfulness

Old Testament pre-exilic prophets

The prophets are usually divided up into two large categories, those who prophesied before the exile (586 BC) and those who prophesied during and after the exile. We will further divide the pre-exilic prophets into two smaller categories.

Prophets to the northern kingdom, Israel

The earliest of the writing prophets addressed the sins of the northern kingdom of Israel. Amos, Hosea, Isaiah, and Micah called Israel to repentance. It was a time of great prosperity, but it was also a time of ruthless economic injustice. The poor were trampled under the feet of the rich. In the religious sphere, idolatry was rampant among the people. Israel and its leaders did not obey the prophets' call for a return to God. Israel was then conquered by the Assyrians.

Prophets to the southern kingdom, Judah

After the northern kingdom fell, Isaiah and Micah continued to prophesy to Judah, along with the prophets Zephaniah, Jeremiah, Nahum, Obadiah, and Habakkuk. Daniel and Ezekiel were taken captive in the first and second waves of Babylonian aggression. Ezekiel prophesied to Judah and to the Jews who were with him in Babylon. Judah experienced periods of revival under Hezekiah and Josiah, but eventually Judah fell away from God just as Israel had done. Idolatry became the norm. They too were removed from their homeland and exiled.

Old Testament post-exilic prophets

After seventy years of exile, the Jews were allowed to return to Judah and Jerusalem. They returned with great expectations of God's blessings. They anticipated a time of prosperity and success. Ezekiel had promised a time of fruitfulness (Ezekiel 34). Isaiah had prophesied a population explosion (Isaiah 54). Jeremiah had declared that the son of David would regain the throne (Jeremiah 23). The Jews also expected that the nations would come and serve God at Jerusalem (Isaiah 49). However, their expectations were disappointed, and they began to doubt the promises of God. The post-exilic prophets Haggai and Zechariah arose with a message of encouragement. They inspired the Jews to rebuild their temple and to believe in God's promises. The rebuilding of the temple, Zechariah said, is 'not by might, not by power, but by my Spirit says the Lord of hosts' (Zech. 4.6).

After the time of revival inspired by Haggai and Zechariah, the people lapsed into another period of spiritual decline. God raised up Malachi to preach a new message of repentance. He called Israel back to the Mosaic Covenant and back to a life of faithfulness.

Keys to interpreting Old Testament prophecy

The following keys are useful in interpreting prophecy.
1. Determine the type of prophetic speech employed. Is it a judgment speech or a salvation speech?

2. Study the message in light of its historical context. What is the sin being addressed? What are the Israelites being asked to do?
3. Does the prophecy include a prediction of future events? If so, is the prediction conditional or unconditional? Has it already been fulfilled?
4. Examine any figurative language to determine the meaning of any symbolism.
5. Look for any reference to Jesus Christ. Some passages are directly messianic, such as Mic. 5.2 (on Jesus' birth in Bethlehem) and Mal. 4.5 (on Elijah as Christ's forerunner). Other passages serve only as analogies, for example, Hos. 11.1 (the calling of Jesus out of Egypt).
6. Do not force the passage to fit into your prophetic schemes. Proof-texting is a dangerous practice that prevents us from hearing the real message of the biblical text.
7. Use the principle of analogy to compare the prophetic word to your life and to the modern church (see Chapter 10). All of the themes found in the prophets have relevance to our own day. For example, God calls us to live faithfully under his covenant. The warnings of judgment and the promises of salvation all speak to the modern Christian just as they did to the ancient Israelites. Social injustice and immorality are just as pronounced today as they were in the Old Testament times. Finally, idolatry is a prevalent sin today. Christians should not honor or love anything above God. To do so is idolatry.

Daniel and Revelation

Apocalyptic literature

A special category of prophecy is called apocalyptic literature. The word 'apocalyptic' means 'unveiling' or 'revealing.' Apocalyptic literature has a heavy interest in events of the last days, and it tells its story with extensive use of symbolism. Apocalyptic literature is a preview of the end that shows how God will overthrow the present ruling powers and set up his eternal kingdom. Thus, apocalyptic is highly theological in its message. The books of Daniel and Revelation are classified as apocalyptic literature. These books, with their monsters and cataclysms, are both fascinating and perplexing.

Interpretation of symbols

The first step in understanding Daniel and Revelation is to realize that their symbolism must be interpreted much like the figurative language that we discussed in Chapter 4. The symbols that are used in Daniel and Revelation can have various meanings. The interpreter must determine which meaning applies within the given context. We begin by examining the biblical background of the symbols. For example, the visions in the book of Daniel include four beasts. We are told that these beasts represent four world empires and their leaders. We can expect, therefore, that the beasts in the book of Revelation may also represent human kingdoms and their rulers.

We must be very careful, however, because symbols can carry different meanings. For example, the lion is used in the Bible to symbolize the tribe of Judah, Jesus Christ, and Satan. We must depend upon the context to help us determine the meaning of the symbol.

Keys to interpreting Daniel and Revelation

Most of the rules for interpreting prophetic literature also apply to the interpretation of apocalyptic literature. In addition, the following guidelines may be helpful:
1. Outline the structure of the passage or book.
2. Note what elements are emphasized and which are less important. Observe any repetitions.
3. List the possible functions and meanings of the symbols.
4. Observe the theological message of the text. The future elements of an apocalyptic text are not an end in themselves. The purpose is to turn the reader toward God.
5. Apply the message to our present-day situation. Daniel and Revelation present a powerful theological message to the people of God, especially during difficulty times. We are living in a day of great uncertainty, international conflicts, economic upheaval, and religious persecution. The themes of Daniel and Revelation are important for the Church of today. Like Daniel, we can live faithfully and hopefully in the face of opposition. In the midst of crisis we can live in light of the the end, because we know that the end is controlled by God. The book of Revelation also tells us that God is in control. He holds the keys in his hand and

he holds the churches in his hand. The Church must maintain its witness even in the midst of suffering. God will finally put all things under his feet and establish his eternal kingdom where we will find joy and peace.

Some Bible scholars say that Old Testament prophecies may have a 'double meaning.' (Cf. Isa. 7.14). The first meaning is immediate and may be understood by the ancient audience. The second meaning is in the distant future. These second meanings are often Messianic and may not understood even by the prophet himself. However, this idea of 'double meaning' is too simplistic, too mechanical, too rationalistic. It is the nature of *all* of the Word of God, not just prophecies, to be filled with future possibilities. These future possibilities may be seen in the way the prophets reinterpreted the Law of Moses. The openness of Scripture to reinterpretation by the Holy Spirit may be seen as well in the way the Old Testament is used in the New Testament. Through the Holy Spirit, who is the author of Scripture, all of Scripture is open to a fresh articulation.

The Word of God is dynamic. We affirm authority of Scripture; it is the living and active Word of God. God through his Spirit takes the words which he spoke many years ago and through the Spirit He gives a new application which was not apparent to the original readers. This is not 'New Hermeneutic,' when the meaning comes out of the reader. It is not new or created meaning, but because of continuing experience with the God our eyes can be opened to something that was closed before.

For Review and Study

1. What are the two common misconceptions about prophecy?
2. How does the prophetic call and commission show that the prophets were messengers?
3. What is the messenger formula? What is its significance?
4. How did the prophets' encounter with God cause them to embody the passions of God?
5. What is the purpose of predictive prophecy?
6. Discuss the prophetic demand for covenant faithfulness.
7. List the two basic types of prophetic speech.
8. Explain how the prophets' use of poetry creates difficulties for interpretation.

9. List at least three of the prophets and their symbolic actions.
10. List five important events in Israel's history.
11. Name a few of the sins of Israel and Judah during the pre-exilic period.
12. Discuss the ministry of the post-exilic prophets.
13. List three of the seven keys to interpreting old Testament prophecy.
14. Describe apocalyptic literature.
15. How do we determine the meaning of symbols in the books of Daniel and Revelation?
16. Explain how we should apply the message of Daniel and Revelation to our present-day situation.

13

A STEP-BY-STEP GUIDE TO SYSTEMATIC BIBLE STUDY

We began our study by showing the importance of sound hermeneutics. We learned that the rules of hermeneutics help us to understand the Bible. Hermeneutics provides rules and guidelines so that we may interpret the Bible correctly and avoid incorrect and dangerous interpretations. Next, we examined the basic general principles for interpretation. Then we looked at guidelines for interpreting specific types of biblical material including figures of speech, wisdom literature, poetry, parables, narrative, and prophecy. We will now give our attention to a step-by-step procedure for the interpretation of Scripture.

Approaches to Bible study

Before we examine the Bible study process, we will consider three insufficient approaches to Bible study.

1. The inactive approach
Some Bible readers never really study the Bible. Instead, they simply rely on the interpretations of others. They do not take time to examine the Scripture for themselves, but they listen to what others have to say and accept their conclusions and interpretations without question. It is important that we listen to our pastor and our teachers, but God expects us to study his Word for ourselves. We should *meditate* on the Word of God (Josh. 1.8). We should *delight* in it (Ps.

1.2). We should *rejoice* in it (Ps. 19.8). We should *obey* it (Ps. 119.4). We should *hide* it in our hearts (Ps. 119.11). Also, we should *pray for understanding* (Ps. 119.18-19, 73). We should *examine* the Scriptures (Ps. 119.6). We should *search* Scriptures (Jn 5.39; Acts 17.11). We should *study* the Scriptures (2 Tim. 2.15). We should *know* the Scriptures (2 Tim. 3.15). We should *be equipped* with the Scriptures (2 Tim. 3.17). Every Christian should study the Bible regularly.

The reactive approach

The second insufficient method is what I call the reactive approach. In this approach, we search for Scriptures out of a reaction to our felt needs. If we are sick, we read passages that indicate hope for healing; if we are depressed, we read passages that bring cheer. On the market today are books of Scriptures for men, Scriptures for women, Scriptures for teenagers, and various other categories. This approach is important and valuable at certain times, but it is not enough. We must take the time and make the effort to study the whole Bible.

The proof-text approach

The third insufficient approach is the proof-text approach. This refers to the use of the Bible to support and prove our own ideas. Rather than reading the Bible openly and listening to the message of the Scriptures, we are tempted to search for ways to prove a particular doctrine or idea. Like the two previous approaches, this one has some value, but it is not complete. Certainly, we should search the Scriptures to find support for our doctrines and practices. However, we should not approach the Scripture with a closed mind. We must allow the Word of God to speak to us and challenge our thinking. These three insufficient approaches to Bible study are limited, and they do not give us a full understanding of the Scriptures.

The exegetical approach

A deeper and more helpful way of studying Scripture is called the exegetical approach. Exegesis is the study of the Bible through the use of established rules and principles. We have studied these rules and principles throughout this book.

However, as we look at the process for exegesis, we should be reminded that the Holy Spirit is our teacher and the Church is our context (see Chapter 2). Hermeneutical rules and principles are helpful, but mastery of these rules does not guarantee that we will arrive at the correct interpretation. Therefore, at all times, we must pray for wisdom and understanding. We must open our hearts to the voice of the Holy Spirit so that we can hear 'what the Spirit is saying' to us and to the Church (Rev. 2.7). Also, we should conduct all of our study as an act of worship. When we come before God to hear his Word, we should come with thanksgiving, praise, and adoration (see Chapter 1).

In the sections that follow, we will pull together all that we have studied, and we will offer a step-by-step method for studying the Bible.

Outline of the exegetical process

The three major steps for effective Bible study are (1) observation, (2) interpretation, and (3) application. The following outline is a brief overview of the process. A more detailed explanation will come afterward.

1. Observation
First, observe the facts in the text.
a. Examine the context of your passage.
    (1) Survey the entire book in which your passage is found. You cannot exegete a passage without knowing the message of the whole book. Read as an investigator. List the important facts, but be familiar with everything possible.
    (2) Survey the whole section in which your passage is found. What comes immediately before and immediately after your passage? How does the passage reflect, respond, or relate to the surrounding verses and chapters?
b. Determine the genre of your passage.
In other words, is this poetry or prose? Is it a Gospel or an epistle? Is it narrative? Is it wisdom literature? Is it apocalyptic?
c. Study the historical background.
What is known and pertinent concerning when the book was written, where it was written, to whom and by whom it was written? What period(s), event(s), and situation(s) of Israel's

history are important to the proper understanding of the book and why?
  d. *Outline the content.*
  What are the apparent divisions and subdivisions of the passage? What distinguishes these parts? What holds them together?

Interpretation

Interpretation includes determining what the author is saying, how it is universally significant, or if any generalizations or principles should be noted.
  a. *Look for patterns.*
  What are the prominent themes, words, repetitions, contrasts, or symbolisms, and how do they function in the passage? What is the perspective, style, mood? What is the progression, development, climax, focal point?
  b. *Look for themes.*
  c. *Investigate the meanings of important words.*
  (1) Compare different Bible translations
  (2) Study any words that are significant, ambiguous, or theologically important
  d. *Consider the genre of your passage.*
  As part of step 1, you determined the genre. Now you will interpret the passage with that knowledge in mind. Each type of writing requires a specific set of questions that we bring to the text.
  (1) Examine any figurative language.
  (2) Study any poetic forms.
  (3) Explore any narratives.
  (4) Analyze any prophecies.
  e. *Consult study Bibles and commentaries.*
  f. *Contemplate the theological significance of your passage.*
  What does it say about God, Christ, the Holy Spirit, humanity, sin, salvation, or the return of Jesus?

Application

How might this passage be speaking beyond its own day even unto our own? How should this text impact all Christians everywhere? How does this text impact one's personal life? What issues surface through a study of this text? What response is being called for?

Detailed instructions for exegetical Bible study

We will now look at a detailed explanation of the three-step process for effective Bible study: (1) observation, (2) interpretation, and (3) application.

1. Observation

Observation is the process of perceiving the facts of the text. We observe any characters, speakers, or listeners. We observe the setting, the time, and the topics under discussion. Facts are always the actual data contained within the text, such as who did what, precisely what they did, why they did it, and what is said about it. One should make a list of all the important things found in the book and try to be as familiar with the material as possible.

Examine the context of your passage.

Part of observation is to place the passage in its context. Read the surrounding Scriptures. Seek to place your passage within the context of what comes before it and after it. Every passage of Scripture must be interpreted in light of the message of the chapter and book in which it appears.

Survey the entire book in which your passage is found.
The Bible is made up of sixty-six books, and each book was written as a unit. It would not make sense to pick up a magazine and read a few lines from the middle of an article then a few lines from the end. To understand an article, we start reading at the beginning and proceed to the end.

The books of the Bible were written in the same way. The books of the Bible were designed to be read from beginning to end. For example, Paul began the book of Ephesians with a greeting, followed by his discussion that moves forward with emphasis on his major points. He fully intended that the reader or the listener should begin with the introduction and proceed all the way through to the end.

You cannot exegete a passage without knowing the message of the whole book. Therefore, read the entire book and make observations about the book as a whole. As you read, you should have a Bible dictionary at hand so that you can find the meaning of difficult words. However, you should not yet consult commentaries or the ideas of other people. Just sit down and read through a book of the Bible without distractions.

As you read, you should take note of the structure of the book. What are the major sections and their themes? Also, what is the theological purpose of the book? What is the apparent message or distinctive aim of the book as a whole?

Survey the section where your passage is found.
Pay attention to what comes immediately before your passage and what comes immediately after it. Determine where your passage begins and ends. What is happening in the immediate context? What is God doing and saying? How does the passage reflect, respond, or relate to the surrounding verses and chapters? To the book as a whole? To the surrounding historical and sociological situations? To the themes, patterns, and traditions found elsewhere in the Old Testament or in the ancient world?

Determine the genre of your passage.

Define the form of writing that characterizes this particular passage. In other words, is this poetry or prose? Is it a letter or an epistle? Is it narrative? Is it a gospel? Is it apocalyptic? Once this answer is decided, you will know more properly how to interpret the passage.

If it is an epistle, you should observe the apparent reason for which it was written. Is there a heresy in view? Are there questions being asked? Are there practical problems being addressed? If it is a story, you will observe the characters, setting, events, and conflicts. If it is poetry, you will note the structure and figurative language. If it is prophecy, you will examine the symbolism and the message.

Study the historical background.

After discovering the form of writing, or the genre of the passage, then you should study the historical context. Note points of geography. Look for historical references, cultural references, and religious references that will shed light on the message. For example, Ruth 1.1 tells us, 'There was a man who lived in the days of the judges.' Therefore, we know the era when this narrative took place.

It occurred during the time of the judges. Later we learn that the man and his family migrated from Israel to the land of Moab. The mention of Moab tells us the geographical background of the book.

Discover what is known and pertinent concerning when the book was written, where it was written, to whom and by whom it was written. What period(s), event(s), and situation(s) of Israel's history are important to the proper understanding of the book and why?

Outline the content.

After reading your passage and the book in which it is located, you should chart and outline the book. This should not be done in an artificial fashion but in a manner that follows the natural progressions found in the book. For example, when we read the book of Genesis, we see a certain phrase repeated over and over. The phrase is, 'These are the generations of ...' as in 'These are the generations of Noah', 'These are the generations of Adam', and 'These are the generations of Terah.' This repetition indicates something important to the structure of the book because each occurrence begins a new section. Other books are structured according to different strategies and divisions of the text. When outlining the book, we must remember that the chapter divisions are not a part of the original text, and sometimes they are not accurate signals for dividing up the text.

Example of the outline process: Colossians

The best way to outline an epistle is to list each verse then combine verses into paragraphs. The paragraphs can then be joined to form larger sections. We start with the verses, then paragraphs, and then sections and build larger and larger divisions until we have charted the whole book. The paragraphs in Colossians can be listed as follows.

- Greetings (1.1-2)
- Thanksgiving for the readers (1.3-8)
- Prayer for the readers (1.9)
- The preeminence of Christ and his work (1.12-20)
- Encouragement to continue in the Gospel (1.21)
- Paul's own ministry in the Gospel (1.22-24)

- A warning: Christ is all we need (2.1-5)
- Christians should walk freely in newness of life (2.6-15)
- Freedom from legalism (2.16-19)
- Freedom from the old way of life (2.20)
- The new life is to seek things above (3.1-4)
- Freedom from the old man and his actions (3.5-11)
- The new man and his actions (3.12-17)
- The Christian's relationships with others (3.18-25)
- Request for prayer (4.2)
- Mention of Paul's friends (4.7-17)
- Closing salutation (4.18)

The paragraphs above can then be combined to form the following sections of Colossians:

- Growth in Genuine Christianity (1.3-11)
- The Preeminence of Christ (1.12-29)
- The Sufficiency of Christ (2.1-15)
- Freedom From Legalism (2.16-23)
- The New Life (3.5-17)
- Relationship to the Unconverted (4.2-6)
- Greetings From Friends (4.7-17)

By joining the related sections together, we arrive at a basic two-part structure for Colossians:

- The Preeminence and the Sufficiency of Christ (1-2)
- Living Under the Lordship of Jesus Christ (3-4)

It seems obvious from this brief study that the major theme of Colossians is that *Jesus Christ is sufficient to free us for new life in him.*

Interpretation

The second major part of the exegetical process is the interpretation. This interpretation is informed by your survey of the whole book and of the context in which your passage is found.

Look for patterns.

After reading your passage several times, take note of any patterns that you have observed. What are the prominent words, repetitions, contrasts, or symbolisms? How do they function in the passage?

What is the progression, development, climax, and focal point? Patterns to look for include.

(1) Comparison and contrast
For example, at the end of Colossians 2 and the beginning of Colossians 3, Paul contrasts life and death. He tells his readers, 'You were dead, but now you are alive in Christ' (2.13). He then states, 'If you have been raised up with Christ, keep seeking the things above' (3.1). Formerly, they were dead without Christ, but now they are alive in Christ and should pursue those things that contribute to life.

Other examples include Rom. 5.12-19, where Adam is contrasted to Christ. In Lk. 7.36-50, Simon the Pharisee is contrasted to the sinful woman. In Galatians 5.16-25, the works of the flesh are contrasted to the fruit of the Spirit.

(2) Repetition
We should pay close attention to words and themes that are repeated. John's Gospel repeats words like 'world,' 'light,' and 'darkness.' These and other words such as 'witness' and 'believe' are all repeated in the Gospel of John. This repetition highlights the importance of those ideas. In Mt. 5.21-48, Jesus repeats the phrase, 'You have heard it said.' Jesus used this pattern frequently, and these repetitions reveal a unit of thought within a particular book.

The number of times a word appears may indicate its importance to the theme of the book. For example, the word 'priest' is found 38 times in the book of Hebrews and only 3 other times in the Pauline and General Epistles. This emphatic repetition suggests that the priesthood of Christ is one of the major themes of Hebrews. Similarly, the word 'holy' is found in the book of Leviticus 109 times but only 6 times in Genesis. There is no doubt that one of the aims of Leviticus is to teach the concept that we should be holy as God is holy (Lev. 20.26).

(3) Movement from the general to the particular
The movement from a general statement to particular examples is found often in passages where teaching is in focus. For example, Jesus says, 'Beware of doing your righteous deeds before men, to be seen by them. Otherwise you have no reward from your Father in heaven' (Mt. 6.1). After this general warning, he gives particular

examples of 'righteous acts,' including giving alms, prayer, and fasting. In Lk. 3.8-9, John the Baptist demands that his hearers bring forth fruits of repentance, and then he talks about particular examples. In 1 Cor. 12.1, Paul mentions spiritual gifts, and then he names them.

(4) Movement from the particular to the general

Also in the teaching passages, the speaker may begin with particular examples and then state a general principle based upon the stated examples. In Mt. 5.21-47, Jesus states several moral examples, then he concludes with the generalization, 'Be perfect, even as your Father in heaven is perfect.'[67]

Look for themes.

Along with the patterns mentioned above, we should look for themes, ideas, and motifs that may be prominent in the book and passage. For example, the theme of the trinity is evident in 1 Corinthians 12. Paul states, 'There are diversities of gifts, but the same *Spirit*. There are differences of ministries, but the same *Lord*. And there are diversities of activities, but it is the same *God* who works all in all' (1 Cor. 12.4-6, emphasis added). We note that Paul moves from the *Spirit*, to the *Lord*, then to *God*. It seems important that the spiritual gifts are associated not just with the Holy Spirit, but with the entire trinity.

By listing the themes, we are able to determine the main concerns of the passage. In other words, what is the message of the passage? For example, the book of 2 Corinthians presents an entirely different theme from that of Philippians. In 2 Corinthians, Paul is defending his apostleship, protecting himself and his honor against those who have accused him falsely. In the book of Philippians, however, Paul is very joyous, very encouraged. It appears that Paul has a very close and loving personal relationship with the people of Philippi. We should ask the following questions:

- What response is expected from the readers?
- What are the readers expected to do?
- What can we learn from the way the details are arranged?

---

[67] For a detailed study of these patterns and more, see Walter L. Liefeld, *New Testament Exposition: From Text to Sermon* (Grand Rapids, MI: Zondervan, 1984).

- What is going on in the writer's or reader's situation as reflected in this text?
- Is a particular doctrine being emphasized?

Investigate the meaning of important words.

In any biblical passage, we will find words that deserve detailed study. The Appendix lists a number of helpful resources for your study of Hebrew and Greek words.

(1) How to study biblical words
Word studies should include these four steps:

- Consult a dictionary for the range of meanings.
  Words can have a variety of meanings, and the dictionary will list all of the possible meanings.

- *Examine the occurrences of the word throughout the Bible.*
  Look especially at contexts that are similar to the passage you are studying. Seeing the word used in context will give you a deeper understanding of the word.

- *Examine the occurrences of the word in your passage and book.*
  Give priority to the meaning that you find in the immediate context and book. The word will often mean the same thing throughout one particular book.

- *Determine the meaning that best fits the context.*
  While all of the steps above will contribute to your decision, you should choose the meaning that best fits into the flow of the passage where it occurs.

Remember that a word will not have all of its meanings within a single context; it will have only one meaning.[68] Therefore, you should never bring all the meanings of a single word into one situation. You should look at the context and determine the most likely meaning in that particular context.

(2) How to choose which words to study
You can investigate the meanings of as many words as your time permits; however, you should begin with the following categories.

---

[68] In rare cases, an author may use the literary device called 'double meaning,' which is used for poetic effect. See D.A. Carson, *Exegetical Fallacies* (Grand Rapids, MI: Baker, 2nd edn, 1996).

- Study words that appear differently in various translations.

As you know, our Bible has been translated from the original languages of Hebrew, Aramaic, and Greek. We should compare Bible translations and compile of a list of the words that are translated differently. For example, compare these translations of Mt. 28.18. Jesus says,

> All *power* is given unto me (KJV)
> All *authority* has been given to Me (NKJV)
> All *authority* has been given to Me (NASB)

The two newer translations use the word 'authority,' while the older translation uses the word 'power.' By consulting a good study Bible, commentary, or Strong's concordance, we learn that the underlying Greek word is *exousia*, which should be translated 'authority.'

- Study ambiguous words.

A biblical passage may contain words whose meanings are unclear to the reader, words that are difficult to understand, or words which today carry a meaning that is different from years past. Any word that causes difficulty is worthy of examination.

- Study words that are important to the passage.

Certain words may contribute heavily to the meaning of your passage. These crucial words are deserving of study. For example, while discussing the person and work of Christ in Colossians 1.9-18, Paul calls Jesus the 'firstborn of all creation.' The word 'firstborn' is important in establishing the nature of Jesus Christ. A study of the word suggests that it signifies 'preeminence.' In Heb. 2.1 we read, 'Therefore we ought to give the more earnest heed to the things which we have heard, lest at any time we should let them slip' (KJV). The word 'slip' is significant for the meaning of the verse. A study of the word shows that it means 'drift away'; therefore, the verse is warning us not to drift away from the Gospel that we have heard. In Rom. 1.17, where Paul says 'the just shall live by faith,' it would be helpful to study the words 'just' and 'faith.' These two words are significant to an understanding of the passage.

- Study words that are theologically significant.

Some words carry more theological significance than other words. Significant theological words occur more frequently in the New Testament, particularly the epistles. Examples of theological terms include righteousness, salvation, redemption, justification, sanctification, and grace. For example, Jesus says of himself, 'The Son of Man did not come to be served, but to serve, and to give his life a ransom for many' (Mt. 20.28). The word 'ransom' is an important theological term. A study of the word shows that it is a variation on the word 'redemption' and that it is first used in reference to salvation from sin in Ps. 130.7-8.

Consider the genre of your passage.

Is your passage a story, a proverb, a parable, an epistle? Is it wisdom literature, poetry, or narrative? Is it a prophetic or apocalyptic passage? Each type of writing requires a specific set of questions that we should ask the text. Depending upon the genre, your study should include the following.

(1) Examine any figurative language.
Figurative language is found in all types of biblical literature; however, it is far more prevalent in the poetic books. Take note of any figures of speech, including metaphors, similes, hyperboles, and personifications. You may wish to refer back to Chapter 4 where we discussed the interpretation of figurative language.

(2) Study any poetic forms.
Poetry will include a large amount of figurative language, and it will call for other considerations as well. We noted earlier that poetry is intended to move the heart rather than inform the mind. If your passage contains poetry, you should consider its impact upon the heart and the feelings of the reader. Poetry will attempt to paint a picture in the mind of the reader. What kind of picture does it paint in your mind? Remember as well that biblical poetry uses parallelism of lines in which two lines combine to form a verse (see Chapter 9).

(3) Analyze any narratives.
If your passage tells a story, then it is narrative, and you should follow the process that is set forth in Chapter 10. Most of the Bible is narrative. Narrative books include Genesis, Exodus, Numbers, Deuteronomy, Joshua, Judges, Ruth, Samuel, Kings, Chronicles, Ezra, Nehemiah, Esther, Matthew, Mark, Luke, John, and Acts.

When interpreting narrative, you should ...
- Listen to the words of the narrator.
- Follow the events of the plot.
- Pay attention to the descriptions of the characters.
- Examine the point of view.
- Consider the setting of the story.

In addition to the basic elements of narrative (listed above), you should be alert for other common literary devices that may appear in the narrative, such as imagery, tone, poetic justice, paradox, dramatic irony, and allusions to other Scriptures.

(4) Explore any prophecies.
If your passage includes any prophetic material, you should review the guidelines found in Chapter 11, 'Interpreting Prophecy.' In order to understand prophecy, you will need to examine the historical context, analyze any prophetic symbols, and determine the theological message of the prophetic word.

Consult study Bibles and commentaries.

Until now, you have conducted your study mostly on your own. Your final step in interpretation should be to consult commentaries and other scholarly resources. Sometimes the commentaries will confirm your own findings, and at other times they will include observations and insights that you have not previously considered. When reading commentaries, you should note any different interpretations and the arguments that attend each interpretation. You should observe any outstanding insights or quotations.

Contemplate the theological significance of your passage.

Throughout your study, you may have observed a number of theological insights from your passage. At this point you should read through the passage once more and note any theological points that stand out. You may find it helpful to ask the following questions of your passage.

1. Consider how this biblical text informs our theology,
    especially as it relates to one of the following topics:
    a. The nature and character of God: omniscience, omnipotence, omnipresence, holiness, love, wisdom, goodness, grace, mercy, compassion, faithfulness, truthfulness, justice, self-

existence, immutability, invisibility, incomprehensibility, mystery, etc.;
   b. The plan and purpose of God;
   c. Doctrines such as salvation, sanctification, Holy Spirit, sin, healing, eschatology, ecclesiology, anthropology;
   d. The nature of revelation and/or doctrine of Holy Scripture.
   e. Finally, are there any theological issues which do not fit the traditional categories of systematic theology?
2. Identify aspects of this passage that may create tension.
   Regarding our theology or practice, what part of this text tends to make us uncomfortable or requires discernment. How does this tension and struggle with the text feed our spiritual growth?
3. Explore how this text forms and shapes our affections and desires.
   That is, how does it transform the heart? How does it sanctify us? Observe the rhetorical structure and language of the text, and describe any affections/emotions that are provoked and brought to the surface by the literary devices in the text or by the text as a whole. Does the text generate gratitude, love, compassion, courage, hope, joy, or a combination of these?
4. Describe how this text contributes to spirituality.
   Explain how the text relates to one of the following topics:
   a. Spiritual disciplines (such as prayer, fasting, witnessing, testimony, giving, study, etc.)
   b. Worship
   c. The Community of faith (Body of Christ)
   d. The divine–human relationship
   e. Spiritual formation
   f. Ministry formation and practice
   g. The sacraments

Application

Third, apply the message. In seeking to apply the message of the text to people today, four steps can be helpful.

Face the issues.

How is life informed, formed, or transformed by this passage? What response is being called for? How might this passage be speaking beyond its own day even unto our own? List the issues in your life that surfaced in your study of the text. Describe the impact of the study on your life.

Deal with the challenges.

Second, you must deal with any personal tensions created by your study. Where do you find yourself at odds with the message of the text? Where is the struggle focused? Where is the difficulty revealed?

Address behavior.

Finally, you should address specific behavior. How should you fulfill the meaning of this passage in your personal life? How should you change your life in response to this text? In what ways should the Church be challenged by this passage?

Construct a lesson plan or sermon.

Once your study is finished, you are prepared to carry the message of God's Word to other people in the form of a lesson or sermon. The lesson or sermon should take the application of this passage and present it to others in a form that will challenge them and encourage them to be faithful (2 Tim. 2.2).

Biblical Commands and Cultural Context

There are times when making application can be difficult, even though we affirm that the Bible is God's inspired Word, and it is relevant for every culture in every age. The Apostle Paul tells us that the Bible is useful for 'teaching, for reproof, for correction, for training in righteousness' (1 Tim. 3.16 NASB). Therefore, the Bible teaches us right from wrong, good from evil, and holy from unholy. The Psalmist writes, 'Your word is a lamp to my feet and a light to my path' (Ps. 119.105 NKJV).

Although all Christians agree that the Bible is our source for moral guidance, they do not agree on which commands of the Bible are timeless laws and which commands apply only to a specific cultural context. The Bible was written within certain cultures, but some ancient cultural practices are not necessarily requirements for us today. For example, are we required to greet each other 'with a holy kiss' (Rom. 16.16)? Should women be forbidden to wear pearls (1 Tim. 2.9)? Are all men required to lift their hands when they pray (1 Tim. 2.8)?

The cultural gap became clearer for me when I was invited to Seoul, Korea to teach at the Church of God Bible college. I experienced a dramatic culture shock! The social customs were different from those in America. The food was different. The language was different. Even the worship service was different. Everyone removed their shoes when they entered the church, and they put on house slippers. I preached in house slippers! Furthermore, the Korean manner of prayer was much quieter than what I had witnessed in American churches.

The culture gap that I experienced in Korea is similar to the culture gap that exists between the Bible and today's society – different languages, different foods, different social customs, different governments, different traditions, and different lifestyles. Unfortunately, some people today are using that cultural gap to undermine biblical morality. A large segment of contemporary society has decided that biblical morals are no longer relevant. We are like the Israelites in the time of the judges, when 'everyone did what was right in his own eyes' (Judg. 21.25 NKJV). One evening of watching television will reveal that lying, drunkenness, promiscuity, adultery, pride, envy, and greed have become acceptable behavior. However, the Bible teaches that these actions and attitudes are sinful in any culture and in any age. These sins must not be practiced by the followers of Jesus Christ (Gal. 5.19-21).

The task of the Church is to apply the teachings of Scripture to each succeeding generation. That means that we must be able to discern which parts of the Bible are timeless commands and which parts are temporary cultural practices. According to Jesus, all of God's moral law is summarized in two great commandments: 1. 'You shall love the Lord your God with all your heart, with all your soul, and with all your mind,' and 2. 'You shall love your neighbor as yourself' (Mt. 22.37-39 NKJV; see also Deut. 6.5 and Lev. 19.18). These two great commandments are expanded further in the Ten Commandments. God also gave to Israel a series of additional laws that applied the Ten Commandments to Israel's cultural context. The biblical stories, prophecies, and New Testament letters are examples of how God's people applied God's moral laws to their unique situations. For example, the Corinthian church faced particular moral challenges that were different from those found in the

Philippian church. The Apostle Paul addressed the moral issues of each church from the perspective of the Ten Commandments. As we study these biblical examples, our moral conscience is shaped and formed so that we can discern right from wrong.

However, the question still remains: How do we determine which biblical commands apply to us, and which are limited to their historical context? I suggest seven important guidelines that help us to judge which biblical commands are eternal and which are temporary.

1. The Old Testament ceremonial laws are no longer in force.

Although Christianity arose from Judaism, certain Old Testament commands are not binding upon Christians (Gal. 6.15; Col. 2.11). For example, the sacrifices, circumcision, the Sabbath day, and food laws are part of the ritual law from the Old Covenant that was fulfilled in Jesus Christ. The Apostles and other Church leaders met in Jerusalem and decided, with the guidance of the Holy Spirit, that it was not necessary for Christians to observe 'the law of Moses' (Acts 15.5-29). The decision of the Jerusalem Council is confirmed by the book of Hebrews, which declares that the Old Covenant has been replaced by the New Covenant, for the Old Covenant has passed away (Heb. 8.13). Therefore, it is no longer necessary for believers to keep the Old Testament ceremonial laws because they have been fulfilled in Christ. They are the 'shadow,' but Christ is the 'reality' (Heb. 10.1).

2. God's moral laws are universal and permanent.

God's permanent moral laws are summarized in the Ten Commandments. Although Christians are not 'under the law' as a means of salvation, we are still required to live righteously (Rom. 6) and to keep God's commandments (1 Jn 5.2). The New Testament instructs believers to obey the Ten Commandments, and any biblical command that is derived from the Ten Commandments must be followed today (except for the commandment to keep the Sabbath day, which is the only one of the Ten Commandments that is not repeated in the New Testament; see Rom. 14.5-6; Col. 2.16-17). The believer's obligation to obey God's moral law is affirmed by all major Christian denominations. Leaders such as Martin Luther, John Calvin, and John Wesley unanimously agreed that the Ten

Commandments display the perfect righteousness of God and serve as a guide to Christian morals.[69]

3. Permanent moral laws have a consistent biblical witness.

Whenever we read a command in the Bible, we can ask if that command is consistent throughout the Bible. If not, then it is probably a culturally limited command. For example, the command of Jesus, 'sell all you have and give to the poor' (Mt. 19.21), is directed only to one individual. It is not found elsewhere in Scripture. Paul's instruction that single people should remain unmarried (1 Cor. 7.8) does not correspond to other biblical teaching on marriage and is valid only in the specific situation of the Corinthian church. However, the command to avoid sexual immorality is consistent throughout Scripture; therefore, it is a timeless moral law.

4. Jesus Christ is our model.

Jesus lived as our example, that we 'should follow in his steps' (1 Pet. 2.21; see Jn 13.15). The more that we study the life of Jesus and the teachings of Jesus, the more we will become like Jesus. As we seek to know and love Jesus, we will be increasingly able to imitate his example. Jesus taught that genuine morality is deeper than just obedience to a list of rules; it comes from attitudes of the heart. Therefore, not only is adultery a sin, but lustful thoughts are also sinful (Mt. 5.28). Not only is murder a sin, but hatred is also sinful (1 Jn 3.15).

5. The Christian community helps us to distinguish between the timeless and the temporary.

If the Church throughout history has held consistently to a certain moral position, then that position is probably legitimate. Furthermore, whenever we are struggling with a moral dilemma, we should consult with other Christians and prayerfully discuss the issues (see Acts 15).

6. The Holy Spirit aids our discernment of right and wrong.

Jesus promised, 'when He, the Spirit of truth, has come, he will guide you into all truth' (Jn 16.13 NKJV). The decision of the

---

[69] See Martin Luther, *A Commentary on St. Paul's Epistle to the Galatians*, 1535; John Calvin, *Institutes of the Christian Religion*, 1536; and John Wesley, 'The Original, Nature, Property, and Use of the Law', about 1763.

Jerusalem Council is confirmed by James' statement, 'for it seemed good to the Holy Ghost' (Acts 15.28). Moreover, our ability to know right from wrong is sharpened as we continue to live in obedience. Thus, the Apostle Paul declares, 'Walk in the Spirit, and you shall not fulfill the lust of the flesh' (Gal 5.16 NKJV). The closer we are to God, the easier it is to understand the moral laws; but people who are living in disobedience will find it difficult to grasp the commandments of God. According to Jesus, a willing heart leads to understanding. He said that whoever wants to do God's will 'shall know concerning the doctrine, whether it is from God' (Jn 7.17 NKJV). Those who wish to justify their immoral behavior by appealing to cultural context are unable to know the truth (2 Tim. 3.7).

7. The ultimate test of any commandment is the law of love.

As we stated earlier, Jesus explained that all of God's timeless moral laws are commandments to love. Whenever we read a biblical command, we must ask how it expresses love for God and/or love for neighbor. For example, we can easily see how the commands of Paul to the Colossians are expressions of love that apply to us today. Paul writes, 'put off all these: anger, wrath, malice, blasphemy, filthy language out of your mouth. Do not lie to one another ... put on tender mercies, kindness, humility, meekness, longsuffering; bearing with one another, and forgiving one another ... But above all these things put on love, which is the bond of perfection' (Col. 3.8-15 NKJV).

I realize that these guidelines do not answer every question, and they do not solve every problem. However, God has given us his Word and his Spirit to lead us into truth. It is important that we walk in the light that God has given to us (1 Jn 1.7). Where God's moral law is clear, we should stand firm; and where we find some uncertainty, we must follow Paul's advice to let each person have their own convictions (Rom. 14.5-23).

Although the Old Testament is addressed specifically to the Hebrew people, it is God's Word to all people, everywhere, and in every time period. Israel was called by God to be a 'light to the nations' and to bring blessing and salvation to all people (Gen. 12.3; Isa. 2.3; 49.6; Ps. 67.2; 96.1-13), and Israel's light continues to shine by means of the Scriptures.

For Review and Study

1. Explain the exegetical approach.
2. Describe the three major steps for effective Bible study.
3. What is the process for examining the context of your passage?
4. Why is it important to determine the genre of your passage?
5. How is the historical background important in Ruth chapter one?
6. Describe four types of patterns that may be found in the Bible.
7. Explain the four steps for studying biblical words.
8. Describe the four categories of words that we should study.
9. What are the four points that we should follow when considering the genre of the passage?
10. What should we look for when consulting commentaries?
11. How do we determine the theological significance of the passage?
12. Explain the four steps that we should follow when applying the message of the text to people today.
13. What are the guidelines for applying biblical commands to our contemporary context?

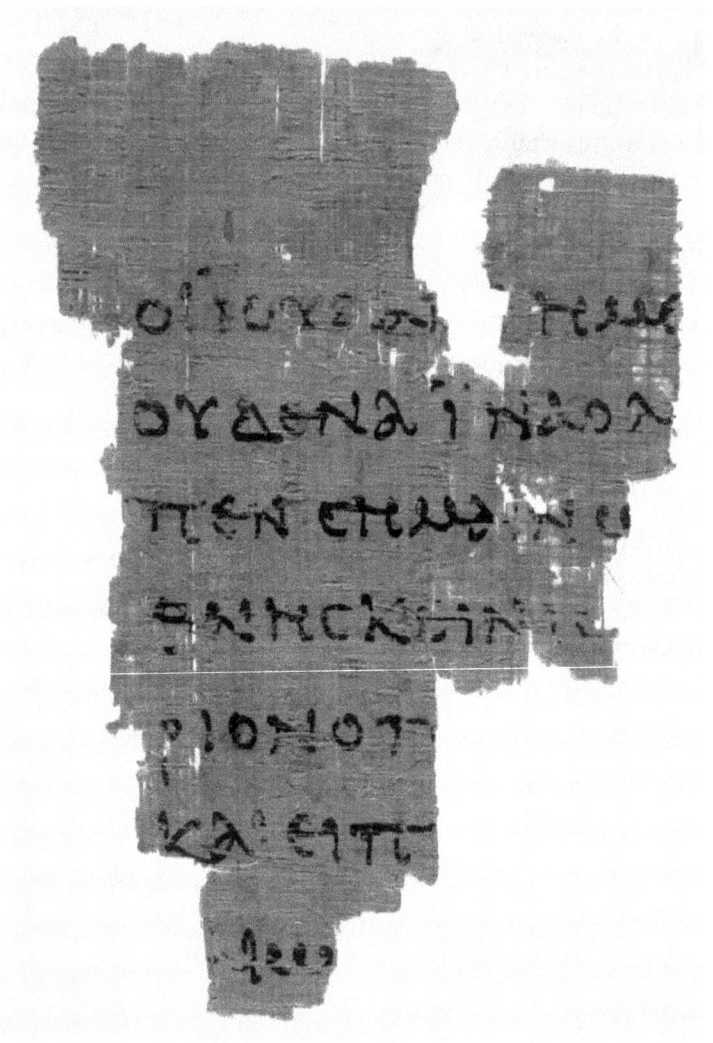

Oldest New Testament Fragment
John 18.31 — Written about AD125

14

From Research to Presentation

Converting Research into a Lesson or Sermon

The guide to biblical study found in the previous chapter sets forth a method for deep research and for personal reflection on the biblical text. After completing your research, it is necessary to compile and organize your results into a lesson or sermon that you can share with others. A lesson or expository sermon should follow the outline of the passage and should have a central theme or thesis. The main points should support your thesis and should be stated in a manner that is creative and interesting.

I recommend that Bible lessons be presented in four steps that are based on the well-known 4MAT learning process (Meaning, Content, Experiment, Creative application).[70] Each step serves as a stage in the learning process, and each step also addresses the different learning styles of students. Step one is an introduction to the lesson and may include group discussion. Step two is the basic content of the Scripture lesson. Steps three and four bring the lesson to bear upon the Christian life, the church, and the world. The last two steps can be times of discussion that provide for more extensive student participation and interaction. The teacher should be at liberty to spend as much time as necessary on each step, depending upon the needs and desires of the students. Also, teachers are

---

[70] For sermon outlines, I recommend Charles W. Koller, *How to Preach Without Notes* (Grand Rapids, MI: Baker, 2007).

encouraged to create their own learning activities that are appropriate for the students and to their particular context.

The four learning steps may be described as follows.

1. Setting the Direction

(For a sermon, this would be called the introduction.)
The purpose of the first step is to stimulate student interest in the topic. In this step we answer the question, 'Why do we need to study this lesson?' Teachers can feel free to lead a discussion that brings to the surface the life needs of the students in relation to the lesson at hand. Initial discussions can be based upon the teacher's own context or upon the suggested Discussion Starters that are offered in the book. The overall goal is to involve the students and their personal testimonies so that they become deeply engaged in the topic at hand. The challenges faced by each student will resonate with other members of the group, and a sense of community will develop.

2. Hearing the Word of God

The second step is to present the basic Bible lesson (or sermon). Here we answer the questions, 'What do we learn from this Scripture passage, and how are we transformed by it?' The lesson is presented according to an approach to Scripture that recognizes the guidance of the Holy Spirit, the role of experience, the relationality of truth, and the importance of God's dealings with humanity (the story of Scripture). Thus, the Bible is more than a roadmap or list of principles; instead, it is God's living, dynamic Word that continues to speak to God's people in new and creative ways.

3. Connecting with the Scripture

(For a sermon, this would be called your conclusion.)
The purpose of the third step is to apply the Scripture to our churches and to our lives as Christians. We answer the question, 'How does this lesson pertain to us?' In this step, we submit our lives to the Holy Spirit. We must be open to the convicting power of the Holy Spirit, who will challenge, confront, and transform the believer who is hungry for God and willing to hear God's voice. The goal of Bible study includes not just the acquisition of

information, but the acknowledgment that each of us is held accountable for what we hear in Scripture.

4. What if … ?

This final step is a creative process that seeks to answer the question, 'How can we build upon the foundation laid in this lesson?' In other words, the lesson serves as a base for generating new and imaginative ideas that move beyond the basic applications that are discovered in step three. How do we live in the presence of God? How do we demonstrate the love of God to the world? In light of our Bible lesson, what is God calling us to do?

For more information on teaching with the students' learning styles in mind, see Marlene D. Lefever, *Learning Styles: Reaching Everyone God Gave You to Teach* (Colorado Springs, CO: David C. Cook, 2002).

Example of a Lesson/Sermon (in abbreviated form)

The Passionate Pursuit of God's Glory

Biblical Text: Psalm 63

I. Setting the Direction (Introduction)

Have you ever experienced the glory of God? When I use the term 'glory of God', I am referring to the manifestation of God's awesome presence. The prophets Isaiah and Ezekiel saw the glory of the Lord in Spirit-inspired visions (Isaiah 6 and Ezekiel 1-3).

As believers, we desire to see God's glory, to recognize it, and to appreciate it. The psalmist David loved God's glory, desired God's glory, and yearned for God's glory to be manifested. When God's kingdom comes in its fullness, then God's glory will be clearly seen throughout the earth.

The clearest and most important manifestation of God's glory came to us through God's personal appearance in human form. We read in the Gospel of John, 'And the Word became flesh and dwelt among us, and we beheld his glory, the glory as of the only begotten of the Father, full of grace and truth' (Jn 1.14).

We, too, desire to see God's glory; and, like the biblical characters, we may experience the glory in a variety of ways. Like Moses, we can see the divine glory in God's grace and compassion. Furthermore, like Jesus' disciples, we can see God's glory in the signs and wonders that Jesus continues to perform in the midst of his church today.

(THESIS STATEMENT) If we desire to experience God's glory, then we must seek after God. Moses said, 'you will seek the LORD your God, and you will find him if you seek him with all your heart and with all your soul' (Deut. 4.29).

Discussion Starters

> How were Isaiah and Ezekiel affected by their visions of God's glory?

> How do healings, miracles, and spiritual gifts bear witness to God's glory today?

Describe your most powerful experience of the glory of God.

II. Hearing the Word of God

A. The Biblical Text

(At this point, I would read Psalm 63)

B. The Lesson

Psalm 63 is a passionate prayer, an articulation of deep spiritual longing; and it is an example of Pentecostal spirituality. The longing for God expressed in Psalm 63 represents to me the passionate pursuit of God that is generated by Pentecostal spirituality, a spirituality that Steven Jack Land has characterized as 'a passion for the kingdom', which is 'ultimately a passion for God' (Land, pp. 2, 97).

1. Longing for God's Presence (verses 1-2)

A passion for God is evident in the first words of the psalmist: 'God, you are my God'. The entire psalm, therefore, is grounded upon David's personal relationship with God. God had said to Israel, 'I will be your God and you will be my people' (Lev. 26.12). The relationship is one of covenant. Therefore, if we desire to see God's glory manifested in our midst, we must start with our relationship with God. Every day, when we wake up, we should say, 'Oh, God you are my God today'. He is not just the God of David, he is our God. He is my God and your God. We can come into his presence to worship him.

2. Praise for God's Kindness (verses 3-5)

Immediately after his prayer for God's presence, David breaks forth in joyous praise. 'My lips shall praise You', he declares to God, 'Because Your lovingkindness is better than life'. The word 'lovingkindness' is a translation of the word *ḥesed,* which refers to God's love, loyalty, faithfulness, kindness, and mercy that come to the believer because of God's covenant. It is God's unbreakable commitment to his covenant. Therefore, David is saying that God's covenant commitment to his people is more precious than life itself.

3. Remembrance of God's Faithfulness (verses 6-8)

The third section of Psalm 63 recalls the past benefits of David's relationship to God. The psalmist asserts that just as God has been faithful to him, he has been faithful to God by remembering God and meditating upon God, two activities that signal deep devotion and commitment.

4. Rejoicing in God's Covenant Protection (verses 9-11)

This final section of the psalm displays a mood of confident hope for the future. The psalmist is confident that justice will prevail, that evil will be punished, and that God's people 'shall glory' in their covenant relationship with God.

These final verses of Psalm 63 imply that we must reaffirm our hope in the Lord's soon return. At the return of Jesus, the wicked will be punished; those who are faithful to God will rejoice in God's protection; and the kingdom of God will manifest itself as a kingdom of justice and righteousness.

C. Connecting with the Psalm (Questions for discussion)

(If you are constructing a sermon, you would place a conclusion here rather than questions for discussion.)

What are the signs that we have lost our passion for the presence of God?

What steps can we take to restore our love for God's glory?

Discuss a time when the Lord was your help and your support.

How do we maintain hope for the future?

Share which part of this psalm gives you the most cause to praise God.

What if ... ? (Creative and imaginative ideas)

What if we prayerfully evaluate our spiritual desires in light of Psalm 63?

What if we extend God's kindness and love to someone who needs help?

Now, come up with your own 'What if ... ?'

Converting Research into an Academic Exegesis Paper

The guide to biblical study found in the previous chapter sets forth a method for research. After completing your research, it is necessary to compile and organize your results into the format that is required by your teacher. An exegetical paper should follow the outline of the passage and should be presented in a verse-by-verse or section-by-section format. If you are able to use the biblical languages, you should do so extensively in the exegesis.

Your exegesis should have the following components, outlined as follows:
 I. Introduction
 II. Translation of the Biblical Text
 III. Structure and Genre
 IV. Exegesis
  A. The exegetical section should have as many points as is required by the passage's structure.
  B. etc.
 V. Theological Implications
 VI. Conclusions

Example of an Exegetical Paper (in abbreviated form)

Psalm 63: Longing for God

I. Introduction

Psalm 63 is a passionate prayer, an articulation of deep spiritual inclinations. It is an expression of the psalmist's intense desire to encounter God and to experience God's presence.

In this constructive and integrative study, I examine Psalm 63 through the lens of Pentecostal spirituality. I will present an affective Pentecostal hearing of Psalm 63 that emerges from my location within the Pentecostal community. Then I will suggest ways in which Psalm 63 can contribute to the affective formation of the Pentecostal church of today.

II. A Translation of Psalm 63

 (A translation of Psalm 63 is inserted here. If you have studied Hebrew, the translation should be your own.)

III. Structure and Genre of Psalm 63

The structure of Psalm 63 is unclear,[71] and scholars have divided the psalm in a variety of ways.[72] I suggest a four-part structure, beginning after the superscription (v. 1):

1. Longing for God's Presence (vv. 2-3).
Verses 2-3 hold together as an introduction that establishes the overall topic of the psalm as the psalmist's intention to passionately and habitually pursue the presence of God.

2. Praise for God's Covenant Loyalty (vv. 4-6).
The second section, like the first, includes an affirmation that is expressed syntactically with a verbless clause ('you are my God' and 'your kindness is better than life'). The verbless clauses are followed by statements of future intent ('I will seek you' and 'my lips will praise you'). Each verb in this section is a *yiqtol* and should be translated as future tense.

3. Remembrance of God's Faithfulness (vv. 7-9).
The third section (vv. 7-9) is held together by a focus upon remembrance of God's actions in the past.[73] Verses 7-8 consist of two compound sentences, each of which begins with a *qatal* verb and is followed by a habitual *yiqtol*.[74]

4. Rejoicing in God's Covenant Protection (vv. 10-12).[75]
The fourth section turns to the eventual downfall of the psalmist's enemies, and all of the verbs are *yiqtols* that should be translated as future tense.

Like the laments, Psalm 63 begins with a direct address to God (v. 2), and it includes other elements that are common to the

---

[71] Cf. Michael Wilcock, *The Message of Psalms 1–72: Songs for the People of God* (Downers Grove, IL: InterVarsity Press, 2001), I, p. 222.

[72] James Limburg, *Psalms* (Louisville, KY: Westminster John Knox Press, 1st edn, 2000), pp. 208-10, divides the psalm into three parts: vv. 1-4, body and soul; vv. 5-8, remembering; and vv. 9-11, rejoicing.

[73] Cf. Susanne Gillmayr-Bucher, 'David, Ich und der König: Fortschreibung und Relecture in Psalm 63', in Josef M. Oesch, Andreas Vonach, and Georg Fischer (eds.), *Horizonte biblischer Texte: Festschrift für Josef M. Oesch zum 60. Geburtstag* (Göttingen: Vandenhoeck & Ruprecht, 2003), pp. 71-89 (76).

[74] Cf. Gillmayr-Bucher, 'David, Ich und der König', p. 74.

[75] Gillmayr-Bucher, 'David, Ich und der König', p. 76, agrees that vv. 10-12 hold together as a unit.

laments: a mention of enemies (v. 9), a promise to praise God (v. 11), and a statement of trust (v. 7). Consequently, a number of scholars have classified Psalm 63 as an individual lament.[76]

IV. Exegesis of Psalm 63

Our overview of the text, structure, and genre of Psalm 63 reveals a number of affective components that intersect with Christian spirituality.

A. Longing for God's Presence (vv. 2-3)

A passion for God is evident in the first words of the psalmist: 'God, you are my God'.[77] The entire psalm, therefore, is grounded upon the certainty of the divine human relationship;[78] 'the emphatic "my God" expresses the covenantal bond with all its assurances'.[79]

B. Gratitude (vv. 4-6)

Following upon the moving articulation of his unquenchable longing for God's presence, the psalmist breaks forth in joyous praise. 'I will praise you', he declares to God, 'because your kindness (חסד) is better than life'. Before Psalm 63, human life in its fullness, enjoyed in covenant with God, was understood as the ultimate benefit of God's covenant loyalty (חסד).[80]

In celebration of God's faithful love, the psalmist pledges to 'praise' God, to 'bless' God, and to 'lift up' his hands to God in worship. Lifting up the hands is the 'customary attitude of the worshipper in prayer ... a sign of an expectant trust that one's empty hands will be "filled" with divine blessings'.[81] This elaborate praise will not be offered briefly or intermittently; it will continue

---

[76] Nancy L. DeClaissé-Walford, *Introduction to the Psalms: A Song from Ancient Israel* (St. Louis, MO: Chalice Press, 2004), p. 147.

[77] Kraus, *Psalms 60-150*, p. 17, argues that אלהים אלי אתה אשחרך should be rendered, 'God, my God, you – I seek you', so that אתה functions to add emphasis (Cf. Gen. 49.8). However, it is clear that in its four other occurrences (Pss. 22.11; 118.28; 140.7; cf. also Ps. 31.15, אלהי אתה), the phrase אלי אתה should be translated 'you are my God', and I would argue that it carries the same meaning here.

[78] Briggs and Briggs, *Psalms*, II, p. 72.

[79] John Eaton, *The Psalms: A Historical and Spiritual Commentary with an Introduction and New Translation* (London: T & T Clark International, 2003), p. 235.

[80] *CDCH*, p. 126, defines חסד as 'loyalty, faithfulness, kindness, love, mercy', a quite broad definition.

[81] Anderson, *The Book of Psalms*, I, p. 457.

throughout the psalmist's 'life'. He promises to bless the Lord 'in perpetual worship'.[82]

C. Trust and Commitment (vv. 7-9)

The third section of Psalm 63 continues to express thankfulness, but the tone transitions to a mood of deep trust and commitment to God. While vv. 4-6 declare the present and future value of God's immeasurable kindness, vv. 7-9 recall the past benefits of the psalmist's relationship to God. The psalmist asserts that just as God has been faithful to him, he has been faithful to God by remembering (זכר) God and meditating (הגה) upon God, two activities that signal deep devotion and commitment.

The psalmist remembers that, with God as his 'help', he shouted for joy underneath the covering of God's 'wings', which represent God's 'protection'.[83] He remembers further that he 'stuck close' to God and that God supported him. The phrase 'stuck close' is difficult to translate into English. The verb דבק means 'to cling, to cleave, to stick to' (cf. Gen. 2.24), but in combination with אחרי, it apparently means to 'pursue or follow very closely behind'.[84] Metaphorically, it signifies 'loyalty, affection, etc.'[85] Israel is commanded to 'cling' to Yahweh (Deut. 10.20; 13.5; Josh. 23.8; Ps. 119.31). While the psalmist 'stuck close' to God, God 'upheld' him with his powerful 'right hand'.

D. Confident Hope (vv. 10-12)

This final section of the psalm registers a mood of confident hope for the future. The section unfolds through a contrast between the psalmist's enemies and 'the king'. The enemies, who seek 'to ruin'[86] the psalmist, will 'go into the depths of the earth', and they will become the 'prey of foxes'.[87] The king, however, will rejoice in God,

---

[82] Briggs and Briggs, *Psalms*, II, p. 73.
[83] Anderson, *The Book of Psalms*, I, p. 458.
[84] *HALOT*, I, p. 209.
[85] *BDB*, p. 179. Cf. Tate, *Psalms 51-100*, p. 128.
[86] The Hebrew for 'ruin' is actually a noun, prefixed with a preposition that suggests purpose: 'They seek my life for the purpose of ruin'. See *DCH*, p. 450, and *HALOT*, II, p. 1427.
[87] *HALOT*, II, 1445, define שועל as 'fox'. So *BDB*, but they add, 'perhaps also jackal' (p. 1048).

along with all those who swear allegiance to God, because the mouths of the deceivers 'will be stopped'.

The last section of Psalm 63 is a fitting conclusion to this psalm of reorientation. The psalmist has admitted his sense of separation from God's presence (v. 2) and his need to be satisfied by God's kindness (v. 6). He has remembered (v. 7) times when he needed God's help (v. 8) and God came to his aid. In this final strophe, he acknowledges the ongoing presence of dangerous enemies who threaten his safety. Nevertheless, his past experiences of God's presence (v. 3), God's covenant loyalty (v. 4), and God's tender care (v. 9) have generated a renewed confidence in God's faithfulness. The psalmist is convinced that God's people will prevail in the end.

V. Theological Implications

Psalm 63 is a passionate expression of the psalmist's spiritual longings after God. These longings are suggestive of the affective component of Christian spirituality in general and Pentecostal spirituality in particular. I find that the psalmist's 'hunger' and 'thirst' for God is consistent with Pentecostals' passion for God and that the desire to encounter God in the sanctuary is consistent with the goals of Pentecostal worship.

Chris Green insists that 'Pentecostal spirituality is nothing if not a *personal* engagement' with God.[88] Although I am most familiar with North American Pentecostalism and do not claim to speak for all Pentecostals, my associations with Pentecostals in Latin America, Africa, Australia, Asia, Europe, and the UK lead me to conclude that a passionate affective spirituality is common to all Pentecostals.[89]

The psalmist's longing for the manifestation of God's 'power and glory' can be compared to Pentecostalism's 'holy desire for God himself'.[90] This longing for God is described repeatedly in early Pentecostal literature. For example, Alice Flower writes, 'All I seemed to sense was a deep craving for the overflowing of his love

---

[88] Chris E.W. Green, *Toward a Pentecostal Theology of the Lord's Supper: Foretasting the Kingdom* (Cleveland, TN: CPT Press, 2012), p. 289 (emphasis original).

[89] Regarding Korean spirituality, see Julie C. Ma, 'Korean Pentecostal Spirituality: A Case Study of Jashil Choi', *AJPS* 5.2 (2002), pp. 235-54.

[90] Daniel Castelo, 'Tarrying on the Lord: Affections, Virtues and Theological Ethics in Pentecostal Perspective', *JPT* 13.1 (2004), p. 53.

in my heart. At that moment it seemed I wanted Jesus more than anything in all the world'.[91]

VI. Conclusions

In his article on 'Community and Worship', Jerome Boone argues that the 'single most important goal of any Pentecostal worship service is a personal encounter with the Spirit of God'.[92] This encounter will often include the manifestation of spiritual gifts and the worshipers will experience 'the Spirit as transformational power'.[93]

If the Pentecostal movement is to maintain its vitality from generation to generation, it must periodically reclaim the spiritual passion that we find demonstrated in Psalm 63. I would suggest the following ways in which Psalm 63 can help to shape the spirituality of the Pentecostal movement both now and in the future.

1. Spiritual formation should include the nurture and development of the affect.
2. Churches must provide frequent and open-ended opportunities for prayer.
3. In our practice of the Pentecostal life and ministry, we must become hungry and thirsty for God, desperate for God's presence.
4. The Church must reaffirm its eschatological hope.
5. Pentecostals face the danger of seeking out experiences rather than seeking God for God's sake.
6. The Christian community must recover the practice of testimony. Psalm 63 is directed to God, but it is a song that is meant to be heard by the congregation, and as such, it functions as testimony. The recounting of the psalmist's own longing for God is an implicit challenge to the hearer to pursue God with the same fervent intensity and with the same unreserved yearning.

For examples of biblical exegesis, see the following books:

Lee Roy Martin, *Judging the Judges: Pentecostal Theological Perspectives on the Book of Judges* (Cleveland, TN: CPT Press, 2018).

Lee Roy Martin, *The Spirit of the Psalms: Rhetorical Analysis, Affectivity, and Pentecostal Spirituality* (Cleveland, TN: CPT Press, 2018).

---

[91] Alice Reynolds Flower, 'My Pentecost', *AGH* 20 (Winter 1997-98), p. 18; excerpted from her *Grace for Grace: Some Highlights of God's Grace in the Daily Life of the Flower Family* (Springfield, MO: privately published, 1961).

[92] Boone, 'Community and Worship', p. 137.

[93] Boone, 'Community and Worship', p. 138.

Hebrew Aleppo Codex (written by hand in AD 920)

APPENDIX

Resources for Hebrew and Greek Word Studies

HEBREW

These resources are useful if you have NOT studied Hebrew.

Brown, Francis *et al.*, *The New Brown-Driver-Briggs-Gesenius Hebrew and English Lexicon* (Peabody, MA: Hendrickson Publishers, 1979). Keyed to Strong's numbers – online at BibleHub.com.

Harris, R. Laird, Gleason Archer, and Bruce Waltke (eds.), *Theological Wordbook of the Old Testament* (2 Vols.; Chicago: Moody Press, 1980). This has a word index keyed to Strong's numbers.

Mounce, W. D. *Mounce's Complete Expository Dictionary of Old and New Testament Words* (Grand Rapids, MI: Zondervan, 2006) ISBN: 9780310591504

Wigram, George (ed.), *The New Englishman's Hebrew Concordance*. Hendrickson Publishers, 1996. This book lists the biblical verses where each Hebrew word appears. Keyed to Strong's numbers – online at BibleHub.com.

These resources are important if you have studied Hebrew.

Botterweck, G. Johannes and Helmer Ringgren, *Theological Dictionary of the Old Testament* (Grand Rapids: Eerdmans, 1974-).

Clines, David, *Dictionary of Classical Hebrew* (Sheffield: Sheffield Academic Press, 1993-).

Holladay, William (ed.), *A Concise Hebrew and Aramaic Lexicon of the Old Testament* (Grand Rapids: Eerdmans, 1988).

Jenni, Ernst and Claus Westermann (eds.), *Theological Lexicon of the Old Testament* (3 Vols.; Peabody, MA: Hendrickson Publishers, 1997).

Köhler, Ludwig, *The Hebrew and Aramaic Lexicon of the Old Testament* (2 vols.; Leiden: E. J. Brill, Study edn, 2001).

VanGemeren, Willem A. (ed.), *New International Dictionary of Old Testament Theology and Exegesis* (5 Vols.; Grand Rapids: Zondervan, 1997).

GREEK

These resources are useful if you have NOT studied Greek.

Kittel, Gerhard, Gerhard Friedrich, and G. W. Bromiley, *Theological Dictionary of the New Testament [Abridged Edition]* (Grand Rapids, MI: Eerdmans, 1985). ISBN: 0802824048

Brown, Colin, *The New International Dictionary of New Testament Theology* (3 vols.; Grand Rapids, MI: Zondervan Pub. House, 1975). The 3-volume set is available at abebooks.com for $50 or less.

Mounce, W. D. *Mounce's Complete Expository Dictionary of Old and New Testament Words* (Grand Rapids, MI: Zondervan, 2006) ISBN: 9780310591504

Wigram, G. V. (1985). *The Englishman's Greek Concordance*: Numerically coded to Strong's Exhaustive concordance. Grand Rapids, MI, Baker Book House. Available on biblehub.com.

These sources are important if you have studied Greek.

Alford, Henry, *Alford's Greek Testament: An Exegetical and Critical Commentary* (4 vols.; Grand Rapids, MI: Guardian Press, 1976).

Bauer, W., W. Arndt, et al. (2000). *A Greek-English lexicon of the New Testament and other early Christian literature*. Chicago, University of Chicago Press. 0226039331 (acid-free paper).

Kittel, Gerhard, Geoffrey William Bromiley, and Gerhard Friedrich, *Theological Dictionary of the New Testament* (trans. G. Bromiley; 10 vols.; Grand Rapids, MI: Eerdmans, 1964).

Alford, Henry, *Alford's Greek Testament: An Exegetical and Critical Commentary* (4 vols.; Grand Rapids, MI: Guardian Press, 1976). Available online at www.studylight.org.

Friberg, B., T. Friberg, *et al.* (1981). *Analytical Greek New Testament: Greek text analysis*. Grand Rapids, Mich., Baker Book House. ISBN: 0801034965.

Liddell, H. G., R. Scott, *et al.* (1996). *A Greek-English lexicon*. Oxford. New York, Clarendon Press; Oxford University Press. ISBN: 0198642261.

Louw, J. P., and Eugene Albert Nida, *Greek-English Lexicon of the New Testament: Based on Semantic Domains* (2 vols.; New York: United Bible Societies, 2nd edn, 1989).

Mounce, W. D. (1993). *The Analytical Lexicon to the Greek New Testament*. Grand Rapids, MI, Zondervan. ISBN: 0310542103.

Nicoll, W. Robertson *et al.*, *The Expositor's Greek Testament* (New York: Dodd, Mead, 1897). Available online at www.studylight.org.

Robertson, A.T., and Wesley J. Perschbacher, *Word Pictures of the New Testament* (Grand Rapids: Kregel Publications, Rev. edn, 2004). Available online at www.studylight.org.

Rogers, Cleon L. Jr., Cleon L. Rogers III, and Fritz Rienecker, *The New Linguistic and Exegetical Key to the Greek New Testament* (Grand Rapids, MI: Zondervan, 1998).

Silva, Moisés, *New International Dictionary of New Testament Theology and Exegesis* (Grand Rapids, Michigan: Zondervan, 2nd edn, 2014). Update of Colin Brown's, *NIDNTT*.

Spicq, C. and J.D. Ernest (1994). *Theological Lexicon of the New Testament.* Peabody, Mass., Hendrickson. 1565630351.

BIBLIOGRAPHY

Álvarez, Miguel, *Pasión Por La Palabra: Hacia Una Hermenéutica Latina* (Centro Estudios Latinos Suplementos Académicos 4; Cleveland, TN: CEL Publicaciones, 2017).
—, 'Contextualización De La Hermenéutica Latina', *HECHOS – Una Perspectiva Pneumatológica* 1.1 (2019), pp. 3-18.
—, *Hermeneutica: Palabra, Espiritu Y Comunidad* (Cleveland, TN: CPT Press, 2021).
Archer, Kenneth J., *A Pentecostal Hermeneutic: Spirit, Scripture and Community* (Cleveland, TN: CPT Press, 2009).
Arrington, French L., *Exploring the Declaration of Faith* (Cleveland, TN: Pathway Press, 2003).
Bailey, Mark L., 'The Kingdom in the Parables of Matthew 13', *Bibliotheca sacra* 155.617 (1998), pp. 29-38.
Balz, Horst, and Gerhard Schneider, *Exegetical Dictionary of the New Testament* (3 vols.; Grand Rapids, MI: Eerdmans, 1990).
Barth, Karl, *The Word of God and Theology* (trans. Amy Marga; New York: T&T Clark, 2011).
Barth, Karl, *Church Dogmatics: Volume I. The Doctrine of the Word of God* (trans. G.W. Bromiley; New York: T&T Clark, 1936).
Bavinck, Herman, *Reformed Dogmatics* (trans. John Vriend; 4 vols.; Grand Rapids, MI: Baker Academic, 2003).
Berkouwer, G.C., *Holy Scripture* (trans. Jack B Rogers; Studies in Dogmatics; Grand Rapids, MI: Eerdmans, 1975).
Brueggemann, Walter, *The Bible Makes Sense* (Atlanta, GA: John Knox Press, 1977).
Brunner, Emil, *The Christian Doctrine of God. Dogmatics: Vol. 1* (trans. Olive Wyon; Dogmatics; Wipf and Stodk: Eugene, OR, 2014).
D.A. Carson, *Exegetical Fallacies* (Grand Rapids, MI: Baker, 2nd edn, 1996).
Castelo, Daniel, and Robert W. Wall, *The Marks of Scripture: Rethinking the Nature of the Bible* (Grand Rapids, MI: Baker Academic, 2019).
Castelo, Daniel, and Robert W. Wall, 'Scripture and the Church: A Précis for an Alternative Analogy', *Journal of Theological Interpretation* 5.2 (2011), pp. 197-210.
Conn, Charles W., *The Bible: Book of Books* (Workers' Training Course; Cleveland, TN: Pathway Press, 1961).

Cremer, Hermann, *Biblisch-theologisches Wörterbuch der neutestamentlichen Gräcität* (Gotha: Friedrich Andreas Perthes, 1866).
Danker, Frederick W., Walter Bauer, and William Arndt, *A Greek-English Lexicon of the New Testament and Other Early Christian Literature* (Chicago: University of Chicago Press, 3rd edn, 2000).
Danker, Frederick W., and Kathryn Krug, *The Concise Greek–English Lexicon of the New Testament* (Chicago: The University of Chicago Press, 2009).
Danker, Frederick W., Walter Bauer, and William Arndt, *A Greek-English Lexicon of the New Testament and Other Early Christian Literature* (Chicago: University of Chicago Press, 3rd edn, 2000).
Doerksen, Vernon D., 'The Interpretation of Parables', *Grace Theological Journal* 11.2 (1970), pp. 3-20.
Ehrman, Bart D., *The New Testament: A Historical Introduction to the Early Christian Writings* (New York: Oxford University Press, 1997).
Green, Chris E.W., *Sanctifying Interpretation: Vocation, Holiness, and Scripture* (Cleveland, TN: CPT Press, 2nd edn).
Land, Steven Jack, Pentecostal Spirituality: A Passion for the Kingdom (Cleveland, TN: CPT Press, 2010).
Liddell, Henry G., George Scott, *A Greek-English Lexicon* (Oxford: Clarendon Press, 1940).
Longman, Tremper, *Literary Approaches to Biblical Interpretation* (Foundations of Contemporary Interpretation; V. 3; Grand Rapids, Mich.: Academie Books, 1987).
Louw, J.P., and Eugene Albert Nida, *Greek-English Lexicon of the New Testament: Based on Semantic Domains* (2 vols.; New York: United Bible Societies, 2nd edn, 1989).
Macchia, Frank D., 'Theology, Pentecostal', in Stanley M. Burgess and Ed M. Van der Maas (eds.), *The New International Dictionary of Pentecostal and Charismatic Movements* (Grand Rapids, MI: Zondervan, Rev. and expanded edn, 2002), pp. 1120-41.
—, *Introduction to Theology: Declaring the Wonders of God* (Foundations for Spirit-Filled Christianity; Grand Rapids, MI: Baker Academic, 2023).
Martin, Lee Roy, 'Hearing the Book of Judges: A Dialogue with Reviewers', *Journal of Pentecostal Theology* 18.1 (2009), pp. 30-50.
— (ed.), *Pentecostal Hermeneutics: A Reader* (Leiden: Brill, 2013).
Masenya, Madipoane J., 'African Womanist Hermeneutics : A Suppressed Voice from South Africa Speaks', *Journal of Feminist Studies in Religion* 11 (1995), pp. 149-55.
Montague, George T., *Understanding the Bible: A Basic Introduction to Biblical Interpretation* (New York: Paulist Press, 1997).

Montanari, Franco, Madeleine Goh, and Chad Schroeder (eds.), *The Brill Dictionary of Ancient Greek* (Leiden: Brill, 2015).
Moore, Rickie D., 'Canon and Charisma in the Book of Deuteronomy', *Journal of Pentecostal Theology* 1 (1992), pp. 75-92.
—, 'Deuteronomy and the Fire of God: A Critical Charismatic Interpretation', *Journal of Pentecostal Theology* 7 (1995), pp. 11-33.
—, '"And Also Much Cattle": Prophetic Passions and the End of Jonah', *Journal of Pentecostal Theology*.11 (1997), pp. 35-48.
Osborne, Grant R., *The Hermeneutical Spiral: A Comprehensive Introduction to Biblical Interpretation* (Downers Grove, Ill.: InterVarsity Press, 1991).
Pinnock, Clark H., 'The Work of the Holy Spirit in Hermeneutics', *Journal of Pentecostal Theology* 2 (1993), pp. 3-23.
Pinnock, Clark H., and Barry L. Callen, *The Scripture Principle: Reclaiming the Full Authority of the Bible* (Grand Rapids, Mich.: Baker Academic, 2nd edn, 2006).
Poirier, John C., *The Invention of the Inspired Text: Philological Windows on the Theopneustia of Scripture* (The Library of New Testament Studies; New York: T&T Clark, 2021).
—, 'Is 'All Scripture … Inspired'? The Meaning of θεόπνευστος in 2 Timothy 3.16' (Paper presented at the 39th Annual Meeting of the Society for Pentecostal Studies; Seattle, WA; March 2013).
Ramm, Bernard L., *Protestant Biblical Interpretation: A Textbook of Hermeneutics* (Grand Rapids, MI: Baker, 3d rev. edn, 1970).
Ryrie, Charles C., *A Survey of Bible Doctrine* (Chicago: Moody Press, 1972).
Tate, W. Randolph, *Biblical Interpretation: An Integrated Approach* (Peabody, MA: Hendrickson Publishers, 1991).
Thayer, Joseph Henry, *A Greek-English Lexicon of the New Testament: Being Grimm's Wilke's Clavis Novi Testamenti* (New York: Harper & Brothers, 1889).
Thomas, John Christopher, 'The Word and the Spirit', in *Ministry & Theology: Studies for the Church and Its Leaders* (Cleveland, TN: Pathway Press, 1996)
—, 'Women, Pentecostalism and the Bible: An Experiment in Pentecostal Hermeneutics', *Journal of Pentecostal Theology* 5 (1994), pp. 41-56.
Wiles, J. Ben, *A Believing People* (Living What We Believe; Cleveland, TN: Church of God Adult Discipleship, 2018).
Zuck, Roy B., *Basic Bible Interpretation* (Wheaton, IL: Victor Books, 1991).

Isaiah 34.1-36.2
The Great Isaiah Scroll, written about 200 BC on leather parchment

www.ingramcontent.com/pod-product-compliance
Lightning Source LLC
Chambersburg PA
CBHW072344100426
42738CB00049B/1603